THE SPIRIT OF CHRISTMAS
COOKBOOK

You'll always have the holiday recipes you need when you add this handy volume to your kitchen library! The Spirit of Christmas Cookbook *features 337 of the most delicious recipes from our first five annual holiday guidebooks, and it can help you plan a scrumptious menu for a holiday open house, a mid-morning brunch, or a traditional family dinner. And of course, there are recipes for delectable goodies, as well as delightful desserts to satisfy everyone's sweet tooth. Ideas abound for gift-giving, too. Each yummy treat, appetizer, side dish, main course, and more in this terrific collection has been tried, tested, and proven delicious. And we show them in full-color photographs to ensure successful results for you and a very merry celebration for one and all. May your holiday season be filled with good food and grand company!*

LEISURE ARTS, INC.
Little Rock, Arkansas

THE SPIRIT OF CHRISTMAS
COOKBOOK

EDITORIAL STAFF

Vice-President and Editor-in-Chief: Anne Van Wagner Childs
Executive Director: Sandra Graham Case
Executive Editor: Susan Frantz Wiles
Publications Director: Carla Bentley
Creative Art Director: Gloria Bearden
Production Art Director: Melinda Stout

FOODS
Foods Editor: Celia Fahr Harkey, R.D.
Assistant Foods Editor: Jane Kenner Prather
Test Kitchen Home Economist: Rose Glass Klein
Test Kitchen Assistants: Nora Faye Spencer Clift
and Leslie Belote Dunn

EDITORIAL
Associate Editor: Linda L. Trimble
Senior Editorial Writer: Robyn Sheffield-Edwards
Editorial Associates: Tammi Williamson Bradley,
Terri Leming Davidson, and Darla Burdette Kelsay
Copy Editor: Laura Lee Weland

ART
Book/Magazine Art Director: Diane M. Hugo
Senior Production Artist: Brent Jones
Production Artist: M. Katherine Yancey

ADVERTISING AND DIRECT MAIL
Senior Editor: Tena Kelley Vaughn
Copywriters: Steven M. Cooper, Marla Shivers, and
Marjorie Ann Lacy
Assistant Copywriter: Dixie L. Morris
Designer: Rhonda H. Hestir
Art Director: Jeff Curtis
Production Artists: Linda Lovette Smart and
Leslie Loring Krebs
Publishing Systems Administrator: Cindy Lumpkin
Publishing Systems Assistant: Gregory A. Needels

BUSINESS STAFF

Publisher: Bruce Akin
Vice-President, Finance: Tom Siebenmorgen
Vice-President, Retail Sales: Thomas L. Carlisle
Retail Sales Director: Richard Tignor
Vice-President, Retail Marketing: Pam Stebbins
Retail Customer Services Director: Margaret Sweetin
General Merchandise Manager: Russ Barnett

Distribution Director: Ed M. Strackbein
Executive Director of Marketing and Circulation:
Guy A. Crossley
Circulation Manager: Byron L. Taylor
Print Production Manager: Laura Lockhart
Print Production Coordinator: Nancy Reddick Baker

We would like to extend our thanks to Kay Wright, Micah McConnell, Christy Kalder, and Susan Warren Reeves, R.D., for their contributions as former editors, consultants, and production assistants for foods in the *Spirit of Christmas* volumes from which we chose our recipes.

Library of Congress Catalog Card Number 95-81880
International Standard Book Number 0-942237-79-X

TABLE OF CONTENTS

TABLE OF CONTENTS
(Continued)

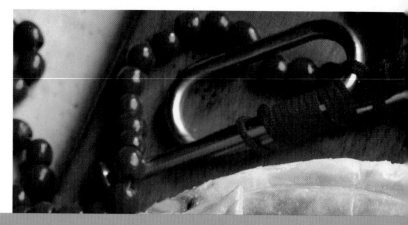

MERRY BRUNCH

After working up an appetite opening gifts and wading through piles of wrapping paper and ribbons, your loved ones will enjoy this hearty mid-morning fare. Every recipe is a tummy-pleasing delight! Whether you make all of these tasty dishes for a large gathering or pick a few of your favorites for a more intimate group, you'll serve up a very merry Christmas brunch.

A robust combination of meat, spinach, eggs, and cheese is hidden beneath a flaky crust in Hearty Brunch Pie. Holly leaves and colorful berries made from dough make a festive garnish.

HEARTY BRUNCH PIE

CRUST

2½ cups all-purpose flour
½ teaspoon salt
¾ cup plus 2 tablespoons butter,
  chilled and cut into pieces
⅓ cup ice water

FILLING

1 pound ground turkey
½ pound mild pork sausage
5 eggs
2 packages (10 ounces each)
  frozen chopped spinach,
  thawed and squeezed dry
4 cups (16 ounces) shredded
  mozzarella cheese
1 cup ricotta cheese
1 teaspoon salt
¼ teaspoon ground black pepper
1 egg yolk
1 tablespoon water

  Red liquid food coloring to garnish

Preheat oven to 375 degrees. For crust, sift flour and salt together in a medium bowl. Using a pastry blender or 2 knives, cut butter into flour mixture until mixture resembles coarse meal. Sprinkle ice water over dough, mixing quickly just until dough forms a soft ball. On a lightly floured surface, use a floured rolling pin to roll out ⅔ of dough into a 16-inch-diameter circle. Press dough into a greased 9-inch springform pan. Do not trim edges of dough. Reserve remaining dough for top crust.

For filling, brown turkey and sausage in a large skillet. Drain well and transfer to a large mixing bowl. Stir in 5 eggs, spinach, cheeses, salt, and pepper. Spoon filling into springform pan. Fold edge of crust over filling. For top crust, roll out remaining dough to ¼-inch thickness. Cut out a 9-inch-diameter circle. Mix egg yolk with water in a small bowl; brush on edge of bottom crust. Place top crust over filling and brush yolk mixture over entire top.

To garnish, cut holly leaves from dough scraps and arrange on top of pie. Add 1 teaspoon red food coloring to about 2 tablespoons dough scraps. Form small balls and place in center of holly leaves. Brush garnish with yolk mixture. Bake 1 hour 15 minutes. Cool 10 minutes in pan; remove sides of pan.
Yield: 10 to 12 servings

Dusted with confectioners sugar, Raisin-Eggnog French Toast is a traditional treat with new holiday style.

RAISIN-EGGNOG FRENCH TOAST

12 slices raisin bread, dry and firm
2 cups prepared eggnog
½ cup butter or margarine

  Confectioners sugar to serve

Cut bread into 1-inch-wide strips, trimming crusts from any long edges of strips. Pour eggnog into a shallow bowl and dip each strip of bread into eggnog, turning each strip over to coat well. Melt butter in a skillet over medium heat. Cook strips of bread on both sides until golden brown. Sprinkle with confectioners sugar to serve.
Yield: about 12 servings

CHOCOLATE-SOUR CREAM COFFEE CAKE

CAKE

- 1 cup butter or margarine, softened
- 2 cups granulated sugar
- 2 eggs
- 2 cups all-purpose flour
- 1 1/2 teaspoons baking powder
- 1/2 teaspoon salt
- 1 cup sour cream
- 1/2 teaspoon vanilla extract

TOPPING

- 1 cup chopped pecans
- 2 tablespoons granulated sugar
- 1 teaspoon ground cinnamon

CHOCOLATE GLAZE

- 1/2 cup semisweet chocolate chips
- 1/4 cup butter or margarine

Preheat oven to 350 degrees. For cake, cream butter and sugar in a large bowl until fluffy. Add eggs, beating until smooth. In a medium bowl, combine flour, baking powder, and salt. Gradually add dry ingredients to creamed mixture, blending well. Gently fold in sour cream and vanilla.

For topping, combine pecans, sugar, and cinnamon in a small bowl.

For chocolate glaze, melt chocolate chips and butter in a small saucepan over low heat, stirring until smooth. Sprinkle 2 tablespoons topping in bottom of greased and floured 9-inch tube pan. Spoon half of cake batter into pan. Sprinkle 4 tablespoons topping over batter and drizzle half of glaze over topping. Spoon remaining batter into pan and sprinkle with remaining topping. Reserve remaining glaze. Bake 1 to 1 1/4 hours or until a toothpick inserted in center of cake comes out clean. Cool in pan. Transfer to a serving plate. Reheat remaining glaze and drizzle over cake.

Yield: about 16 servings

Layered with a yummy streusel and chocolate filling, this Chocolate-Sour Cream Coffee Cake is indescribably delicious.

Sherried Fruit Cobbler *(left)* is a mouth-watering mixture of apples, pineapple, peaches, pears, and apricots with brown sugar and sherry. The Cheesy Garden Casserole features a creamy medley of vegetables, eggs, and cheese beneath a layer of toasted bread crumbs.

SHERRIED FRUIT COBBLER

COBBLER
1 can (16 ounces) peach halves, drained
1 can (16 ounces) pear halves, drained
1 can (16 ounces) apricot halves, drained
1 can (15 1/2 ounces) sliced pineapple, drained
1 jar (6 ounces) maraschino cherries, drained
1 can (21 ounces) apple pie filling
1/2 cup butter
1/2 cup firmly packed brown sugar
2 tablespoons all-purpose flour
1 teaspoon ground cinnamon
1/2 teaspoon ground nutmeg
1/4 teaspoon ground allspice
1 cup cooking sherry

TOPPING
1/4 cup butter
1 cup graham cracker crumbs

For cobbler, arrange drained fruit and pie filling in a 3-quart casserole dish. Melt butter in a medium saucepan over low heat. Stir in the next 5 ingredients. Stirring constantly, slowly add sherry and cook over medium heat until thickened. Pour over fruit. Cover and chill 8 hours or overnight.

Allow cobbler to come to room temperature. Preheat oven to 350 degrees and bake 20 to 25 minutes or until bubbly.

For topping, melt butter in a small saucepan and stir in graham cracker crumbs. Spread crumbs evenly over cobbler and bake 5 minutes longer or until crumbs are dark brown.
Yield: about 10 servings

CHEESY GARDEN CASSEROLE

1 cup diced potato (about 1 medium potato)
1 cup diced zucchini squash (about 1 medium squash)
1 cup diced carrots (about 3 medium carrots)
1/2 cup diced onion (about 1 medium onion)
1 cup water
1/4 cup all-purpose flour
2 cups milk
1/2 cup butter or margarine, divided
1 teaspoon salt
1/4 teaspoon celery seed
1/4 teaspoon ground black pepper
4 hard-cooked eggs, thinly sliced
1/2 cup shredded sharp Cheddar cheese
1/4 cup plain bread crumbs

Preheat oven to 400 degrees. In a large skillet, cook potato, squash, carrots, and onion in water over medium-high heat until soft; drain. Reduce heat to medium and return vegetables to skillet. Sprinkle flour over vegetables; stir to blend. Add milk, 1/4 cup butter, salt, celery seed, and pepper. Cook 10 to 15 minutes, stirring occasionally, until thickened. Pour half of vegetable mixture into a greased 9-inch glass pie plate. Top with sliced eggs and pour remaining vegetable mixture over eggs. Sprinkle cheese over vegetable mixture. Melt remaining 1/4 cup butter in a small saucepan and stir in bread crumbs. Sprinkle bread crumbs evenly over cheese. Bake 15 to 20 minutes or until cheese is bubbly.
Yield: 8 to 10 servings

Note: Casserole may be assembled 1 day in advance. Cover unbaked casserole and refrigerate. If refrigerated, bake uncovered 25 to 30 minutes or until cheese is bubbly.

These delicious Pecan Biscuits *(top)* are easy to prepare with packaged baking mix. Chock-full of cheese and bacon, savory Quiche Muffins make nifty little breakfast tidbits.

PECAN BISCUITS

2¹/₂ cups biscuit baking mix
¹/₂ cup chopped pecans
1 cup whipping cream
2 tablespoons butter or margarine, melted

Preheat oven to 450 degrees. In a large bowl, combine baking mix and pecans. Add cream and stir just until a soft dough forms. On a lightly floured surface, use a floured rolling pin to roll out dough to ¹/₂-inch thickness. Use a floured 2-inch biscuit cutter to cut out dough. Transfer biscuits to a greased baking sheet and brush tops with melted butter. Bake 7 to 10 minutes or until light brown.
Yield: about 2 dozen biscuits

QUICHE MUFFINS

1 container (16 ounces) cottage cheese
3 egg whites
5 eggs
¹/₄ cup buttermilk
¹/₄ cup all-purpose flour
1 teaspoon baking powder
¹/₄ teaspoon salt
2 cups (8 ounces) shredded sharp Cheddar cheese
10 slices bacon, cooked and crumbled
2 green onions, chopped

Preheat oven to 400 degrees. Place cottage cheese in a food processor fitted with a steel blade and process until smooth. Transfer to a large bowl. Process egg whites in food processor until foamy. Add next 5 ingredients and process until smooth. Add egg mixture to cottage cheese. Stir in Cheddar cheese, bacon, and onions. Fill greased large muffin tins ²/₃ full and bake 12 to 15 minutes or until edges are lightly browned.
Yield: about 10 muffins

11

BRUNCH EGGS

1/2	cup butter, divided
1	cup minced green onions, including tops
1/4	cup all-purpose flour
2 1/2	cups milk
1	cup (4 ounces) shredded Cheddar cheese
1/4	cup sherry
3/4	teaspoon seasoned salt
1/2	teaspoon dry mustard
1/4	teaspoon curry powder
1/4	teaspoon ground white pepper
1/4	teaspoon cayenne pepper
18	eggs
1	cup water
2	tablespoons vegetable oil
	Salt and ground black pepper
1/2	cup chopped green onions, including tops

In a saucepan, melt 1/4 cup butter. Add 1 cup minced green onions and sauté until soft. Remove from heat and blend in flour. Stirring slowly, cook over medium heat 2 minutes. Remove from heat; gradually stir in milk. Return to heat and cook until thickened. Add cheese and stir. Remove from heat; add sherry, seasoned salt, dry mustard, curry powder, white pepper, and cayenne pepper. Cool.

Beat eggs with water. Scramble eggs in remaining 1/4 cup butter and oil in a large skillet until barely set. Salt and pepper to taste. Butter two 2-quart casseroles. Pour a small amount of sauce into bottom of each casserole. Spoon scrambled eggs into casseroles and cover with remainder of sauce. Cover and bake in a preheated 275-degree oven 1 hour. Sprinkle with chopped green onions.
Yield: about 12 servings

GOLDEN BREAKFAST PUNCH

2	tea bags
2	cups boiling water
3	cups freshly squeezed orange juice
2	cups freshly squeezed lemon juice
1 1/2	to 2 cups granulated sugar
1	quart dry white wine
1	cup vodka

Place tea bags in boiling water and steep 5 minutes. Remove tea bags. Add juices and sugar; stir until sugar is dissolved. Cool. Stir in wine and vodka; chill. Serve over ice ring in punch bowl or in glasses filled with ice.
Yield: about 3 quarts punch

TOMATOES STUFFED WITH SPINACH AND ARTICHOKES

6	large tomatoes
1/2	cup chopped green onions, including tops
1/2	cup plus 3 tablespoons butter or margarine, divided
2	packages (10 ounces each) frozen chopped spinach
	Salt
1	can (14 ounces) artichoke hearts, drained and chopped
1	cup sour cream
1	teaspoon Worcestershire sauce
3	drops hot pepper sauce
3/4	cup grated Parmesan cheese, divided

Wash tomatoes, remove stems, and scoop out seeds; turn upside down to drain.

In a large skillet, sauté onions in 1/2 cup butter. Cook spinach according to package directions; lightly salt and drain. Add spinach, artichoke hearts, sour cream, Worcestershire sauce, and pepper sauce to onions. Stir in 1/2 cup cheese. Stuff tomatoes with spinach mixture and sprinkle with remaining 1/4 cup cheese; dot with remaining 3 tablespoons butter. Bake in a preheated 350-degree oven 20 minutes or until thoroughly heated.
Yield: about 6 servings

BROCCOLI ROULADE WITH HAM

CREAMED HAM

3	tablespoons butter
3	tablespoons all-purpose flour
3/4	cup chicken broth
2	tablespoons sherry
1	teaspoon Dijon-style mustard
	Salt and ground black pepper
1/2	cup half and half
1 1/2	cups diced boiled or baked ham
1	can (4 ounces) sliced mushrooms, drained

BROCCOLI ROULADE

4	packages (10 ounces each) frozen chopped broccoli
1/2	cup dry bread crumbs
6	tablespoons butter, melted
	Pinch of ground nutmeg
	Salt and ground black pepper
4	eggs, separated
8	tablespoons grated Parmesan cheese, divided

For creamed ham, melt butter in a medium saucepan. Remove from heat and add flour. Stirring slowly, cook over medium heat 2 minutes. Remove from heat; gradually stir in broth, sherry, and mustard. Salt and pepper to taste. Return to heat and cook until mixture thickens. Add half and half, ham, and mushrooms; continue cooking until thoroughly heated. Keep warm while preparing broccoli roulade.

For broccoli roulade, cook broccoli according to package directions; drain. Cool and finely chop. Butter a 10 1/2 x 15 1/2 x 1-inch jellyroll pan and line with waxed paper. Butter waxed paper well and sprinkle with bread crumbs. In a large mixing bowl, combine broccoli, melted butter, and nutmeg; salt and pepper to taste. Beat in egg yolks, one at a time, blending thoroughly after each addition. Beat egg whites until soft peaks form; fold into broccoli mixture. Turn into prepared pan and smooth top. Sprinkle with 4 tablespoons cheese. Bake in a preheated 350-degree oven 12 to 16 minutes or until center feels barely firm when touched.

Place a sheet of buttered waxed paper over the top of the broccoli mixture and invert onto a large baking sheet. Carefully peel away waxed paper. Spread creamed ham over broccoli mixture. Beginning with one long side, gently roll up broccoli mixture. Sprinkle with remaining 4 tablespoons cheese.
Yield: about 12 servings

(Top) Our spirited Golden Breakfast Punch is a tangy combination of tea and freshly squeezed fruit juices. Keep it frosty cold with a colorful ice ring made with kumquats and herbs, then serve it in canning jars to bring an authentic country touch to the table.

(Bottom) This hearty fare is designed to satisfy country-style appetites: Brunch Eggs *(clockwise from top)*, Tomatoes Stuffed with Spinach and Artichokes, and Broccoli Roulade with Ham.

SWEET POTATO MUFFINS

2 cups all-purpose flour, sifted
2 teaspoons baking powder
1 teaspoon salt
$1/2$ teaspoon baking soda
$1 1/4$ teaspoons ground cinnamon
$1/2$ teaspoon ground nutmeg
1 cup cooked, mashed sweet potatoes
1 cup granulated sugar
$1/2$ cup milk
2 eggs
$1/4$ cup butter, melted
$3/4$ cup chopped pecans

Sift together flour, baking powder, salt, baking soda, cinnamon, and nutmeg; set aside. In a mixing bowl, combine sweet potatoes, sugar, milk, and eggs. Add dry ingredients and melted butter; mix until well blended. Stir in pecans. Fill greased muffin cups half full. Bake in a preheated 350-degree oven 20 minutes or until a toothpick inserted in center of muffin comes out clean.
Yield: about 24 muffins

SUGARED BACON

$1/2$ cup firmly packed light brown sugar
4 egg yolks
10 teaspoons Worcestershire sauce
5 teaspoons prepared mustard
20 thin slices bacon
2 cups fine bread crumbs

Beat brown sugar, egg yolks, Worcestershire sauce, and mustard until well blended. Dip bacon in mixture and roll in crumbs. Place bacon on a broiler pan. Bake in a preheated 250-degree oven 20 minutes or until brown and crispy.
Yield: 20 slices bacon

CRANBERRY BREAKFAST RINGS

2 packages dry yeast
$3 1/2$ to $4 1/2$ cups all-purpose flour, divided
$1 1/4$ cups granulated sugar, divided
1 teaspoon salt
1 cup milk
$1/2$ cup butter or margarine
$1/4$ cup water
2 eggs, beaten
1 teaspoon grated lemon rind
1 jar (14 ounces) cranberry-orange sauce, divided
1 cup chopped walnuts
2 teaspoons ground cinnamon
$1/2$ cup butter or margarine, melted and divided
Frosting (recipe follows)

In a large bowl, combine yeast, $1 1/4$ cups flour, $1/2$ cup sugar, and salt. Set aside.
In a saucepan, combine milk, $1/2$ cup butter, and water; heat until warm. Add to dry ingredients and beat until smooth. Add eggs and $1 1/4$ cups flour, beating again until mixed. Stir in remaining flour and lemon rind. Cover and refrigerate until ready to shape rings.
To make rings, turn dough onto a lightly floured surface and divide in half. Use a floured rolling pin to roll out half of dough into a 14 x 7-inch rectangle. Spread half of cranberry-orange sauce over dough. Combine remaining $3/4$ cup sugar, walnuts, and cinnamon; sprinkle half of mixture over dough. Drizzle with $1/4$ cup melted butter. Beginning with one long side, roll up dough and seal edges. With seam edge down, place dough in a circle on a greased baking sheet. Press ends together to seal. Cut slits two-thirds of the way through ring at 1-inch intervals. Repeat process with remaining half of dough. Cover rings and let rise in a warm place until doubled in size (about 1 hour).
Bake in a preheated 375-degree oven 20 to 25 minutes or until bread sounds hollow when tapped. Frost if desired.
Yield: 2 breakfast rings

FROSTING
1 cup confectioners sugar
2 tablespoons warm milk
$1/2$ teaspoon vanilla extract

Mix all ingredients until smooth; drizzle over rings.

PUMPKIN YEAST BISCUITS

We filled our biscuits with slivers of smoked turkey. You could also use country ham or thin sausage patties.

2 packages dry yeast
$1/2$ teaspoon granulated sugar
$1/2$ cup warm water
1 cup milk, scalded and cooled
1 cup canned pumpkin
1 cup firmly packed light brown sugar
$1/2$ cup butter, melted
6 to 7 cups all-purpose flour
2 teaspoons salt
2 teaspoons pumpkin pie spice
1 teaspoon ground ginger

Dissolve yeast and granulated sugar in warm water. Let stand until bubbly.
In a large mixing bowl, combine yeast mixture, milk, pumpkin, brown sugar, and melted butter. Add flour, salt, pumpkin pie spice, and ginger. Stir until a soft dough forms. Knead on a floured surface until dough is smooth and elastic (about 10 to 12 minutes). Place dough in a greased bowl, turning once to coat. Cover and let rise until doubled in size (about 2 to 3 hours).
On a lightly floured surface, use a floured rolling pin to roll out dough to $1/2$-inch thickness. Cut out biscuits with a floured $1 1/2$-inch biscuit cutter. Place biscuits close together on a greased baking sheet. Cover and let rise until doubled in size (about 1 hour).
Bake in a preheated 350-degree oven 25 minutes or until golden brown.
Yield: about 50 biscuits

A delicious Cranberry Breakfast Ring adds a festive touch to the table. For munching, there are Sweet Potato Muffins *(in tin)*, Pumpkin Yeast Biscuits filled with slices of smoked turkey, and crispy strips of Sugared Bacon *(not shown)*.

(Left) Orange Ambrosia with Holiday Wine Sauce adds heavenly flavor to a meal. *(Right)* Spicy Gingerbread is a luscious ending for a holiday party. When you bake this dessert in a ring mold, you can serve the ice cream from a crock placed inside the ring.

ORANGE AMBROSIA WITH HOLIDAY WINE SAUCE

10 to 12 oranges, peeled and sliced
 1 cup shredded coconut, lightly toasted
 2 packages (4 ounces each) instant vanilla pudding mix
1 1/3 cups milk
 1 cup freshly squeezed orange juice, chilled
 1/2 cup sherry
 1 cup whipping cream, whipped
Grated rind of 1 orange

Layer orange slices and coconut in a large serving bowl. Combine pudding mix, milk, orange juice, and sherry. Beat until smooth. Set aside 5 minutes. Fold whipped cream and orange rind into pudding mixture. Sauce may be poured over fruit mixture or served in a separate bowl.
Yield: about 12 servings

SPICY GINGERBREAD

 1/2 cup vegetable shortening
 1/2 cup granulated sugar
 1 egg
2 1/2 cups all-purpose flour
 1 teaspoon baking powder
 1 teaspoon ground ginger
 1 teaspoon ground allspice
 1 teaspoon ground cloves
 1 teaspoon ground cinnamon
 1/2 teaspoon salt
 1 cup molasses
 1 cup boiling water
 2 tablespoons grated orange rind

Lemon custard ice cream to serve

In a large mixing bowl, cream shortening and sugar until well blended. Add egg and beat. Sift flour, baking powder, ginger, allspice, cloves, cinnamon, and salt; add to creamed mixture, blending well. Add molasses, water, and orange rind; stir just enough to blend ingredients. Pour into a greased and floured 10-inch ring mold or a 9 x 13-inch baking pan. Bake in a preheated 375-degree oven 30 minutes. Cool before unmolding. Serve with lemon custard ice cream.
Yield: about 12 servings

CANDIED PINEAPPLE COOKIES

- ½ cup butter or margarine
- ⅓ cup firmly packed brown sugar
- ¼ cup apple juice
- 2 tablespoons molasses
- 2 cups all-purpose flour
- 2 teaspoons ground cinnamon
- ½ teaspoon baking soda
- 1 package (4 ounces) candied pineapple, finely chopped
- ½ cup chopped walnuts

Preheat oven to 350 degrees. In a large bowl, cream butter and brown sugar until fluffy. Add apple juice and molasses, beating until smooth. In a medium bowl, sift together flour, cinnamon, and baking soda. Stir dry ingredients into creamed mixture. Stir in candied pineapple and walnuts. Shape dough into a ball, cover, and refrigerate 1 hour.

On a lightly floured surface, use a floured rolling pin to roll out dough to ¾-inch thickness. Use a floured 1-inch biscuit cutter to cut out dough. Transfer cookies to a greased baking sheet. Bake 12 to 15 minutes or until light brown.
Yield: about 4 dozen cookies

CHILLED ASPARAGUS MOUSSE

- ¼ cup butter or margarine
- ¼ cup all-purpose flour
- 1½ cups milk, warmed
- ½ cup whipping cream, warmed
- ¼ cup water
- 1 envelope unflavored gelatin
- 1 tablespoon Dijon-style mustard
- 1 teaspoon dried dill weed
- 1 teaspoon salt
- 1 teaspoon lemon juice
- ½ teaspoon ground black pepper
- 2 packages (8 ounces each) frozen asparagus spears, thawed and drained well

Large tomato to garnish

Melt butter in a medium saucepan over medium heat; stir in flour. Cook about 2 minutes or until light brown. Add milk and cream, stirring constantly until sauce is thick and smooth. Remove from heat. In a small saucepan, combine water and gelatin over low heat, stirring until gelatin is dissolved. Stir gelatin mixture, mustard, dill weed, salt, lemon juice, and pepper into sauce. Using a food processor fitted with a steel blade, process asparagus until finely chopped. Stir asparagus into sauce. Pour mixture into a greased 2-quart mold. Chill overnight.

To remove from mold, dip in hot water up to rim of mold and invert onto a serving plate.

For tomato rose garnish, remove peel from tomato in 1-inch-wide strips. Roll 1 piece of peel into a cone shape, then surround with another piece. Continue with remaining pieces of peel until rose is desired size. Secure with a toothpick and place on top of mousse.
Yield: 12 to 14 servings

SUNRISE MIMOSAS

- 2½ cups cranberry juice
- 1½ cups orange juice
- ¾ cup vodka

Orange slices to garnish

Pour cranberry juice, orange juice, and vodka into a blender and mix. Pour over ice cubes. Garnish with an orange slice on rim of each glass.
Yield: 5 to 6 servings

Sunrise Mimosas *(from left)* are an eye-opening blend of orange and cranberry juices spiked with vodka, and Candied Pineapple Cookies are loaded with fruit and nuts. Elegant Chilled Asparagus Mousse is enhanced with a hint of dill.

SANTA'S SWEETSHOP

*Y*ummy homemade confections always add sweet fun to the holiday season. As Christmas draws closer, youngsters and the young at heart all eagerly await the sampling of delicious treats fresh from the kitchen. Our assortment of cookies and candies is so tempting and luscious, you'll think we borrowed the recipes from Santa's own sweetshop at the North Pole. These scrumptious goodies will surely become Yuletide favorites!

Cut in the shape of trees and coated with colorful icing, these buttery Christmas Lemon Cookies have lots of holiday appeal. Silvery dragées make pretty "ornaments" for the trees.

CHRISTMAS LEMON COOKIES

COOKIES

- 1 cup butter or margarine, softened
- 1/2 cup granulated sugar
- 1 teaspoon grated dried lemon peel
- 2 1/2 cups all-purpose flour

ICING

- 2 1/4 cups confectioners sugar
- 5 tablespoons milk
  Red and green paste food coloring

  Dragées to decorate

For cookies, cream butter, sugar, and lemon peel in a large bowl until fluffy. Stir in flour; knead dough until a soft ball forms. Cover and chill 30 minutes.

Preheat oven to 300 degrees. On a lightly floured surface, use a floured rolling pin to roll out dough to 1/4-inch thickness. Use a tree-shaped cookie cutter to cut out dough. Transfer cookies to a greased baking sheet. Bake 20 to 25 minutes or until cookies are light brown. Cool on wire rack.

For icing, mix confectioners sugar and milk together in a medium bowl (icing will be thin). Divide icing evenly into 3 small bowls. Tint 1 bowl red, 1 bowl green, and leave 1 bowl white. Pour icing over tops of cookies, smoothing with a spatula. Decorate with dragées. Allow icing to harden. Store in an airtight container.
Yield: about 3 dozen 5-inch cookies

BUTTER PECAN COOKIES

- 1/2 cup plus 2 tablespoons butter, softened and divided
- 1 1/2 cups coarsely chopped pecans
- 1/2 cup granulated sugar, divided
- 6 tablespoons firmly packed brown sugar
- 1 egg
- 1/2 teaspoon vanilla extract
- 1 1/2 cups all-purpose flour
- 1/2 teaspoon baking soda
- 1/2 teaspoon salt

Preheat oven to 375 degrees. In a large skillet, melt 2 tablespoons butter over medium heat. Stir in pecans and cook 10 to 15 minutes or until nuts are dark brown. Remove from heat and stir in 2 tablespoons granulated sugar. Cool to room temperature.

Cream remaining 1/2 cup butter, remaining 6 tablespoons granulated sugar, and brown sugar in a large bowl until fluffy. Beat in egg and vanilla. Sift next 3 ingredients into a small bowl. Add dry ingredients to creamed mixture, stirring until a soft dough forms. Fold in pecans. Drop by tablespoonfuls onto a greased baking sheet. Bake 8 to 10 minutes or until edges are brown. Cool on wire rack. Store in an airtight container.
Yield: about 2 dozen cookies

Sent special delivery from the North Pole, brown-sugary Butter Pecan Cookies are packed with nuts.

Kids of all ages will love these goodies: Lightly sweetened Christmas Honey Grahams are cut in holiday shapes, and Peanut Butter Crunch Balls are studded with colorful candies. Cashew Toffee is topped with semisweet chocolate.

CHRISTMAS HONEY GRAHAMS

1½ cups whole-wheat graham flour
1 cup all-purpose flour
½ cup vegetable shortening
⅓ cup firmly packed brown sugar
¼ cup honey
¼ cup vegetable oil
3 tablespoons cold water
1 teaspoon baking soda
1 teaspoon ground cinnamon
½ teaspoon salt

Combine all ingredients in a large bowl; knead dough until a soft ball forms. Cover and refrigerate 30 minutes.
Preheat oven to 425 degrees. On a lightly floured surface, use a floured rolling pin to roll out dough to ¼-inch thickness. Use desired cookie cutters to cut out dough. Transfer cookies to an ungreased baking sheet and prick with a fork. Bake 7 to 10 minutes or until golden brown. Cool on baking sheet (cookies will become crisp as they cool). Store in an airtight container.
Yield: about 1½ dozen 5-inch cookies

PEANUT BUTTER CRUNCH BALLS

4 cups miniature marshmallows
½ cup butter or margarine
½ cup smooth peanut butter
3 cups round toasted oat cereal
1 cup unsalted peanuts
1 cup red and green candy-coated chocolate pieces

In a medium saucepan, melt marshmallows, butter, and peanut butter over low heat, stirring constantly until smooth. Remove from heat. Cool 15 minutes.
In a large bowl, mix cereal, peanuts, and candy-coated chocolate pieces. Pour syrup over cereal mixture, stirring until evenly coated. Roll mixture into 2-inch balls and cool completely on waxed paper. Store in an airtight container.
Yield: about 3 dozen crunch balls

CASHEW TOFFEE

40 unsalted saltine crackers
1 cup butter or margarine
1 cup firmly packed brown sugar
2 cups chopped unsalted cashews
1 package (12 ounces) semisweet chocolate chips

Preheat oven to 400 degrees. Arrange a single layer of crackers with sides touching in the bottom of a foil-lined 11 x 17-inch shallow baking pan. In a small saucepan, combine butter and brown sugar over medium heat. Cook, stirring constantly, until syrup reaches hard ball stage (250 to 268 degrees). Remove from heat and stir in cashews. Pour syrup over crackers and bake 5 minutes. Remove from oven and sprinkle chocolate chips evenly over crackers. As chocolate melts, spread evenly over candy. Refrigerate 30 minutes or until candy hardens. Break candy into pieces. Store at room temperature in an airtight container.
Yield: about 1 pound of candy

These rich cookies offer old-fashioned goodness, especially when you serve them in quaint baskets, wooden bowls and trays, and napkin-lined grapevine wreaths: Clove Cookies *(clockwise from top left)*, Triple Chip Cookies, Caramel Graham Crackers, Date Bars, and Cream Cheese Preserve Cookies.

CLOVE COOKIES

- 1/2 cup butter or margarine, melted
- 1 cup granulated sugar
- 1 teaspoon vanilla extract
- 1 egg
- 1 cup all-purpose flour
- 1 teaspoon ground cloves

Stir butter and sugar together; add vanilla. Beat in egg until mixture is smooth. Stir flour and cloves together; blend with butter mixture. Drop teaspoonfuls of dough 2 inches apart onto lightly greased baking sheets. Bake in a preheated 350-degree oven 8 to 10 minutes or until lightly browned. Cool slightly before removing from baking sheets.
Yield: about 4 dozen cookies

DATE BARS

- 1 cup butter or margarine, softened
- 2 1/3 cups firmly packed dark brown sugar
- 3 eggs
- 1 1/2 teaspoons vanilla extract
- 3 cups all-purpose flour
- 1 teaspoon baking powder
- 1/2 teaspoon baking soda
- 3 cups pitted dates, coarsely chopped
- 1 cup chopped pecans

Cream butter and brown sugar until light and fluffy. Beat in eggs, one at a time. Stir in vanilla. Combine flour, baking powder, and baking soda; gradually add to creamed mixture. Stir in dates and pecans. Spread batter in a greased 13 x 9 x 2-inch baking pan. Bake in a preheated 375-degree oven 25 minutes. Cool in pan and cut into bars.
Yield: about 2 dozen bars

CARAMEL GRAHAM CRACKERS

- 24 2 1/2-inch cinnamon graham cracker squares
- 1/2 cup margarine
- 1/2 cup butter
- 1 cup firmly packed light brown sugar
- 1 cup chopped pecans

Line a 15 1/2 x 10 1/2 x 1-inch jellyroll pan with foil; cover with single layer of graham crackers. Mix margarine, butter, and brown sugar in a saucepan; bring to a boil and cook 2 minutes. Pour mixture over crackers; sprinkle pecans on top. Bake in a preheated 350-degree oven 12 minutes. Cut into triangles while warm.
Yield: about 4 dozen cookies

CREAM CHEESE PRESERVE COOKIES

- 1 package (8 ounces) cream cheese, softened
- 1 cup unsalted butter, softened
- 2 cups all-purpose flour
  Grated rind of 1/2 lemon **or** dash of lemon juice
  Blackberry, apricot, and strawberry preserves

Beat cream cheese and butter together until well blended. Add flour and lemon rind; mix well. Shape into four balls of equal size; wrap in plastic wrap and refrigerate until firm.

Roll out one ball at a time between two sheets of plastic wrap to 1/4-inch thickness. Cut out with 2 1/2-inch round scalloped-edge cookie cutter. Place cookies on ungreased baking sheets. On one half of each cookie, use a 1-inch-wide heart-shaped cookie cutter to cut out heart 1/4 inch from edge (refer to photo on facing page). Place a small amount of preserves on the other half of each cookie. Fold each cookie in half and press edges together. Bake in a preheated 375-degree oven 15 to 20 minutes or until slightly puffed and just beginning to brown. Cool slightly before removing from baking sheets.
Yield: about 4 dozen cookies

TRIPLE CHIP COOKIES

- 1 cup butter or margarine, softened
- 1 1/2 cups firmly packed light brown sugar
- 1/2 cup granulated sugar
- 2 eggs
- 2 teaspoons vanilla extract
- 2 cups all-purpose flour
- 1 teaspoon baking soda
- 1/2 teaspoon baking powder
- 1/2 teaspoon salt
- 1 1/2 cups semisweet chocolate chips
- 1 cup peanut butter chips
- 3/4 cup butterscotch chips

Cream butter and sugars. Beat in eggs and vanilla. Combine flour, baking soda, baking powder, and salt; gradually add to creamed mixture. Stir in chips. Drop heaping teaspoonfuls of dough onto greased baking sheets. Bake in a preheated 350-degree oven 10 to 12 minutes or just until done. Do not overbake.
Yield: about 6 dozen cookies

Date Pinwheels are easy-to-make refrigerator cookies that have all the good, spicy flavor of Grandma's traditional version.

DATE PINWHEELS

- 1/2 cup butter or margarine, softened
- 1 cup firmly packed brown sugar
- 1 egg
- 1 1/2 teaspoons vanilla extract
- 2 cups all-purpose flour
- 1/2 teaspoon baking soda
- 1/2 teaspoon salt
- 1/2 teaspoon ground cinnamon
- 1/4 teaspoon ground nutmeg
- 1 package (8 ounces) chopped dates
- 1/2 cup water
- 1/4 cup granulated sugar
- 1/4 teaspoon ground cinnamon

In a large bowl, cream butter, brown sugar, egg, and vanilla. In a separate bowl, combine flour, baking soda, salt, 1/2 teaspoon cinnamon, and nutmeg. Stir flour mixture into creamed mixture. Cover and refrigerate dough at least 2 hours or until well chilled.

In a saucepan, combine dates, water, granulated sugar, and 1/4 teaspoon cinnamon over low heat. Cook, stirring constantly, until thickened; cool.

Preheat oven to 350 degrees. Divide dough into three equal parts. Roll each third of dough into a rectangle 8 x 10 inches and 1/4-inch thick. Spread one third of date mixture over each rectangle. Starting with one long end, roll up dough. Cut into 1/2-inch-thick slices. Place on lightly greased baking sheets. Bake 14 to 16 minutes or until lightly browned. Cool on wire racks.
Yield: about 5 dozen cookies

Santa will love these treats on Christmas Eve: Checkerboard Walnuts *(left)* are luscious bites of coconut covered with vanilla or chocolate candy coating, and Raspberry Nut Bars have a jam filling.

CHECKERBOARD WALNUTS

    2 cups flaked coconut
  ¹/₂ cup granulated sugar
    2 tablespoons light corn syrup
  ¹/₈ teaspoon salt
    1 egg white
  ¹/₄ teaspoon coconut extract
   24 walnut halves
    4 ounces chocolate-flavored
       almond bark
    4 ounces vanilla-flavored
       almond bark

In a large saucepan, combine coconut, sugar, corn syrup, and salt. Cook over medium heat, stirring constantly, 5 to 6 minutes or until candy thickens and coconut is light brown. Whisk egg white in a small bowl until foamy. Add egg white to coconut mixture. Stirring constantly, cook 5 to 6 minutes longer or until mixture becomes stiff and very sticky. Remove from heat and stir in coconut extract. Cool to room temperature.

Dip fingers in cold water and shape coconut mixture into 1-inch balls. Place on waxed paper; press 1 walnut half on top of each coconut ball. Refrigerate 1 hour or until firm.

Melt chocolate and vanilla almond bark in separate small saucepans following package directions. Dip bottom half of each candy in chocolate or vanilla bark, completely covering coconut. Return to waxed paper and cool completely. Store at room temperature in an airtight container.
Yield: about 2 dozen candies

RASPBERRY NUT BARS

  1¹/₂ cups butter or margarine,
         softened
      2 cups granulated sugar
      2 egg yolks
      1 teaspoon vanilla extract
      4 cups all-purpose flour
  1¹/₃ cups finely chopped pecans
      1 jar (12 ounces) raspberry
         preserves

Preheat oven to 350 degrees. In a large bowl, cream butter and sugar until fluffy. Beat in egg yolks and vanilla. Mix in flour and pecans, stirring until a soft dough forms. Divide dough in half. Press half of dough into a greased 9 x 13-inch glass baking dish. Spread preserves evenly over dough. Place remaining dough on a sheet of waxed paper. Dust with flour and use a floured rolling pin to roll out dough to a 9 x 13-inch rectangle. Place dough over preserves, patching if necessary to completely cover preserves. Bake 40 to 45 minutes or until golden brown. Cool completely in dish. Cut into 1 x 3-inch bars. Store in an airtight container.
Yield: about 3 dozen bars

HAZELNUT LACE COOKIES

- ½ cup butter or margarine, softened
- ½ cup firmly packed brown sugar
- 2 tablespoons dark rum, divided
- 2 tablespoons whipping cream
- ⅓ cup semisweet chocolate chips
- ¼ cup all-purpose flour
- ¼ teaspoon salt
- ⅛ teaspoon baking soda
- 1 cup quick-cooking oats
- ½ cup flaked coconut
- ½ cup finely chopped hazelnuts

  Purchased tube red decorating icing

Preheat oven to 350 degrees. In a large bowl, cream butter and brown sugar until fluffy. Beat in 1 tablespoon rum. In a small saucepan, heat cream to boiling over medium heat. Reduce heat to medium-low. Stir in remaining rum and simmer 2 to 3 minutes. Remove from heat; add chocolate chips and stir until mixture is smooth. Beat chocolate mixture into creamed mixture until smooth. In a large bowl, sift flour, salt, and baking soda together. Stir dry ingredients into chocolate mixture. Fold in oats, coconut, and hazelnuts. Drop batter by rounded teaspoonfuls 4 inches apart onto a greased baking sheet. Use fingers to press each cookie into a 2-inch circle. Bake 8 minutes (cookies will be soft). Remove from oven and cool on pan 5 minutes. Cool completely on a wire rack. Decorate with icing. Allow icing to harden. Store in an airtight container.
Yield: about 3½ dozen cookies

MACADAMIA NUT TARTS

CRUST
- 1½ cups butter or margarine, softened
- ⅔ cup granulated sugar
- 2½ teaspoons grated dried lemon peel
- 3 cups all-purpose flour
- ½ cup cornstarch
- ½ teaspoon salt

TOPPING
- ½ cup plus 2 tablespoons butter or margarine
- ½ cup firmly packed brown sugar
- ⅓ cup honey
- 3 cups macadamia nuts
- 2½ tablespoons whipping cream

Preheat oven to 350 degrees. For crust, cream butter, sugar, and lemon peel in a large bowl until fluffy. In a medium bowl, sift together next 3 ingredients. Stir dry ingredients into creamed mixture, mixing just until dough is crumbly. On a lightly floured surface, use a floured rolling pin to roll out dough to ¼-inch thickness. Use a 3-inch biscuit cutter to cut out dough. Transfer dough to greased 2½-inch-diameter tart pans. Prick with a fork. Bake 16 to 18 minutes or until light brown. Cool in pan 10 minutes; turn onto a wire rack to cool completely.

A hint of rum makes these delicate Hazelnut Lace Cookies *(top)* extra special. Macadamia Nut Tarts feature caramel-coated nuts heaped in pastry shells.

For topping, combine first 3 ingredients in a medium saucepan. Stir constantly over medium-high heat until mixture comes to a boil. Boil 1 minute, without stirring, until mixture thickens and large bubbles begin to form. Remove from heat; stir in nuts and cream. Spoon about 2 tablespoons mixture into each tart crust. Cool completely.
Yield: about 20 tarts

APPLE SPICE COOKIES

     1   cup vegetable shortening
 2 1/2   cups granulated sugar
     1   cup dark molasses
 4 1/2   cups all-purpose flour
     2   tablespoons baking soda
     2   teaspoons salt
 1 1/2   teaspoons ground cinnamon
     1   teaspoon ground cloves
     1   teaspoon ground ginger
   1/2   teaspoon ground nutmeg
   1/2   cup milk
         Granulated sugar
         Apple jelly

Preheat oven to 350 degrees. Cream shortening and sugar until fluffy. Add molasses and blend well. In a medium bowl, combine flour, baking soda, salt, cinnamon, cloves, ginger, and nutmeg. Alternately stir dry ingredients and milk into creamed mixture, blending well after each addition. Shape dough into 1-inch balls. Roll balls in sugar and place on ungreased baking sheets. Make a small indentation with thumb in the top of each ball. Use a teaspoon to place a small amount of apple jelly in each indentation. Bake 8 to 10 minutes. Cookies will be very soft, but will harden as they cool. Remove from sheets and cool on wire racks.
Yield: about 7 dozen cookies

Baskets and antique cookware make interesting containers for serving fresh-baked cookies like these: Peanut Butter Surprises *(clockwise from top left)* are enhanced by the chocolaty goodness of chopped peanut butter cups. Apple Spice Cookies, baked with a dollop of apple jelly, are full of old-fashioned taste. Almond Fingers, dipped in chocolate and chopped almonds, are elegant and extra delicious. Raspberry preserves and chocolate chips make a scrumptious combination in Raspberry Thumbprint Cookies. Milk chocolate chips pair up with butterscotch chips to make terrific Chocolate Butter Brickle Bars.

CHOCOLATE BUTTER BRICKLE BARS

 1 1/2   cups all-purpose flour
   3/4   cup firmly packed brown sugar
   1/2   cup plus 2 tablespoons butter or
         margarine, softened and divided
   1/2   teaspoon salt, divided
     1   cup butterscotch chips
   1/4   cup light corn syrup
     1   tablespoon water
     1   cup chopped pecans
     1   cup milk chocolate chips

Preheat oven to 375 degrees. In a medium mixing bowl, combine flour, brown sugar, 1/2 cup butter, and 1/4 teaspoon salt. Press mixture into a 13 x 9 x 2-inch baking pan. Bake 10 minutes or until golden.

While crust is baking, combine butterscotch chips, corn syrup, remaining 2 tablespoons butter, water, and remaining 1/4 teaspoon salt in a small saucepan over low heat; stir until smooth. Remove from heat and stir in pecans. While crust is still warm, spread mixture over top of crust. Allow to cool completely.

Melt chocolate chips and spread over butterscotch layer. Chill 10 minutes or until chocolate is set. Cut into bars.
Yield: about 2 dozen bars

RASPBERRY THUMBPRINT COOKIES

   1/2   cup butter or margarine, softened
   1/4   cup firmly packed brown sugar
   1/4   cup granulated sugar
     1   teaspoon vanilla extract
   1/2   teaspoon salt
 1 1/2   cups all-purpose flour, sifted
     2   tablespoons milk
   1/3   cup miniature semisweet
         chocolate chips
         Raspberry preserves

Preheat oven to 375 degrees. In a medium mixing bowl, cream butter, sugars, vanilla, and salt until light and fluffy. Blend in flour and milk. Stir in chocolate chips. Shape dough into 1-inch balls and place on ungreased baking sheets. Make a small indentation with thumb in the top of each ball. Use a teaspoon to place a small amount of raspberry preserves in each indentation. Bake 10 to 12 minutes. Remove from sheets and cool on wire racks.
Yield: about 3 dozen cookies

PEANUT BUTTER SURPRISES

     1   cup butter or margarine, softened
     1   cup crunchy peanut butter
   3/4   cup firmly packed brown sugar
   3/4   cup granulated sugar
     2   eggs
 1 1/2   teaspoons vanilla extract
 2 1/2   cups all-purpose flour
     1   teaspoon baking powder
     1   teaspoon baking soda
   1/2   teaspoon salt
     2   cups coarsely chopped miniature
         peanut butter cups

Preheat oven to 350 degrees. Cream butter, peanut butter, sugars, eggs, and vanilla until fluffy. Sift flour, baking powder, baking soda, and salt together. Gradually stir dry ingredients into creamed mixture. Stir in chopped peanut butter cups. Drop by heaping teaspoonfuls onto ungreased baking sheets. Bake 12 to 15 minutes or until lightly browned. Remove from sheets and cool on wire racks.
Yield: about 5 dozen cookies

ALMOND FINGERS

     1   cup butter or margarine, softened
   1/2   cup firmly packed brown sugar
   1/2   cup granulated sugar
     1   egg yolk, lightly beaten
   1/2   teaspoon vanilla extract
   1/2   teaspoon almond extract
 2 1/4   cups all-purpose flour
     1   package (6 ounces) semisweet
         chocolate chips
     1   cup finely chopped almonds

Preheat oven to 350 degrees. Cream butter and sugars together until fluffy. Beat in egg yolk and extracts. Stir in flour. Shape teaspoonfuls of dough into 2-inch-long rolls. Place on lightly greased baking sheets. Bake 10 to 12 minutes or until very lightly browned around the edges. Remove from sheets and cool on wire racks.

Melt chocolate chips. Dip ends of each cookie 1/2 inch into melted chocolate. Roll ends in chopped almonds. Allow chocolate to harden.
Yield: about 5 dozen cookies

MARMALADE COOKIES

- 2 cups all-purpose flour
- 1 teaspoon baking powder
- 1 cup butter or margarine, chilled and cut into pieces
- 1 cup finely ground almonds
- 3/4 cup granulated sugar
- 2 tablespoons lemon juice
- 1/2 cup orange marmalade
- 6 ounces chocolate-flavored almond bark

Preheat oven to 375 degrees. In a large bowl, sift flour and baking powder together. With a pastry blender or 2 knives, cut butter into flour mixture until mixture resembles coarse meal. Stir in next 3 ingredients; knead dough until a soft ball forms. Cover and chill 1 hour.

On a lightly floured surface, use a floured rolling pin to roll out dough to 1/8-inch thickness. Use a 3-inch round cookie cutter to cut out 48 cookies. Transfer cookies to a greased baking sheet and bake 10 to 12 minutes or until lightly browned. Cool on baking sheet.

Spread marmalade on half the cookies; top with remaining cookies. In a small saucepan, melt almond bark following package directions. Dip half of each sandwich cookie into almond bark. Cool on waxed paper.

Yield: 2 dozen cookies

CHERRY CORDIAL FUDGE

- 3/4 cup milk
- 2 cups granulated sugar
- 2 ounces unsweetened baking chocolate
- 2 tablespoons light corn syrup
- 2 tablespoons butter or margarine, cut into small pieces
- 1 jar (6 ounces) maraschino cherries, drained and halved
- 2 teaspoons vanilla extract

In a medium saucepan, combine first 4 ingredients. Cook over medium heat, stirring constantly, until mixture is smooth and comes to a boil. Reduce heat to low, cover pan, and boil 2 to 3 minutes. Uncover and stir to blend ingredients. Continue to boil uncovered, without stirring, until syrup reaches soft ball stage (234 to 240 degrees). Remove from heat. Add butter; do not stir until syrup cools to 110 degrees. Add cherries and vanilla, stirring until mixture thickens and is no longer glossy. Pour into greased 8-inch square pan. Chill until firm; cut into 1-inch squares.

Yield: about 5 dozen pieces of fudge

Light up the season with these fruity delights: Spread with orange marmalade and dipped in chocolate, Marmalade Cookies *(in tin)* taste as good as they look. Tiny Apricot Foldovers have a sweet filling of dried fruit, and Cherry Cordial Fudge is a rich blend of chocolate and maraschino cherries.

APRICOT FOLDOVERS

FILLING
- 1 cup chopped dried apricots
- 1 cup firmly packed brown sugar
- 1/2 cup water
- 2 tablespoons all-purpose flour

PASTRY
- 2 1/2 cups all-purpose flour
- 1/2 teaspoon salt
- 3/4 cup plus 2 tablespoons butter or margarine, chilled and cut into pieces
- 1 package (3 ounces) cream cheese, cut into pieces
- 1/3 cup ice water

For filling, mix all ingredients together in a medium saucepan over medium heat and bring to a boil. Cook, stirring constantly, 8 to 10 minutes or until filling thickens. Cool completely.

Preheat oven to 350 degrees. For pastry, sift flour and salt together into a medium bowl. Using a pastry blender or 2 knives, cut butter and cream cheese into flour until mixture resembles coarse meal. Sprinkle ice water over dough, mixing quickly just until dough forms a soft ball. On a lightly floured surface, use a floured rolling pin to roll out dough into a 1/4-inch-thick rectangle. Use a pastry wheel to cut dough into 2-inch squares. Transfer dough to a greased baking sheet. Spoon about 1 teaspoon of filling into the center of each square. Fold dough in half diagonally over filling to form a triangle; use a fork to crimp edges together. Bake 15 to 20 minutes or until golden brown. Cool completely on a wire rack. Store in an airtight container.

Yield: about 4 dozen cookies

CHOCOLATE BRANDY DROPS

- 1 cup butter or margarine, softened
- 1 cup confectioners sugar
- ¹/₂ cup granulated sugar
- 1 cup semisweet chocolate chips, chilled
- 3 cups all-purpose flour
- 1¹/₂ cups brandy
- 1 cup finely chopped pecans

Preheat oven to 350 degrees. In a large bowl, cream butter and sugars until fluffy. In a food processor fitted with a steel blade, process chocolate chips until finely chopped. Add chocolate and remaining ingredients to creamed mixture, stirring until a soft dough forms. Drop by teaspoonfuls onto a greased baking sheet. Bake 12 to 15 minutes or until light brown. Cool completely on a wire rack. Store in an airtight container.

Yield: about 3 dozen cookies

SCOTCHIES

- 1 cup butter or margarine, softened
- 1 cup confectioners sugar
- 2¹/₂ cups all-purpose flour
- 6 tablespoons Scotch whiskey
- ¹/₂ cup butterscotch chips, chilled
- 1 cup finely chopped pecans
  Confectioners sugar

Preheat oven to 350 degrees. In a large bowl, cream butter and sugar until fluffy. Add flour and whiskey, stirring until a soft dough forms. In a food processor fitted with a steel blade, process butterscotch chips until finely chopped. Stir chopped chips and pecans into dough. Shape tablespoonfuls of dough into crescent shapes and place on a greased baking sheet. Bake 12 to 15 minutes or until lightly browned. Roll cookies in confectioners sugar immediately after removing from oven. Cool completely on a wire rack. Roll in confectioners sugar again.

Yield: about 4¹/₂ dozen cookies

CHOCOLATE-RAISIN TOFFEE

- 1 cup raisins
- ³/₄ cup butter
- 1 cup firmly packed brown sugar
- 1 cup semisweet chocolate chips

Spread raisins evenly on a greased 10¹/₂ x 15¹/₂-inch jellyroll pan. Melt butter and brown sugar in a medium saucepan. Cook over medium heat, stirring constantly, until syrup reaches hard crack stage (300 to 310 degrees). Pour syrup over raisins. Sprinkle with chocolate chips. As chocolate melts, spread evenly over raisins. Cool and cut into 1¹/₂-inch squares. Store at room temperature.

Yield: about 5 dozen pieces of candy

A creamy-crunchy combination, Chocolate-Raisin Toffee *(from left)* is sure to be a favorite any time of the year. Chocolate Brandy Drops will melt in your mouth, and crispy Scotchies are flavored with butterscotch and Scotch whiskey.

Lisa
Liz
Patty
Roberta
Anne
Jan
Susan
Judith
Vicki
Bob
Mike
Scott
Sandy
Ed
Leslie
Lynn
John
Kevin
Tammi
Sandra
Pat
Carol

Mark

Wayne

LOLLIPOPS

Crush pieces of same-color clear, hard candies. Preheat oven to 300 degrees. Place lightly oiled metal lollipop molds on a baking sheet, propping molds level with crumpled aluminum foil. Fill molds with crushed candy. Bake 10 minutes or until candy melts. Remove from oven and insert lollipop sticks into candies. Allow candies to cool. Gently press backs of molds to release candies.

WHITE CHOCOLATE FUDGE

3 cups granulated sugar
3/4 cup butter or margarine
2/3 cup half and half
12 ounces white chocolate
1 jar (7 ounces) marshmallow creme
1 cup coconut
1 cup chopped toasted almonds

Small pieces of candied red and green cherries to decorate

In a large heavy saucepan, combine sugar, butter, and half and half. Bring to a boil over medium heat, stirring constantly. Continue stirring and boil 5 minutes. Remove from heat. Add chocolate and stir until melted. Stir in remaining ingredients. Pour into a greased 13 x 9 x 2-inch pan; cool. Cut into squares. If desired, decorate with pieces of red and green cherries to resemble holly.
Yield: about 45 pieces of fudge

This selection was inspired by visions of Santa's sweetshop: Quick-and-easy Oriental Snack Mix *(from top left)* blends crunchy pretzels and chow mein noodles with golden raisins, peanuts, and vanilla baking chips. Decorated with "holly" made of candied cherries, White Chocolate Fudge is another delectable treat. Your friends will find it hard to believe that these Chocolate Billionaires are homemade! The adorable Santa-shaped Lollipops are easy to make with purchased candies. Colorful tissue paper makes festive wrappers for Honey Taffy, and Chocolate-Covered Cherries are wonderfully rich.

ORIENTAL SNACK MIX

2 cups small pretzels
1 1/2 cups golden raisins
1 cup chow mein noodles
1 cup salted peanuts
11 ounces vanilla baking chips
1 teaspoon vegetable shortening

In a large mixing bowl, combine pretzels, raisins, chow mein noodles, and peanuts. In a heavy medium saucepan, melt baking chips and shortening over low heat. Remove from heat and quickly stir into pretzel mixture. Spread mixture on a lightly greased baking sheet. Refrigerate 10 minutes or until set.
Break candy into bite-size pieces. Store in airtight container.
Yield: about 2 3/4 pounds of candy

CHOCOLATE-COVERED CHERRIES

3 1/2 cups confectioners sugar
1/4 cup butter or margarine, softened
3 tablespoons crème de cacao liqueur
1 tablespoon milk
1 tablespoon vanilla extract
About 60 maraschino cherries with stems, drained and patted dry
6 ounces semisweet chocolate chips **or** vanilla baking chips, divided
6 ounces chocolate- **or** vanilla-flavored candy coating, divided

In a large mixing bowl, combine confectioners sugar, butter, liqueur, milk, and vanilla; chill 1 hour. Mold a small amount of mixture around each cherry, being careful to completely enclose cherry with mixture. Place on baking sheet lined with waxed paper; chill 1 hour.
In the top of a double boiler over simmering water, melt half of desired chocolate and half of candy coating. Dip half of cherries in chocolate mixture and return to waxed paper. Melt remaining chocolate and candy coating; dip remaining cherries. Allow chocolate-covered cherries to sit at room temperature. Check bottoms of cherries and reseal with additional chocolate if necessary. If desired, drizzle tops of cherries with additional melted chocolate. Cover loosely and store in a cool place at least two days to form cordial (do not refrigerate). Store in airtight container.
Yield: about 5 dozen candies

HONEY TAFFY

3 cups granulated sugar
1 cup whipping cream
1 cup honey
1 tablespoon butter or margarine
1/8 teaspoon salt

Combine all ingredients in a large heavy saucepan. Bring to a boil over medium heat, stirring constantly. Continue stirring and cook until mixture reaches soft crack stage (270 degrees on a candy thermometer). Pour mixture onto a cool, buttered surface. Allow mixture to cool slightly (enough so that it can be handled comfortably). Pull taffy into ropes (color will lighten slightly). Break ropes into pieces about 2 inches long. Wrap each piece of candy in waxed paper and twist ends. If desired, wrap red and green tissue over waxed paper.
Yield: about 2 3/4 pounds of candy

CHOCOLATE BILLIONAIRES

1 package (14 ounces) caramels
3 tablespoons water
1 1/2 cups coarsely chopped pecans
1 cup coarsely crushed crisp rice cereal
18 ounces chocolate-flavored candy coating

In the top of a double boiler over simmering water, melt caramels with water. Remove from heat and stir in pecans and cereal. Drop by rounded teaspoonfuls onto lightly greased waxed paper. Chill until firm.
Melt candy coating in a heavy medium saucepan over low heat. Dip candies in candy coating; place on waxed paper and chill until set. Store in airtight container.
Yield: about 4 dozen candies

BIZCOCHITOS

- 1 cup butter or margarine, softened
- 1 cup granulated sugar, divided
- 1 egg yolk
- 1 tablespoon milk
- 2½ cups all-purpose flour
- 4½ teaspoons ground cinnamon, divided
- 2 teaspoons anise seed
- ½ cup white wine

In a large mixing bowl, cream butter, ½ cup sugar, egg yolk, and milk. In a medium bowl, combine flour, 1½ teaspoons cinnamon, and anise seed. Add flour mixture to creamed mixture, stirring until combined. Stir in wine. Wrap dough in plastic wrap and chill 2 hours.

Preheat oven to 350 degrees. On a lightly floured surface, use a floured rolling pin to roll out dough to ⅛-inch thickness. Cut into desired shapes using a 2-inch cookie cutter. Transfer cookies to lightly greased baking sheets and bake 10 to 12 minutes or until edges are very lightly browned.

In a small bowl, combine remaining ½ cup sugar and remaining 3 teaspoons of cinnamon. Coat warm cookies with sugar mixture. Store in airtight container.
Yield: about 8 dozen cookies

BELGIAN NUT COOKIES

- ¾ cup butter, softened
- ⅓ cup granulated sugar
- 1½ cups all-purpose flour
- 1½ cups ground toasted almonds
- 1 teaspoon vanilla extract
- ⅛ teaspoon salt
- 1 cup semisweet chocolate chips
- ½ cup raspberry jam

In a large mixing bowl, cream butter and sugar. Add flour, almonds, vanilla, and salt, stirring just until mixture is combined and forms a dough. Divide dough in half and wrap each half in plastic wrap. Refrigerate 1 hour.

Preheat oven to 350 degrees. Roll out dough to ⅛-inch thickness between two sheets of waxed paper. Remove top sheet of waxed paper. Using a 2½-inch-long fluted tart mold or cookie cutter, cut out dough. Place cookies on lightly greased baking sheet. Bake 10 to 12 minutes or until lightly browned around edges. Cool cookies on baking sheet.

Melt chocolate chips in the top of a double boiler over simmering water. Reserving ¼ cup of melted chocolate, spread a thin layer of chocolate on half of the cookies. Spread remaining half of cookies with a thin layer of raspberry jam. With one chocolate side and one raspberry side together, place two cookies together.

Choose one or all of these international treats to delight cookie lovers: Mexican Bizcochitos *(from left)* have a mild licorice flavor, Belgian Nut Cookies are filled with chocolate and raspberry jam, and French Madeleines are flavored with Grand Marnier liqueur.

Place cookies on waxed paper-lined baking sheet. Drizzle tops of cookies with reserved chocolate. Place cookies in refrigerator to set. Store cookies in airtight container in a cool, dry place.
Yield: about 2 dozen cookies

MADELEINES

- 2 eggs
- ⅛ teaspoon salt
- ½ cup granulated sugar
- ½ cup all-purpose flour
- ½ cup butter, melted and cooled
  Grand Marnier liqueur

Preheat oven to 400 degrees. In a large mixing bowl, combine eggs and salt.

Gradually beat in sugar until mixture is thick and lightens in color (about 5 minutes). Fold flour into egg mixture a few tablespoons at a time. Fold in butter a few tablespoons at a time. Spoon 1 tablespoon of batter into each shell of a greased and floured Madeleine pan. Bake 8 to 10 minutes or until a cake springs back when lightly touched. Immediately remove from molds and cool on wire racks. Sprinkle Madeleines with liqueur.
Yield: about 18 Madeleines

Variation: To make chocolate Madeleines, reduce flour to ⅓ cup and combine flour with 3 tablespoons cocoa. Proceed with recipe as directed.

SUGAR COOKIE ORNAMENTS

- ³/₄ cup confectioners sugar
- ¹/₂ cup butter or margarine, softened
- 1 egg yolk
- 1 teaspoon vanilla extract
- ¹/₂ teaspoon almond extract
- 1¹/₄ cups all-purpose flour
- ¹/₂ teaspoon baking soda
- ¹/₄ teaspoon cream of tartar
- ¹/₈ teaspoon salt

  Purchased tubes of decorating icing, candy sprinkles, and dragées to decorate
  Nylon line (to hang cookies)

In a large mixing bowl, combine confectioners sugar, butter, egg yolk, and extracts, beating until fluffy. In a medium bowl, combine flour, baking soda, cream of tartar, and salt. Stir flour mixture into butter mixture. Wrap dough in plastic wrap. Chill at least 2 hours.

Preheat oven to 350 degrees. On a lightly floured surface, use a floured rolling pin to roll out dough to ¹/₈-inch thickness. Use miniature cookie cutters or patterns to cut out dough. (To use patterns, trace patterns onto tracing paper and cut out. Place patterns on dough and use a sharp knife to cut around patterns.) Transfer cookies to a lightly greased baking sheet. Bake 5 to 7 minutes or until very lightly browned. Use a toothpick to make a hole for hanger in top of each warm cookie. Transfer cookies to a wire rack to cool. Referring to photo, decorate cookies with icing, candy sprinkles, and dragées. Use nylon line to hang cookies from tree.
Yield: about 5 dozen cookies

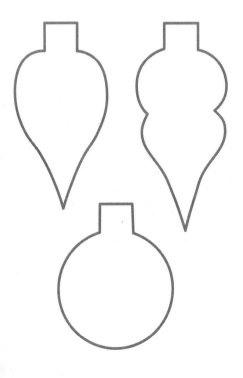

Reminiscent of the days when tree decorations were often cookies or candies, this miniature feather tree adorned with delicious Sugar Cookie Ornaments makes a charming gift or decorative accent. We cut our cookies in the shapes of antique Victorian glass ornaments and decorated them with colorful icing and candy accents.

FILBERT COOKIES

1 cup butter, softened
1 cup granulated sugar
2 cups all-purpose flour
2 teaspoons vanilla extract
¼ teaspoon salt
1 cup finely ground filberts
  Confectioners sugar
  Pastel Glaze (recipe follows)

Cream butter and granulated sugar; stir in flour, vanilla, and salt. Add filberts and mix well. Shape teaspoonfuls of dough into balls. Place balls 1 inch apart on ungreased baking sheets; flatten slightly. Bake in a preheated 300-degree oven 18 to 20 minutes. Cool slightly, then roll in confectioners sugar. Cookies may also be iced with Pastel Glaze.
Yield: about 6 dozen cookies

PASTEL GLAZE
The flavor of our glaze can be changed by substituting orange or lemon juice for the water.

3 to 4 tablespoons hot water
  Red food coloring
2½ cups confectioners sugar, sifted

Add water and food coloring gradually to sugar. (**Note:** Be careful to add only a few drops of color at a time.) Beat mixture until smooth; drizzle or pour over cookies.

ALMOND CRISPS

⅔ cup plus 2 tablespoons finely ground blanched almonds
½ cup granulated sugar
½ cup butter or margarine
2 tablespoons whipping cream
1 tablespoon all-purpose flour

Combine all ingredients in a 10-inch skillet. Cook over low heat, stirring constantly, until butter is melted and mixture is blended. Keep skillet warm over very low heat. Drop heaping teaspoonfuls of mixture 2 inches apart onto a greased baking sheet. (**Note:** Bake only 4 cookies at a time.) Bake in a preheated 350-degree oven 5 minutes or until golden. Use a spatula to loosen and turn cookies over; quickly roll each one around the handle of a wooden spoon. If cookies become too firm to roll, reheat in oven a minute to soften. Cool rolled cookies on wire racks. Repeat until all batter is used, greasing baking sheet each time. Store cookies in an airtight container.
Yield: about 2½ dozen cookies

CREAM CHEESE SPRITZ

1 cup vegetable shortening
1 package (3 ounces) cream cheese, softened
1 cup granulated sugar
1 egg yolk
1 teaspoon vanilla extract
2½ cups all-purpose flour, sifted
½ teaspoon salt
¼ teaspoon ground cinnamon
  Food coloring, if desired

  Dragées to decorate

Cream shortening and cream cheese. Gradually add sugar and mix well. Beat in egg yolk and vanilla. Sift flour with salt and cinnamon; gradually add to creamed mixture. Tint with food coloring, if desired. Fill cookie press and form cookies on ungreased baking sheets. Bake in a preheated 350-degree oven 12 to 15 minutes. Cool before removing from baking sheets. Decorate with dragées.
Yield: about 6 dozen cookies

MINT PATTIES

½ cup butter, melted
1 cup granulated sugar
1 egg
1¾ cups all-purpose flour
1 teaspoon baking soda
1 teaspoon peppermint extract
8 ounces chocolate-flavored candy coating
1 package (6 ounces) semisweet chocolate chips

Beat butter, sugar, and egg together. Combine flour and baking soda; add to butter mixture. Stir in peppermint extract. Drop by teaspoonfuls onto greased baking sheets. Bake in a preheated 350-degree oven 8 to 10 minutes. Remove from baking sheets and cool on wire racks.

Melt candy coating and chocolate chips in the top of a double boiler over simmering water. Drop each cookie into chocolate to coat. Lift out with a fork, wiping excess chocolate from bottom of cookie. Place on waxed paper and allow chocolate to harden.
Yield: about 3 dozen cookies

MERINGUE DELIGHTS

1 egg white
¾ cup firmly packed dark brown sugar
1 tablespoon all-purpose flour
  Pinch of salt
1 cup pecans, chopped

Beat egg white until stiff. Add brown sugar and beat until blended. Stir in flour, salt, and pecans. Drop teaspoonfuls of mixture 2 inches apart onto greased baking sheets. Bake in a preheated 325-degree oven 10 minutes. Cool slightly before removing from baking sheets.
Yield: about 3 dozen cookies

You'll want to bring out your best silver and crystal serving pieces for these elegant cookies: Filbert Cookies *(clockwise from top right)*, Meringue Delights, Cream Cheese Spritz, Almond Crisps, and Mint Patties.

CHAMPAGNE APRICOT CREAMS

1 package (6 ounces) dried
   apricots, diced
1 cup brut champagne
$1/2$ cup butter, softened
$2^1/4$ cups confectioners sugar, sifted
8 ounces chocolate-flavored candy
   coating
1 package (6 ounces) semisweet
   chocolate chips
2 ounces white chocolate for
   garnish

Marinate apricots in champagne at room temperature 1 hour. Drain apricots; set aside.

Beat butter and confectioners sugar until fluffy. Stir in marinated apricots. Transfer mixture to a small bowl; cover and chill overnight.

Shape chilled mixture into 1-inch balls; place on a baking sheet lined with waxed paper. Refrigerate until firm.

Melt candy coating and chocolate chips in the top of a double boiler over simmering water. Working with only 4 or 5 candies at a time (keep remainder refrigerated), dip the candies into the chocolate. Return to refrigerator to allow chocolate to harden.

Melt white chocolate in microwave or in the top of a double boiler over simmering water. Spoon white chocolate into a pastry bag fitted with a small round tip. Pipe decorative lines on tops of candies. Store candies in refrigerator.
Yield: about 40 candies

Surprise Santa with these whimsical Peppermint Stockings. He'll love them — and so will the kids!

PEPPERMINT STOCKINGS

COOKIES
$3^1/4$ cups all-purpose flour
1 tablespoon baking powder
$1/2$ cup butter or margarine, softened
$1^1/4$ cups granulated sugar
1 egg
$2^1/2$ teaspoons peppermint extract
1 teaspoon vanilla extract
$1/4$ cup milk

ICING
1 cup confectioners sugar
2 tablespoons milk
1 tablespoon butter, softened
   Red paste food coloring

Preheat oven to 350 degrees. For cookies, combine flour and baking powder in a medium bowl. In a large bowl, cream butter, sugar, egg, and extracts. Add dry ingredients alternately with milk. On a lightly floured surface, use a floured rolling pin to roll out dough to $1/8$-inch thickness. Using desired cookie cutter, cut out dough. Transfer cookies to a lightly greased baking sheet. Bake 8 to 10 minutes or until very lightly browned around edges. Remove from pans and cool on wire racks.

For icing, beat confectioners sugar, milk, and butter until smooth; tint red. Ice cookies as desired.
Yield: about 3 dozen 3-inch-long cookies

A bite into one of these Champagne Apricot Creams reveals tasty bits of dried apricots that have been marinated in champagne.

The festive look of our Almond Christmas Trees is enhanced by their raspberry jam filling. Whether plain, iced, or decorated, Sugar Cookies are traditional holiday favorites — and they're so much fun to make in your favorite shapes!

ALMOND CHRISTMAS TREES

1¼ cups butter or margarine, softened
²/₃ cup granulated sugar
2 cups all-purpose flour
1½ cups finely ground almonds
1 teaspoon ground cinnamon
¼ teaspoon ground nutmeg
½ teaspoon vanilla extract
½ teaspoon almond extract
Raspberry jam
Confectioners sugar

Cream butter and granulated sugar until light and fluffy. Stir in flour, almonds, cinnamon, nutmeg, and extracts. Wrap dough in plastic wrap and chill 1 hour.

Preheat oven to 375 degrees. Divide dough in half. On a lightly floured surface, use a floured rolling pin to roll out half of dough to ¹/₈-inch thickness. Using a 4½-inch tree-shaped cookie cutter, cut out 24 trees. Place cookies on a lightly greased baking sheet. Roll out remaining half of dough and cut out 24 additional trees. Using a drinking straw, randomly cut a few holes for "ornaments" in second batch of cookies. Place cookies on a lightly greased baking sheet. If there is any extra dough, roll out and cut an even number of trees, making holes in half of them. Bake 8 to 10 minutes or until lightly browned. Remove from sheets and cool on wire racks.

Spread each solid tree with a layer of raspberry jam. Place a tree with holes on top of jam layer and dust with confectioners sugar.
Yield: about 2 dozen cookies

SUGAR COOKIES

½ cup butter or margarine, softened
1 cup granulated sugar
1 egg
1½ teaspoons vanilla extract
½ teaspoon almond extract
2 cups all-purpose flour
½ teaspoon baking powder
¼ teaspoon salt
Icing (recipe follows)

Cream butter and sugar until light and fluffy. Beat in egg and extracts. Sift together dry ingredients. Gradually add dry ingredients to creamed mixture, blending well. Wrap dough in plastic wrap and chill at least 1 hour.

Preheat oven to 400 degrees. On a lightly floured surface, use a floured rolling pin to roll out dough to ¹/₈-inch thickness. Cut out dough using desired cookie cutters. Place cookies on lightly greased baking sheets. Bake 8 to 10 minutes or until edges are lightly browned. Remove from sheets and cool on wire racks.

Ice and decorate cookies, if desired.
Yield: about 3 dozen cookies

ICING

2¼ cups confectioners sugar, sifted
¹/₃ cup milk
½ teaspoon vanilla extract
Red and green food coloring (optional)

Combine all ingredients, blending until smooth. Dip tops of cookies in icing; place on wire racks to dry. If desired, divide remaining icing and add food coloring to icing, stirring to blend well. Spoon into pastry bags fitted with small, round tips. Decorate tops of cookies.

FRUITCAKE CHRISTMAS COOKIES

- 1/2 cup butter or margarine, softened
- 1 cup granulated sugar
- 1 egg, beaten
- 1/2 teaspoon baking soda
- 1/4 cup sour milk
- 1 3/4 to 2 cups all-purpose flour
- 1/2 teaspoon salt
- 3/4 cup chopped candied cherries
- 3/4 cup chopped dates
- 3/4 cup chopped pecans
  Buttercream Frosting (recipe follows)
  Red and green candied cherries to decorate

Cream butter and sugar; stir in egg. Stir together baking soda and sour milk; gradually add to creamed mixture. (**Note:** Milk may be soured by stirring 1 tablespoon lemon juice or vinegar into scant 1/4 cup whole milk.) Combine flour and salt; gradually add to creamed mixture. Stir in fruit and pecans until well blended. Drop teaspoonfuls of dough onto greased baking sheets. Bake in a preheated 350-degree oven 10 to 12 minutes. Cool cookies on wire racks.

Spread Buttercream Frosting on cookies and decorate with red and green cherries.
Yield: about 3 dozen cookies

BUTTERCREAM FROSTING
- 2 cups confectioners sugar
- 2 tablespoons butter or margarine
- 1 tablespoon milk
- 1 teaspoon vanilla extract

Blend all ingredients until smooth. Add more milk or sugar as necessary to achieve spreading consistency.

Here's a collection of cookies to please your country-lovin' heart: White Chocolate Chunk Macadamia Cookies *(clockwise from top left)*, Eggnog Cookies, Cinnamon Bars, Chocolate Gingerbread, Shortbread, and Fruitcake Christmas Cookies *(center)*.

CHOCOLATE GINGERBREAD

- 1/2 cup butter or margarine, softened
- 3/4 cup firmly packed dark brown sugar
- 1/2 cup dark corn syrup
- 1/4 cup molasses
- 1 egg
- 3 cups all-purpose flour
- 1/2 cup cocoa
- 1 teaspoon ground ginger
- 1 teaspoon ground cloves

Cream butter, brown sugar, corn syrup, and molasses. Add egg and beat until well blended. Add flour, cocoa, and spices; stir until blended, adding more flour if necessary to make a stiff dough. Cover and chill at least 1 hour.

On a lightly floured surface, use a floured rolling pin to roll out dough to 1/8-inch thickness. Cut out with desired cookie cutters and place on ungreased baking sheets. Bake in a preheated 325-degree oven 8 to 12 minutes. Cool and remove from baking sheets.
Yield: about 3 dozen cookies

WHITE CHOCOLATE CHUNK MACADAMIA COOKIES

- 1 cup butter or margarine, softened
- 1 cup firmly packed light brown sugar
- 1/2 cup granulated sugar
- 2 eggs
- 1 teaspoon vanilla extract
- 2 1/4 cups all-purpose flour
- 1 teaspoon baking soda
- 1 teaspoon salt
- 1 cup macadamia nuts, coarsely chopped
- 2 cups white chocolate **or** almond bark, broken into bite-size pieces

Cream butter and sugars until light and fluffy. Beat in eggs and vanilla. Combine flour, baking soda, and salt; gradually add to creamed mixture. Stir in macadamia nuts and chocolate. Drop by heaping teaspoonfuls onto greased baking sheets. Bake in a preheated 350-degree oven 10 to 12 minutes. Cool slightly before removing from baking sheets.
Yield: about 6 dozen cookies

CINNAMON BARS

- 1 cup butter or margarine, softened
- 3/4 cup granulated sugar
- 2 cups all-purpose flour, sifted
- 3 teaspoons ground cinnamon
- 1 egg, separated

- 1 teaspoon vanilla extract
- 1 cup chopped pecans

Cream butter and sugar. Combine flour and cinnamon; gradually add to creamed mixture. Stir in egg yolk and vanilla until well blended. Spread dough in a greased 15 1/2 x 10 1/2 x 1-inch-deep jellyroll pan and pat down. Brush egg white on top of dough. Sprinkle pecans over dough; press pecans into dough. Bake in a preheated 300-degree oven 30 minutes. Cut into bars and remove from pan to cool.
Yield: about 2 dozen bars

EGGNOG COOKIES

- 1 cup butter or margarine, softened
- 2 cups granulated sugar
- 1 teaspoon vanilla extract
- 4 eggs
- 3 cups all-purpose flour
- 2 teaspoons baking powder
- 1/2 teaspoon ground nutmeg
- 1/2 teaspoon salt

Cream butter, sugar, and vanilla. Beat in eggs, one at a time. Sift dry ingredients together; gradually add to creamed mixture. Cover and refrigerate several hours.

Drop by heaping teaspoonfuls onto ungreased baking sheets. Bake in a preheated 375-degree oven 6 to 8 minutes or until lightly browned around the edges. Cool slightly before removing from baking sheets.
Yield: about 8 dozen cookies

SHORTBREAD

- 1 cup butter, softened
- 1/2 cup granulated sugar
- 2 1/2 cups all-purpose flour, sifted

Cream butter; gradually add sugar and blend until light and fluffy. Stir in flour until well blended. Cover with waxed paper and chill for several hours.

Work with half of dough at a time and store remainder in refrigerator. Press dough into a cookie mold or use a floured rolling pin to roll out dough on a lightly floured surface to 1/2-inch thickness; cut out with desired cookie cutters. Place on ungreased baking sheets. Bake in a preheated 300-degree oven 30 minutes. Cool slightly before removing from sheets.
Yield: about 3 1/2 dozen cookies

PUMPKIN-WALNUT COOKIES

COOKIES
- 1 cup butter or margarine, softened
- 1 cup granulated sugar
- 1 cup canned pumpkin
- 1 egg
- 1 teaspoon vanilla extract
- 2 cups all-purpose flour
- 1 teaspoon baking powder
- 1 teaspoon ground cinnamon
- ½ teaspoon ground nutmeg
- ½ teaspoon baking soda
- ½ teaspoon salt
- ¼ teaspoon ground allspice
- 1 cup raisins
- 1 cup chopped walnuts

ICING
- 1 cup confectioners sugar
- 1 package (3 ounces) cream cheese, softened
- 2 tablespoons water

Preheat oven to 350 degrees. For cookies, cream butter and sugar in a large bowl until fluffy. Add next 3 ingredients, mixing well. In a medium bowl, sift together next 7 ingredients. Add to creamed mixture, mixing well. Stir in raisins and walnuts. Drop by rounded teaspoonfuls onto a greased baking sheet. Bake 12 to 15 minutes or until lightly browned. Cool on a wire rack.

For icing, combine all ingredients in a small bowl until smooth. Drizzle icing over cooled cookies. Allow icing to harden. Store in an airtight container.
Yield: about 7 dozen cookies

Cut in heart, moon, and star shapes, Santa Cookies decorated with colorful frosting and bits of licorice will delight young and old alike.

SANTA COOKIES

COOKIES
- ½ cup butter or margarine, softened
- ½ cup vegetable shortening
- 1 cup granulated sugar
- 1½ teaspoons vanilla extract
- 3 eggs
- 3½ cups all-purpose flour
- 2 teaspoons cream of tartar

ICING
- 3 cups confectioners sugar
- ¼ cup butter or margarine, softened
- ¼ cup milk
- 1 teaspoon vanilla extract
  Red paste food coloring

  Small pieces of black licorice to decorate

For cookies, cream butter, shortening, sugar, and vanilla in a large mixing bowl. Beat in eggs, one at a time, beating well after each addition. Stir in flour and cream of tartar. Wrap dough in plastic wrap and refrigerate at least 2 hours.

Preheat oven to 425 degrees. On a lightly floured surface, use a floured rolling pin to roll out dough to ⅛-inch thickness. Use star, moon, or heart-shaped cookie cutters to cut out dough. Transfer cookies to lightly greased baking sheets and bake 6 to 8 minutes or until lightly browned around edges. Remove from pans and cool on wire racks.

For icing, combine all ingredients except food coloring in a medium mixing bowl, blending until smooth. Divide icing in half; tint half red. Referring to photo, ice cookies with red icing. Use a pastry bag fitted with a small round tip and filled with white icing to pipe beards and trim. Decorate with small pieces of licorice for eyes.
Yield: about 6 dozen cookies

Pumpkin-Walnut Cookies have a moist, cake-like texture similar to pumpkin bread.

Chock-full of almonds and zippy crystallized ginger, crunchy Gingerbread Toasts are light, flavorful sweets.

GINGERBREAD TOASTS

2 1/2 cups all-purpose flour
 1/4 cup finely minced crystallized
       ginger
 3 teaspoons baking powder
 3/4 teaspoon salt
 1/2 teaspoon ground ginger
 1/4 teaspoon ground cinnamon
 1/2 cup butter or margarine, softened
 3/4 cup granulated sugar
 2 eggs
 1 teaspoon vanilla extract
 2/3 cup blanched whole almonds,
       toasted and coarsely chopped
 2 teaspoons milk
    Granulated sugar

Preheat oven to 375 degrees. Combine flour, crystallized ginger, baking powder, salt, ground ginger, and cinnamon in a medium bowl. In a large bowl, beat butter and sugar until fluffy. Beat in eggs and vanilla. Stir in flour mixture and almonds. Divide dough in half and shape each half into a 12 x 2-inch strip on a foil-lined baking sheet. Smooth surface of each strip. Brush each with milk; sprinkle with sugar. Bake 18 to 20 minutes or until light golden brown and firm to the touch. Remove from oven and reduce temperature to

300 degrees. Place strips on a wire rack and cool 15 minutes.

Place strips on a cutting board and use a serrated knife to cut each strip crosswise on the diagonal into 1/2-inch-thick slices. Place slices on a baking sheet and bake 10 minutes. Turn slices over and bake 10 minutes more. Turn off heat and allow toasts to cool in oven, leaving door slightly ajar.
Yield: about 3 dozen toasts

HOLIDAY SUGAR COOKIES

Our sugar cookies are decorated with colorful frosting made using the Butter Frosting recipe. To give the glazed angels the look of beautiful porcelain, we frosted them with the Pastel Glaze (recipe on page 35; omit red food coloring), and let them dry overnight.

- 1/2 cup butter, softened
- 1/2 cup vegetable shortening
- 1 cup granulated sugar
- 1 1/2 teaspoons vanilla extract
- 3 eggs
- 3 1/2 cups all-purpose flour
- 2 teaspoons cream of tartar
- 1 teaspoon baking soda
  Butter Frosting (recipe follows)

Cream butter, shortening, sugar, and vanilla until light and fluffy. Add eggs, one at a time, beating well after each addition. Combine flour, cream of tartar, and baking soda; gradually add to creamed mixture. Cover and refrigerate several hours.

Work with half of the dough at a time and store remainder in refrigerator. On a lightly floured surface, use a floured rolling pin to roll out dough to 1/4-inch thickness; cut out with desired cookie cutters. Place on lightly greased baking sheets. Bake in a preheated 425-degree oven 6 to 8 minutes or until lightly browned. Store in airtight containers, placing waxed paper between layers of cookies.
Yield: about 5 1/2 dozen cookies

BUTTER FROSTING
- 3 cups confectioners sugar, sifted
- 1/4 cup butter, melted and cooled
- 1/4 cup whipping cream or milk
- 1/2 teaspoon vanilla extract
  Food coloring

Blend sugar and butter. Add whipping cream and vanilla; beat until smooth. Tint frosting with food coloring and decorate cookies.

MEXICAN CHOCOLATE COOKIES

- 1 1/2 cups butter, softened
- 1 3/4 cups granulated sugar
- 2 eggs, slightly beaten
- 3 cups all-purpose flour
- 1 1/2 cups cocoa
- 1 teaspoon ground cinnamon
- 1/2 teaspoon ground black pepper
- 1/4 teaspoon salt
- 4 to 6 ounces semisweet baking chocolate, melted

Cream butter and sugar; add eggs and beat until fluffy. Sift dry ingredients together; gradually add to creamed mixture. Beat until well blended, adding more flour if dough seems too soft. Divide dough into thirds and wrap in plastic wrap; chill at least 1 hour.

On a lightly floured surface, use a floured rolling pin to roll out dough to 1/8-inch thickness; cut out with desired cookie cutters. Place on greased baking sheets. Bake in a preheated 375-degree oven 8 to 10 minutes or until crisp but not darkened. Cool on wire racks; drizzle melted chocolate on cookie tops.
Yield: about 3 dozen cookies

WREATH COOKIES

- 3 tablespoons butter or margarine
- 1/2 cup light corn syrup
- 3/4 teaspoon green liquid food coloring
- 3 tablespoons granulated sugar
- 3 1/2 cups cornflake cereal
  Small red cinnamon candies

In a large saucepan, mix butter, corn syrup, food coloring, and sugar. Cook over medium heat until mixture boils, stirring constantly. Boil 5 minutes, stirring frequently; remove from heat. Add cereal and stir until well blended. Drop mixture by buttered 1/4 cup measure onto waxed paper. Use buttered fingers to shape each portion to resemble a wreath; decorate with cinnamon candies. Let stand until firm. Store in airtight containers.
Yield: about 12 wreaths

LEMON BARS

- 2 1/4 cups all-purpose flour, divided
- 2 1/4 cups confectioners sugar, divided
- 1 cup butter or margarine, melted
- 2 cups granulated sugar
- 4 eggs, slightly beaten
- 1 teaspoon baking powder
- 2 cups coconut
- 1/4 cup plus 3 to 4 tablespoons lemon juice, divided

Combine 2 cups flour and 1/2 cup confectioners sugar. Add melted butter; mix well. Spread mixture in a greased 13 x 9 x 2-inch baking pan. Bake in a preheated 350-degree oven 20 to 25 minutes.

Stir granulated sugar and eggs together. Combine baking powder and remaining 1/4 cup flour; add to sugar mixture. Stir in coconut and 1/4 cup lemon juice. Pour over baked crust. Return to oven and bake 30 minutes; cool.

Combine remaining 1 3/4 cups confectioners sugar and remaining 3 to 4 tablespoons lemon juice; pour over baked mixture. Cut into bars.
Yield: about 2 dozen bars

CHEESECAKE BITES

- 1 cup all-purpose flour
- 1/2 cup chopped pecans
- 1/3 cup firmly packed light brown sugar
- 1/3 cup butter or margarine, melted
- 1 package (8 ounces) cream cheese, softened
- 1/4 cup granulated sugar
- 1 egg
- 2 tablespoons milk
- 1 tablespoon lemon juice
- 1 teaspoon vanilla extract

Combine flour, pecans, and brown sugar in a medium bowl. Stir in melted butter until blended. Reserve 1/3 cup of mixture; press remainder into bottom of a greased 8-inch square baking pan. Bake in a preheated 350-degree oven 12 to 15 minutes. Beat cream cheese and granulated sugar until smooth. Beat in remaining ingredients. Pour over baked crust; sprinkle with reserved pecan mixture. Return to oven and bake 25 minutes. Cool slightly; cut into 2-inch squares.
Yield: about 16 squares

These festive cookies say Christmas in a merry way: Lemon Bars (clockwise from top), Wreath Cookies, Holiday Sugar Cookies decorated with butter frosting or pastel glaze, Cheesecake Bites, and Mexican Chocolate Cookies.

Pretty and pink, Marshmallow-Mint Sandwiches are quick-and-easy treats that children will love.

MARSHMALLOW-MINT SANDWICHES

2 packages (12½ ounces each) fudge-covered graham crackers
2 envelopes unflavored gelatin
1 cup cold water, divided
2¼ cups granulated sugar
1½ teaspoons peppermint extract
1 teaspoon vanilla extract
Red paste food coloring

1 ounce vanilla-flavored candy coating and red paste food coloring to decorate

Line the bottom of an ungreased 13 x 9 x 2-inch baking pan with 36 graham crackers, top sides down. In a large mixing bowl, soften gelatin in ½ cup water; set aside. In a saucepan, combine remaining ½ cup water and sugar. Bring to a boil and boil 2 minutes. Stir sugar mixture into gelatin, blending well. Refrigerate 10 minutes.

Beat gelatin mixture at highest speed of an electric mixer until mixture turns white and becomes thick like meringue. Beat in extracts; tint pink. Pour mixture over crackers. Top mixture with 36 crackers, top sides up. Refrigerate about 1 hour or until set.

Using a sharp knife dipped in hot water, cut into sandwiches using cookie tops as guidelines.

If desired, melt candy coating; tint pale pink. Drizzle candy coating over tops of cookies to decorate. Store at room temperature.
Yield: 36 cookies

COCOA PECAN MERINGUES

4 egg whites
1½ teaspoons vanilla extract
¼ teaspoon cream of tartar
⅛ teaspoon salt
1 cup granulated sugar
½ cup cocoa
1 cup finely ground pecans
Pecan halves

Preheat oven to 200 degrees. Beat egg whites, vanilla, cream of tartar, and salt at high speed until soft peaks form. Beat in sugar, a few tablespoons at a time, until meringue is stiff and shiny. Sift cocoa on top of meringue and carefully fold into mixture. Fold in ground pecans. Drop by heaping teaspoonfuls onto ungreased baking sheets. Place a pecan half on top of each meringue. Bake 1½ hours or until firm and dry. Remove from sheets and cool on wire racks.
Yield: about 3 dozen cookies

COCONUT BELLS

    1 cup butter or margarine, softened
 $1/2$ cup firmly packed brown sugar
 $1/2$ cup granulated sugar
    1 teaspoon vanilla extract
    1 egg
 $2^1/2$ cups all-purpose flour
 $1/2$ teaspoon baking soda
 $1/2$ teaspoon salt
    1 teaspoon ground nutmeg
       Coconut Filling (recipe follows)
       Red and green candied cherry
          halves

Beat butter, sugars, vanilla, and egg in a large bowl until well blended. Stir in flour, baking soda, salt, and nutmeg. Wrap in plastic wrap and chill until firm, about 1 hour.

Preheat oven to 375 degrees. On a lightly floured surface, use a floured rolling pin to roll out dough to $1/8$-inch thickness. Cut out dough using $2^1/2$-inch round cookie cutter. Place on ungreased baking sheets. Place $1/2$ teaspoon Coconut Filling in center of each round. Shape into a bell by folding opposite edges together over filling. Pinch top of bell slightly to make it narrower than bottom of bell. Cut each green cherry half into four strips. Place one green cherry strip at bottom of cookie for stem of clapper. Place a red cherry half at bottom of stem for clapper. Bake 10 to 12 minutes or until lightly browned. Remove from sheets and cool on wire racks.
Yield: about 3 dozen cookies

COCONUT FILLING
 $1/4$ cup firmly packed brown sugar
    3 tablespoons butter or margarine
 $1^1/2$ tablespoons water
 $3/4$ cup confectioners sugar, sifted
    1 can ($3^1/2$ ounces) shredded
          coconut
 $1^1/2$ teaspoons vanilla extract
 $1/3$ cup chopped pecans

In a small saucepan, bring brown sugar, butter, and water to a boil. Remove from heat. Stir in confectioners sugar, coconut, vanilla, and pecans.

Here are two delicious cookies to serve your special Christmas visitors: delicately textured Cocoa Pecan Meringues (*in jar*) and rich Coconut Bells.

HARD CANDY SANTAS AND LOLLIPOPS

    2 cups granulated sugar
    1 cup water
 2/3 cup light corn syrup
    1 teaspoon oil-based flavoring for
       candy making
 1/2 to 1 teaspoon candy coloring
       Purchased lollipop sticks

In a large saucepan, combine sugar, water, and corn syrup over medium-high heat. Without stirring, cook to hard crack stage (300 degrees on a candy thermometer). Remove from heat and stir in flavoring and coloring.

For Santas, use balls of aluminum foil to prop oiled two-piece metal candy molds upright on a baking sheet. Pour mixture into molds. When mixture is hard, but not thoroughly cooled, remove candies from molds.

For molded lollipops, pour mixture into oiled metal lollipop molds. Quickly insert lollipop sticks into indentations before mixture hardens. When mixture is hard, but not thoroughly cooled, remove lollipops from molds.

For round lollipops, pour mixture into 3- to 4-inch circles on an oiled baking sheet. Quickly insert lollipop sticks into circles before mixture hardens. When lollipops are thoroughly cooled, remove from baking sheet.
Yield: about four 3-inch-high Santas, fifteen 1 1/2-inch molded lollipops, or ten round lollipops

This sweet selection contains old-fashioned confections made with modern ease! Our collection includes delicious Peppermint-Orange Patties *(clockwise from top left)* and soft, chewy Gumdrops with a crystallized sugar coating. Our Never-Fail Divinity always turns out right because we substitute marshmallow creme for egg whites! Hard Candy Santas and Lollipops are favorite candies, and Rum-Raisin Fudge is spiked with marinated raisins.

PEPPERMINT-ORANGE PATTIES

    7 cups sifted confectioners sugar
    1 can (14 ounces) sweetened
       condensed milk
 1/2 cup butter, softened
 1 1/2 teaspoons orange extract
 1/2 teaspoon peppermint extract
  14 ounces chocolate-flavored candy
       coating
    8 ounces semisweet chocolate chips
       (about 1 1/3 cups)

In a large mixing bowl, combine first five ingredients. Blend until smooth. Cover and refrigerate mixture overnight.

Use lightly greased hands to shape mixture into 1-inch balls and flatten to make patty shapes. Place patties on a jellyroll pan lined with waxed paper. Freeze patties at least 30 minutes.

In a heavy medium saucepan, melt candy coating and chocolate chips over low heat. Remove chocolate mixture from heat. Working with 1 dozen patties at a time, place each patty on a fork and spoon chocolate mixture over top until covered. Transfer patties to a jellyroll pan lined with waxed paper. Chill until chocolate hardens. Store in an airtight container in a cool place.
Yield: about 8 dozen candies

Variation: To make peppermint drops, eliminate orange extract and increase peppermint extract to 1 teaspoon. Proceed as directed. Shape mixture into 1-inch balls, but do not flatten into patty shapes. Continue with recipe as directed.

RUM-RAISIN FUDGE

    1 cup raisins
 1/2 cup dark rum
 2 1/2 cups granulated sugar
    1 cup evaporated milk
 1/2 cup butter or margarine
    2 cups semisweet chocolate chips
    1 jar (7 ounces) marshmallow
       creme
 1/2 cup chopped pecans
    1 teaspoon rum extract

In a small bowl, combine raisins and rum. Cover and marinate overnight at room temperature.

In a heavy large saucepan, combine sugar, evaporated milk, and butter. Cook over medium heat, stirring constantly, until mixture reaches soft ball stage (238 degrees on a candy thermometer). Remove from heat. Stir in chocolate chips, marshmallow creme, pecans, rum extract, and raisin mixture. Spread mixture into a lightly greased 10 x 8 x 2-inch baking pan. Cool and cut into squares.
Yield: about 4 dozen pieces of fudge

NEVER-FAIL DIVINITY

 1 1/2 cups granulated sugar
 1/2 cup water
    2 tablespoons light corn syrup
 1/8 teaspoon salt
    1 jar (7 ounces) marshmallow creme
 1 1/2 teaspoons vanilla extract
    1 cup chopped pecans

In a large saucepan, combine sugar, water, corn syrup, and salt. Cook over medium-high heat to hard ball stage (250 degrees on a candy thermometer). Place marshmallow creme in a large mixing bowl. Beating constantly, gradually add syrup to marshmallow creme. Beat until stiff peaks form. Beat in vanilla and pecans. Quickly drop by heaping teaspoonfuls onto waxed paper. Store in an airtight container.
Yield: about 2 dozen candies

GUMDROPS

    4 tablespoons unflavored gelatin
    1 cup cold water
 1 1/2 cups boiling water
    4 cups granulated sugar
 1/2 teaspoon desired flavoring: lemon
       extract, orange extract,
       peppermint extract, etc.
    3 to 4 drops desired food coloring
       Granulated sugar

In a large saucepan, soften gelatin in cold water 5 minutes. Stir in boiling water until gelatin is dissolved. Stir in sugar and bring mixture to a boil over medium-high heat. Boil 25 minutes, stirring frequently. Pour mixture into two 8 x 8-inch pans. To each pan add 1/2 teaspoon desired flavoring and desired food coloring (do not add color for clear gumdrops). Stir until combined. Cover and refrigerate pans overnight.

Using a knife dipped in hot water, cut gelatin mixture into 1-inch cubes. Roll in granulated sugar until well coated. Place gumdrops on a sheet of waxed paper and allow to sit at room temperature two days to crystallize. Store in airtight containers.
Yield: about 10 dozen candies

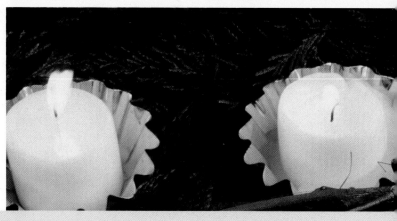

HOLIDAY OPEN HOUSE

Christmas is the perfect time to open our hearts and our homes to friends and family. It's through our hospitality that we are able to give back to those who have blessed our lives over the years. Your guests will rave over every delicious offering — from the hors d'oeuvres to the full-course meals — found in this collection. Enjoy the fun and fellowship that good food can bring during this holiday season!

Creamy garlic-flavored Aioli Dip is delightful with fresh vegetables, seafood, or French bread.

Succulent Chinese Chicken Wings *(left)* are basted with a mixture of soy sauce, horseradish, and plum jam. Cheddar cheese, strawberry jam, bacon, and pecans give Cheese Pockets a sensational taste.

AIOLI DIP

- 3 cloves garlic, minced
- 1/4 cup lemon juice
- 2 egg yolks, beaten
- 1 teaspoon Dijon-style mustard
- 1/4 teaspoon salt
- 1/8 teaspoon ground white pepper
- 1/8 teaspoon cayenne pepper
- 1 1/2 cups olive oil

    See serving suggestions below

In a food processor or blender, purée garlic. Add next 6 ingredients; process until smooth. With the motor running, slowly pour oil into mixture in a steady stream. Continue processing until mixture becomes thick and firm. Chill until ready to serve.

Serve with artichoke hearts, hearts of palm, blanched snow peas, carrots, cauliflower, strips of green pepper, cherry tomatoes, zucchini, hard-cooked eggs, chunks of cooked lobster, cooked shrimp, or chunks of French bread.

Yield: about 2 cups of dip

CHEESE POCKETS

- 1 package (10 ounces) refrigerated pizza dough
- 1/4 cup strawberry jam
- 3/4 cup shredded sharp Cheddar cheese
- 1/4 cup chopped green onion
- 5 slices bacon, cooked and crumbled
- 1/4 cup chopped pecans

Preheat oven to 400 degrees. Unroll pizza dough and cut into 12 equal pieces. Place 1 teaspoon jam on each piece of dough. Top with cheese, green onion, bacon, and pecans. Brush edges of dough with water. Fold dough over filling and seal edges with fork. Place pockets on a lightly greased baking sheet. Bake 12 to 15 minutes or until golden brown. Serve warm.

Yield: 12 pockets

CHINESE CHICKEN WINGS

- 1 1/2 pounds chicken wings, disjointed and wing tips discarded
- 1/2 cup red plum jam
- 3 tablespoons soy sauce
- 2 tablespoons prepared horseradish
- 1 tablespoon prepared mustard
- 3 to 4 drops hot pepper sauce

    Chinese hot mustard to serve

Preheat oven to 425 degrees. Place wings in a single layer on a baking sheet. Combine jam, soy sauce, horseradish, prepared mustard, and pepper sauce; brush generously over wings. Bake 15 to 20 minutes, basting frequently. Serve with Chinese hot mustard, if desired.

Yield: about 20 chicken wings

SAUSAGE AND APPLE APPETIZERS

     2 tablespoons butter or margarine
     1 large onion, chopped
   1/2 cup apple jelly
   1/2 cup firmly packed brown sugar
     2 pounds cocktail-size smoked
        sausages
     3 apples, peeled, cored, and sliced
     2 tablespoons water
     1 tablespoon cornstarch

In a large skillet, melt butter over medium-high heat. Add onion and sauté, stirring constantly, until onion is golden. Stir in apple jelly and brown sugar. Add sausages and reduce heat to medium-low. Cook, stirring occasionally, 20 minutes or until mixture begins to thicken. Add apples, partially cover pan, and cook 10 minutes or until apples are tender. Combine water and cornstarch and stir into mixture in pan. Cook 2 to 3 minutes more or until mixture thickens. Serve warm.
Yield: about 30 appetizers

The fresh-baked goodness of Soft Breadsticks is enhanced by smoky Madeira Cheese Spread.

SOFT BREADSTICKS

 1 1/2 cups warm water
     2 tablespoons granulated sugar
     1 package dry yeast
 1 1/4 teaspoons salt
 4 1/2 cups all-purpose flour
     1 egg
     1 tablespoon water
        Coarse salt or margarita salt

In a large mixing bowl, combine, 1 1/2 cups warm water, sugar, yeast, and 1 1/4 teaspoons salt. Stir to dissolve sugar and yeast; allow to sit 5 minutes. Gradually stir in flour, blending well to make a smooth dough. Turn out dough on a lightly floured surface and knead until smooth and elastic, 8 to 10 minutes. Divide dough into 28 equal pieces. Roll each piece into an approximately 8 x 1/4-inch breadstick. Place on a greased baking sheet.

In a small bowl, combine egg with 1 tablespoon water. Brush mixture over breadsticks and sprinkle with coarse salt. Cover and let rise 25 minutes.

Preheat oven to 425 degrees. Bake 15 to 20 minutes or until brown. Remove from pan and cool on wire rack.
Yield: 28 breadsticks

MADEIRA CHEESE SPREAD

   1/2 cup Madeira wine
   1/3 cup butter, melted
    14 ounces Gouda cheese
     1 cup sour cream
     1 teaspoon salt
   1/8 teaspoon cayenne pepper

In a small bowl, combine wine and butter. In a food processor or blender, combine cheese, sour cream, salt, and cayenne. Process until smooth. With motor running, gradually add wine mixture, blending until smooth. Refrigerate 24 hours before serving to allow flavors to blend.
Yield: about 2 1/2 cups of spread

Apples and brown sugar mingle with smoked sausages to create a special flavor combination in Sausage and Apple Appetizers.

MONTEREY CHEESE CRISPS

You won't believe how easy these are to make. A sprinkling of cayenne pepper gives them an added bite.

- 1 pound Monterey Jack cheese, softened (use only Monterey Jack cheese)
  Cayenne pepper or chili powder

Cut cheese into $1/4$-inch-thick slices, then cut slices into circles using a $1^1/2$-inch round cookie cutter. Place cheese rounds 3 inches apart on an ungreased non-stick baking sheet (cheese will spread while baking). Sprinkle with cayenne or chili powder. Bake in a preheated 400-degree oven 10 minutes or until golden brown. (Do not overbake.) Remove crisps with a spatula and cool on paper towels. Store in airtight containers.
Yield: 36 to 42 crisps

SUGARED WALNUTS

A brown sugar coating makes these crispy nuts a sweet treat for the holidays.

- 8 cups water
- 4 cups English walnut halves
- $1/2$ cup firmly packed light brown sugar
  Vegetable oil

In a large pan, bring water to a boil. Add walnuts and boil for 1 minute. Drain walnuts and rinse in very hot water; drain again. Place warm walnuts in a bowl and add brown sugar. Stir until sugar is melted.

In a heavy skillet, heat 1 inch of oil to 320 degrees on a candy thermometer. Cook 2 cups of walnuts at a time 3 to 4 minutes. (Do not overcook.) Drain on paper towels. Store in airtight containers.
Yield: 4 cups walnuts

(Top) Tangy Glazed Ginger Pork (left) and Marmalade Meatballs will keep your guests coming back for more.

(Bottom left) Meet the call for crunchies with Monterey Cheese Crisps (clockwise from top). Sugared Walnuts and Spicy Pecans are great for snacking on during the holidays.

(Bottom right) Jalapeño peppers and hot, spicy pecans add exciting taste to our Spice Cheese Mold.

GLAZED GINGER PORK

Cooked ahead and served cold, this ginger-flavored pork is an easy dish for entertaining.

- $1/4$ cup soy sauce
- $1/4$ cup dry white wine
- 2 tablespoons honey
- 1 tablespoon freshly grated ginger
- 1 clove garlic, minced
- 1 (3-pound) boneless pork loin roast
- $3/4$ cup currant jelly

  Sweet mustard to serve

For marinade, combine soy sauce, wine, honey, ginger, and garlic. Place roast in marinade. Cover and marinate roast in the refrigerator 6 hours or overnight, turning several times.

When ready to cook, remove roast from container and place on a rack in a shallow baking pan. Insert meat thermometer. Reserve 3 to 4 tablespoons of marinade for glaze; the remainder will be used for basting. Basting several times with marinade during cooking, bake in a preheated 300-degree oven 2 hours or until thermometer reaches 175 degrees.

For glaze, combine 3 to 4 tablespoons reserved marinade with jelly in a small saucepan. Stirring constantly, bring to a boil over medium-high heat; boil 1 minute. Set aside to cool.

After roast is cooked, spoon glaze over meat until it is completely coated. Refrigerate until ready to serve. Slice roast paper thin. Serve with sweet mustard.
Yield: about 50 slices

MARMALADE MEATBALLS

Bake these in batches and freeze for a holiday party.

- 1 egg
- $1/2$ cup water
- 1 pound finely ground chuck
- 1 cup water chestnuts, finely chopped
- $1/2$ cup bread crumbs
- 2 teaspoons horseradish
- $1/4$ teaspoon salt
- $2/3$ cup orange marmalade
- $1/3$ cup water
- 2 tablespoons soy sauce
- 2 tablespoons lemon juice
- 1 clove garlic, finely minced

In a medium bowl, beat egg and $1/2$ cup water. Blend in ground chuck, water chestnuts, bread crumbs, horseradish, and salt.

(**Note:** For tender meatballs, do not overmix.) Shape mixture into balls about $3/4$ inch in diameter. Place meatballs on a foil-lined baking sheet. Bake in a preheated 350-degree oven 30 minutes or until lightly browned.

While meatballs are cooking, make sauce by combining remaining ingredients in a saucepan. Heat slowly, stirring often.

Place cooked meatballs in a serving dish and cover with sauce. If making in advance, place meatballs and sauce in a covered container and refrigerate. Heat slowly before serving.
Yield: about 24 servings

SPICE CHEESE MOLD

This cheese ball is a blend of cheeses with the bite of jalapeño peppers and hot-flavored pecans.

- 2 packages (8 ounces each) cream cheese, softened
- 8 ounces sharp Cheddar cheese, softened
- 8 ounces Monterey Jack cheese with jalapeño peppers, softened
- 3 drops hot pepper sauce
- $1^1/4$ cups Spicy Pecans, chopped and divided (recipe follows)

  Fresh grapes and assorted crackers to serve

In a food processor or blender, combine cheeses and pepper sauce. Process until well blended. Place mixture in a bowl and add $3/4$ cup chopped Spicy Pecans. Form into a large ball or mold in a 1-quart round bowl. Cover tightly and refrigerate overnight.

To serve, remove from refrigerator and garnish with remaining Spicy Pecans. Serve with fresh grapes and assorted crackers.
Yield: 1 cheese ball

SPICY PECANS

- $1/2$ cup butter
- 3 tablespoons steak sauce
- 6 drops hot pepper sauce
- 4 cups pecan halves
  Cajun seasoning

Melt butter in a $15^1/2$ x $10^1/2$-inch jellyroll pan in a preheated 200-degree oven. Add steak sauce and pepper sauce; stir in pecans. Spread pecans on pan and bake 1 hour. Stir often while baking. Drain on paper towels and sprinkle with Cajun seasoning. Store in airtight containers.
Yield: 4 cups pecans

Finger sandwiches filled with juicy beef patties, savory chicken with a hint of white wine, and spicy pork sausage offer hearty holiday fare in the form of Buffet Burgers *(clockwise from top)*, Chicken Puffs, and Stuffed French Loaf.

CHICKEN PUFFS

1/4 cup butter or margarine
1/2 cup boiling water
1/2 cup all-purpose flour
1/4 teaspoon salt
2 eggs
2/3 cup shredded Swiss cheese
1 cup finely chopped cooked
   chicken
1/2 cup chopped almonds
1/3 cup mayonnaise
1/4 cup finely chopped green pepper
1/4 cup finely chopped tomato
2 tablespoons white wine
1/2 teaspoon seasoned salt
1/4 teaspoon ground black pepper

Preheat oven to 400 degrees. In a small saucepan over medium-low heat, melt butter in water. Add flour and salt, stirring until mixture forms a ball. Remove from heat and allow to cool slightly. Add eggs and beat vigorously until smooth. Stir in cheese. Drop dough by heaping teaspoonfuls onto a greased baking sheet. Bake 20 minutes or until golden brown. Remove puffs from oven; cool and split.

Combine remaining ingredients, adding more mayonnaise if needed to moisten. Fill each puff with a heaping teaspoon of chicken mixture.
Yield: about 2 dozen puffs

STUFFED FRENCH LOAF

You'll want to keep this recipe on hand after the holidays to serve with your favorite homemade soups.

1 loaf (16 ounces) French bread
8 ounces spicy bulk pork sausage
1/3 cup chopped onion
1 clove garlic, minced
1 egg
2 tablespoons chopped fresh parsley
1 tablespoon Dijon-style mustard,
   divided
3/4 cup shredded extra-sharp Cheddar
   cheese
1/2 cup grated Parmesan cheese
1/4 cup olive oil
1 teaspoon ground black pepper

Preheat oven to 350 degrees. Slice bread in half lengthwise and slightly hollow out each half, leaving a 1/2-inch-thick layer of bread. Place bread crumbs in container of a blender or food processor and process 15 to 20 seconds or until finely chopped.

Cook sausage, onion, and garlic in a heavy skillet over medium heat until meat is brown; drain. In a large bowl, combine bread crumbs, meat mixture, egg, parsley, and 1 teaspoon mustard; set aside.

Using a blender or food processor, process cheeses, olive oil, remaining 2 teaspoons mustard, and pepper until mixture forms a paste, about 1 minute. Spread cheese mixture evenly over inside of each bread half. Spoon meat mixture into cavity of each bread half. Place bread halves together. Wrap loaf in foil. Bake 30 to 35 minutes or until heated through. Cut into 1-inch-thick slices.
Yield: about 16 servings

BUFFET BURGERS

2 pounds lean ground beef
1 cup soft bread crumbs
1/2 cup chopped onion
1 egg, lightly beaten
1 tablespoon mayonnaise
1 teaspoon garlic salt
1 teaspoon Italian seasoning
1/4 teaspoon ground black pepper
1 1/2 cups shredded mozzarella cheese
20 small square rolls, heated and
   split

Mustard and mayonnaise to serve

Preheat oven to 350 degrees. Combine ground beef, bread crumbs, onion, egg, mayonnaise, garlic salt, Italian seasoning, and pepper; mix well. Press meat mixture into bottom of a 15 1/2 x 10 1/2-inch jellyroll pan to within 1 inch of edges of pan. Bake 20 to 25 minutes; drain. Top meat mixture with cheese and bake 5 to 8 minutes longer or until cheese is melted. Remove from oven and allow to sit (about 5 minutes). Cut meat into 20 squares and place inside split rolls. Serve with mustard and mayonnaise.
Yield: 20 burgers

COLD SHRIMP, ARTICHOKES, AND MUSHROOMS

7 to 8 pounds shrimp, boiled,
   peeled, and deveined
3 cans (14 ounces each) artichoke
   hearts, drained and halved
1 pound fresh mushrooms, sliced
2 cups olive oil
2 cups vegetable oil
1 cup dry sherry
1 cup garlic-flavored vinegar
1 teaspoon salt
3/4 tablespoon Cajun seasoning
3/4 tablespoon hot pepper sauce
   (optional)
1/4 teaspoon cayenne pepper
6 small red onions, thinly sliced

In a large glass bowl, combine shrimp, artichokes, and mushrooms. In a medium bowl, combine remaining ingredients (except onions). Whisk until blended. Pour over shrimp mixture. Cover tightly and refrigerate for 2 to 3 days, stirring occasionally. Several hours before serving, add onions. Place in a glass serving dish.
Yield: about 60 servings

This flavorful medley of Cold Shrimp, Artichokes, and Mushrooms is seasoned with a peppery marinade.

CHEESE CRACKER VEGETABLE DIP

This dip looks especially pretty garnished with a wreath of broccoli and topped with tiny chili pepper "lights."

1²/₃ cups Cheddar cheese snack
       cracker crumbs, divided
3 tablespoons butter or margarine,
       melted
1 carton (16 ounces) sour cream
1 package (3 ounces) cream
       cheese, softened
¼ cup chopped pimientos
¼ cup finely chopped green pepper
2 teaspoons Italian salad dressing
       mix
1 teaspoon Worcestershire sauce
¼ teaspoon cayenne pepper

      Assorted fresh vegetables to serve

Combine 1¹/₃ cups cracker crumbs and melted butter; mix well. Press half of crumb mixture into bottom of a buttered 8-inch round springform pan.

Combine next seven ingredients, blending well. Spread one half of sour cream mixture over cracker crumb crust. Sprinkle remaining buttered cracker crumbs over sour cream mixture; spread remaining sour cream mixture over crumbs. Sprinkle remaining ¹/₃ cup cracker crumbs over top. Cover and refrigerate 6 hours or overnight.

To serve, remove sides of springform pan and serve with assorted fresh vegetables for dipping.
Yield: 15 to 20 servings

SAVORY STUFFED MUSHROOM CAPS

We garnished these yummy appetizers with colorful fresh herbs, chili peppers, and yellow pepper star cutouts.

24 medium fresh mushrooms
½ small onion
2 cloves garlic, minced
3 tablespoons oil
¾ cup shredded Cheddar cheese
½ cup dry bread crumbs
¼ cup butter, melted
1 teaspoon Italian seasoning
½ teaspoon seasoned salt
½ teaspoon ground black pepper
      Dash hot pepper sauce
3 tablespoons butter

Clean mushrooms by wiping with a damp paper towel or cloth. Remove stems and set caps aside. Combine mushroom stems, onion, and garlic in food processor or blender and process until finely chopped. Heat oil in a small skillet. Add mushroom mixture and sauté over medium-high heat 4 to 5 minutes. Return mushroom mixture to processor and add next seven ingredients. Process until smooth, adding additional melted butter if necessary to make a smooth paste. Set aside to cool to room temperature.

Preheat oven to 400 degrees. Heat 3 tablespoons butter in skillet and quickly sauté mushroom caps over high heat 1 to 2 minutes. Place caps on a lightly greased baking sheet and spoon a small amount of stuffing mixture into each cap. Bake for 5 to 10 minutes or until heated through.
Yield: 2 dozen mushrooms

IRISH COFFEE EGGNOG PUNCH

2 cartons (1 quart each) eggnog
¹/₃ cup firmly packed brown sugar
3 tablespoons instant coffee
      granules
½ teaspoon ground cinnamon
½ teaspoon ground nutmeg
1 cup Irish whiskey
1 quart coffee-flavored ice cream

Combine first five ingredients in a large mixing bowl. Beat at low speed with an electric mixer until smooth. Stir in Irish whiskey. Chill 1 to 2 hours.

Pour into a punch bowl. Top punch with scoops of ice cream.
Yield: about 9½ cups of punch

HOT MACADAMIA DIP

The rich flavor of macadamia nuts enhances this creamy dip that is served bubbling hot.

11 ounces (one 8-ounce and one
      3-ounce package) cream cheese,
      softened
2 tablespoons milk
1 jar (2½ ounces) dried chipped
      beef, shredded
¹/₃ cup finely chopped onion
¹/₃ cup finely chopped green pepper
1 clove garlic, minced
½ teaspoon ground black pepper
¼ teaspoon ground ginger
¾ cup sour cream
½ cup coarsely chopped macadamia
      nuts
1 tablespoon butter or margarine

      Crackers to serve

Preheat oven to 350 degrees. Combine cream cheese and milk, blending until completely smooth. Stir in chipped beef, onion, green pepper, garlic, black pepper, and ginger. Fold in sour cream. Pour beef mixture into a glass pie plate or shallow baking dish. In a small skillet, sauté nuts in butter until thoroughly glazed. Sprinkle nuts over beef mixture. Bake 20 to 25 minutes or until heated through. Serve hot with crackers.
Yield: 12 to 15 servings

(Top left) Broccoli flowerets form a wreath of green atop this delectable Cheese Cracker Vegetable Dip.

(Top right) A food processor makes it quick and easy to prepare these Savory Stuffed Mushroom Caps.

(Bottom left) Mellow Irish whiskey, mingled with coffee-flavored ice cream, turns ordinary eggnog into creamy Irish Coffee Eggnog Punch.

(Bottom right) A rich blend of cream cheese and chipped beef, topped with sautéed nuts, makes this Hot Macadamia Dip a heavenly spread for crackers.

(Left) A combination of spinach, parsley, walnuts, and cheeses makes this Layered Christmas Cheese Loaf a luscious holiday spread for French bread. *(Right)* This elegant Blue Cheese Mousse has a delicate taste that's delightful with crackers or gingersnaps.

LAYERED CHRISTMAS CHEESE LOAF

A simple garnish of fresh herbs and pink peppercorns adds a colorful touch to this elegant loaf.

2　packages (8 ounces each) cream cheese, softened
$1/4$　cup butter or margarine, softened
3　tablespoons milk
2　packages (10 ounces each) frozen chopped spinach, thawed and drained
2　cups lightly packed fresh parsley, stems removed
$1/2$　cup chopped walnuts
$1/2$　cup vegetable oil
1　tablespoon fresh lemon juice
2　cloves garlic, minced
1　teaspoon dried basil leaves
1　teaspoon dried oregano leaves
$1 1/2$　cups grated Parmesan cheese

French bread slices to serve

In a mixing bowl, beat cream cheese, butter, and milk until smooth. Set aside.

In a blender or food processor, combine spinach, parsley, walnuts, vegetable oil, lemon juice, garlic, basil, and oregano. Process until smooth. Add Parmesan cheese and blend thoroughly.

Line a $7 1/2$ x $3 1/2$ x 2-inch loaf pan with plastic wrap. Spread one-third of the cream cheese mixture evenly in the bottom of the pan. Top with half of the spinach mixture, spreading evenly. Repeat the layers, ending with the cream cheese mixture. Cover and refrigerate 3 to 4 hours or overnight.

Unmold and carefully remove the plastic wrap. Garnish as desired and serve with slices of French bread.
Yield: 35 to 40 servings

BLUE CHEESE MOUSSE

2　envelopes unflavored gelatin
$1/4$　cup cold water
2　cups sour cream
$1 1/2$　cups small curd cream-style cottage cheese
1　package (4 ounces) crumbled blue cheese

Grapes for garnish
Crackers or gingersnaps to serve

Combine gelatin and cold water in the top of a double boiler, stirring to soften. Place over boiling water and stir until gelatin dissolves. In a blender or food processor, combine gelatin mixture, sour cream, cottage cheese, and blue cheese. Process until smooth. Pour into a lightly oiled $3 1/2$-cup decorative mold or small loaf pan. Chill until firm. Unmold and garnish with grapes. Serve with crackers or gingersnaps.
Yield: 25 to 30 servings

BACON-CHEESE RING

The potent flavors of sharp Cheddar cheese, green onion, and bacon will make this cheese spread a favorite. Top each bite with a small amount of strawberry preserves for a really different treat.

1 package (12 ounces) bacon
1 pound extra sharp Cheddar cheese, shredded
1 bunch green onions, finely chopped
2 cups mayonnaise
1 teaspoon cayenne pepper
1/2 cup toasted slivered almonds

Strawberry preserves and crackers or French bread slices to serve

Fry bacon until crisp. Drain well and crumble into small pieces. In a medium mixing bowl, combine bacon, cheese, green onions, mayonnaise, and cayenne pepper; mix thoroughly. Place almonds in the bottom of an oiled 7-cup ring mold; press cheese mixture into mold. Refrigerate overnight.

Unmold cheese ring onto platter. Place a small custard cup filled with strawberry preserves in the center of the ring. Serve with crackers or French bread slices.
Yield: 20 to 25 servings

DILL DIP WITH CRUDITÉS

1 1/2 cups sour cream
1 1/2 cups mayonnaise
1/4 cup chopped fresh parsley
2 tablespoons lemon juice
3 tablespoons dried salad seasoning
2 tablespoons dried dill weed
2 tablespoons grated onion
1 teaspoon ground black pepper

Assorted fresh vegetables to serve

Combine first eight ingredients; blend well. Chill at least 4 hours to allow flavors to blend. Serve with assorted vegetables for dipping.
Yield: about 3 cups of dip

(Left) Breaking away from the traditional cheese ball is this Bacon-Cheese Ring, a tasty combination of Cheddar cheese and bacon decked with almonds. Strawberry preserves offer a sweet contrast to the sharp Cheddar taste. *(Right)* Crudités — crisp, fresh vegetable pieces — are a refreshing snack when served with our lively Dill Dip.

Rows of roasted almonds and sweet golden chutney give the Curried Almond-Cheese Ball *(left)* its distinctive look. Warmly tucked inside our Crab-Filled Phyllo Triangles are spoonfuls of tender crabmeat mixed with cream cheese and zesty spices.

CURRIED ALMOND-CHEESE BALL

Serve this spicy spread with whole wheat crackers and plenty of mango chutney for a delicious taste treat.

- 2 packages (8 ounces each) cream cheese, softened
- 1 cup mango chutney, divided
- 2 teaspoons curry powder
- 1/2 teaspoon dry mustard
- 1 can (6 ounces) roasted whole almonds, blanched

  Mango chutney and crackers to serve

Combine cream cheese, 1/2 cup chutney, curry powder, and dry mustard. Blend well and place in a small bowl lined with plastic wrap. Refrigerate overnight to allow spices to blend.

Unmold on a serving platter. Cover sides of cheese ball with whole almonds, leaving the top uncovered. Spread remaining 1/2 cup of the chutney over the top. Serve with additional chutney and crackers.
Yield: 12 to 15 servings

CRAB-FILLED PHYLLO TRIANGLES

These sinfully rich appetizers may be prepared one day ahead and reheated before serving.

- 1/3 cup finely chopped green onions
- 1/4 cup butter
- 2 cans (6 ounces each) lump crabmeat, drained
- 2 tablespoons all-purpose flour
- 1 package (8 ounces) cream cheese, softened
- 1/3 cup cocktail sauce
- 2 teaspoons freshly squeezed lemon juice
- 1 teaspoon Worcestershire sauce
- 1 teaspoon dry mustard
- 1/2 teaspoon garlic salt
- 1/4 teaspoon cayenne pepper
- 2 egg yolks
- 1 package (16 ounces) frozen phyllo dough, thawed
- 1/2 cup butter, melted
  Grated Parmesan cheese

In a large skillet over medium heat, sauté green onions in 1/4 cup butter until onions are tender. Stir in crabmeat and sprinkle with flour; cook 2 minutes. In a small bowl, combine next seven ingredients, blending until smooth. Stir into crab mixture, cooking until mixture thickens. Remove from heat and add egg yolks, blending well. Set aside to cool.

Preheat oven to 350 degrees. Remove phyllo dough from the package. Before unrolling, cut dough crosswise into 4 pieces, each approximately 3 inches wide. Unroll each piece. Take one strip of dough from one of the pieces (cover remaining dough with a damp towel to prevent drying) and brush with melted butter. Place a heaping teaspoon of crab filling at one short end of strip. Fold corner of phyllo over filling and continue folding down entire length of strip, creating a triangle. Repeat with remaining strips. Place 1 inch apart on greased baking sheets. Brush with melted butter and sprinkle with Parmesan cheese. Bake triangles 20 to 25 minutes or until golden brown and crisp. Drain on paper towels. Serve warm.
Yield: about 6 dozen triangles

CARAWAY WAFERS

An excellent "nibbler" for parties, these flavor-filled crackers are also perfect served with soups and salads.

- 1 cup all-purpose flour
- 1 teaspoon dry mustard
- 1/4 teaspoon salt
- 1/2 cup shredded Swiss cheese
- 2 teaspoons caraway seed
- 1/2 teaspoon paprika
- 1/4 teaspoon cayenne pepper
- 1/3 cup butter or margarine, softened
- 3 tablespoons cold water
- 1 teaspoon Worcestershire sauce
  Paprika

Preheat oven to 425 degrees. Sift flour, dry mustard, and salt into bowl. Stir in cheese, caraway seed, 1/2 teaspoon paprika, and cayenne. Cut in butter until mixture resembles coarse meal. Add water and Worcestershire sauce; blend with a fork until dough sticks together, adding more water if necessary. Shape into a ball. On a lightly floured surface, roll out dough to 1/8-inch thickness and cut out using a 1 1/2-inch biscuit cutter. Place on an ungreased baking sheet. Sprinkle with paprika. Bake 5 to 7 minutes or until lightly browned.

Yield: about 4 dozen wafers

The crisp, wholesome taste of Caraway Wafers makes them an excellent holiday snack. When served with soups and salads, they're a flavorful complement to the meal.

Bacon, caviar, shredded cheese, and green onions nestle in beds of sour cream atop warm slices of baked new potatoes, making these Potato Coins simple yet savory appetizers.

POTATO COINS

- 2 pounds new potatoes
  Seasoned salt
  Sour cream
  Desired toppings (see below)

Preheat oven to 350 degrees. Wash potatoes. Place potatoes on a baking sheet and cover with aluminum foil. Bake 30 to 45 minutes or until tender.

To serve, slice each potato crosswise into 1/4-inch-thick slices. With a small spoon, scoop out a small portion of the center of each potato slice, creating a small cavity. Sprinkle potatoes with seasoned salt. Fill cavity with sour cream and any of the toppings listed below. Serve warm.

Yield: about 30 slices

TOPPING VARIATIONS
Red, gold, or black caviar
Crumbled bacon
Chopped onion sautéed in butter
Shredded cheeses
Chopped green onion
Fresh herbs

ULTIMATE CHILI DIP

A combination of cheese, beef, and chili seasonings makes this a hearty dip.

    2   pounds ground round
    1   cup chopped onion
    2   cloves garlic, minced
    1   package (2 pounds) processed
          American cheese, cut into pieces
    1   can (16 ounces) undrained chili
          beans
  3/4   cup evaporated milk
    2   packages (1 3/4 ounces each)
          chili seasoning mix
  1/4   cup chopped jalapeño peppers

          Tortilla or corn chips to serve

Cook meat, onion, and garlic in a large Dutch oven over medium heat until meat is brown; drain. Add cheese, beans, evaporated milk, chili seasoning, and jalapeño peppers to meat mixture; stir. Cook over medium heat, stirring often, until thoroughly blended and heated through. Serve warm in a chafing dish with tortilla or corn chips.
Yield: about 10 cups of dip

CRUNCHY SNACK MIX

Here is our version of the traditional cereal snack mix. This mixture freezes well, so it may be made in advance.

  1/2   cup butter or margarine, melted
    1   package Caesar garlic cheese
          salad dressing mix
    1   tablespoon Worcestershire sauce
    1   teaspoon seasoned salt
    4   cups bite-size shredded wheat
          cereal
    3   cups chow mein noodles
    2   cups unblanched whole almonds
    2   cups walnut halves

Preheat oven to 250 degrees. In a small bowl, combine butter, salad dressing mix, Worcestershire sauce, and seasoned salt; stir to blend. In a large bowl, combine the remaining ingredients. Pour butter mixture over cereal mixture, stirring until thoroughly coated. Pour onto a baking sheet and bake 1 hour, stirring every 15 minutes; cool in pan. Store in a tightly sealed container.
Yield: about 11 cups of snack mix

A Christmas party can be a real fiesta when you prepare this spicy Tex-Mex menu: Mexican Quiches *(clockwise from top),* Fuzzy Navel Punch, Crunchy Snack Mix, Tortilla Roll-Ups, and Ultimate Chili Dip.

MEXICAN QUICHES

Green chilies and Monterey Jack cheese add a taste of Mexico to these mouthwatering treats. This recipe freezes well for up to one week. To serve, allow quiches to come to room temperature, then warm in a 325-degree oven.

  1/2   cup butter or margarine, softened
    1   package (3 ounces) cream
          cheese, softened
    1   cup all-purpose flour
    1   cup shredded Monterey Jack cheese
    1   can (4 ounces) chopped green
          chilies
    2   eggs, lightly beaten
  1/2   cup whipping cream
  1/4   teaspoon salt
          Ground black pepper to taste

In a medium mixing bowl, combine butter and cream cheese; blend until smooth. Stir in flour. Shape dough into a ball and wrap in waxed paper. Chill 2 to 3 hours.
Preheat oven to 350 degrees. Divide dough into 24 balls and press into lightly greased cups of miniature muffin pans to form shells. Sprinkle cheese and chilies in the bottom of each pastry shell. Combine eggs, cream, salt, and pepper. Pour over cheese and chilies in pastry shells. Bake 30 to 35 minutes.
Yield: 24 quiches

FUZZY NAVEL PUNCH

Here's a wonderful punch adaptation of the Fuzzy Navel Cocktail. This is a sparkling, flavorful punch that you will want to make all year long.

    9   cups orange juice with pulp
    3   cups peach schnapps
    1   bottle (750 ml) brut champagne,
          chilled
          Crushed ice or ice ring

Combine orange juice, peach schnapps, and champagne. Pour into a punch bowl and add crushed ice or ice ring.
Yield: about 1 gallon of punch

TORTILLA ROLL-UPS

These are so easy to make ahead. Have them waiting in the refrigerator ready to top with our creamy guacamole just before serving.

    1   package (8 ounces) cream
          cheese, softened
  1/3   cup chunky salsa
  1/4   cup chopped green onion
  1/2   teaspoon garlic salt
  1/2   teaspoon chili powder
   12   (6-inch) flour tortillas
          Guacamole (recipe follows)

          Small red chili peppers to garnish

Beat cream cheese until smooth. Add salsa, green onion, garlic salt, and chili powder, mixing well. Spread a heaping tablespoon of the cream cheese mixture on each tortilla. Roll up each tortilla tightly, jellyroll fashion, and place seam side down on a baking sheet. Cover and chill at least 2 hours. Slice each roll into 4 pieces. Top each appetizer with a small amount of Guacamole and garnish with a small red chili pepper. Serve with additional Guacamole.
Yield: 4 dozen roll-ups

GUACAMOLE

    2   ripe avocados, mashed (about
          1 cup)
  1/3   cup mayonnaise
  1/4   cup chopped ripe olives
    2   tablespoons lemon juice
    2   tablespoons grated onion
    1   clove garlic, minced
    1   teaspoon salt
  1/4   teaspoon chili powder
          Dash cayenne pepper

Using a food processor or blender, process all ingredients until creamy. Chill. Use as topping for Tortilla Roll-Ups.

MARMALADE CHEESE TARTS

- 1 cup butter, softened
- 2 cups all-purpose flour
- 1 cup grated sharp Cheddar cheese
- ³/4 cup orange marmalade
- 1 egg, lightly beaten

In a medium mixing bowl, combine butter, flour, and cheese. Knead until well blended. Wrap dough in plastic wrap and refrigerate 1 hour.

Preheat oven to 350 degrees. On a lightly floured surface, use a floured rolling pin to roll out dough to ¹/8-inch thickness. Cut out dough using a 2-inch round cookie cutter. Place about ¹/2 teaspoon marmalade in center of each circle of dough. Fold dough in half and seal edges by pressing with a fork. Transfer tarts to ungreased baking sheets and brush tops with egg. Bake 10 to 15 minutes or until tarts are set and lightly browned. Remove from pans and cool on wire racks.
Yield: about 5 dozen tarts

MARINATED OLIVES

These stuffed olives fortified with vinegar and herbs give an everyday treat a party flavor. The recipe can easily be doubled for larger crowds.

- 1 jar (8 ounces) pimiento-stuffed green olives, drained
- ¹/4 cup tarragon wine vinegar
- ¹/4 cup olive oil
- 1 tablespoon dried chives
- 1 clove garlic, minced
- ¹/4 teaspoon whole black peppercorns

Place olives in a glass container with a lid. Combine remaining ingredients and pour over olives. Secure lid on jar and shake to coat olives well. Marinate at room temperature 2 days, shaking jar daily. Drain before serving.
Yield: about 1 cup of olives

BACON AND LETTUCE STUFFED TOMATOES

- 20 cherry tomatoes
  Salt
- ¹/2 cup finely chopped lettuce
- ¹/3 cup mayonnaise
- 10 slices bacon, cooked and crumbled
- ¹/4 cup chopped green onion
  Salt and ground black pepper to taste

Cut the top off of each tomato. Scoop out pulp and seeds. Salt inside of each tomato. Invert tomatoes and drain 15 minutes.

In a small bowl, combine the remaining ingredients. Fill each tomato with mixture.
Yield: 20 stuffed tomatoes

MINIATURE CORN MUFFINS WITH TURKEY AND RELISH

- 2 cups buttermilk
- 2 eggs
- 1¹/2 cups cornmeal
- ¹/2 cup all-purpose flour
- ¹/4 cup granulated sugar
- 1 teaspoon baking soda
- 1 teaspoon salt
- ¹/4 pound sliced, cooked turkey breast
  Purchased cranberry relish

Preheat oven to 450 degrees. In a medium mixing bowl, beat buttermilk and eggs. Beat in cornmeal, flour, sugar, baking soda, and salt. Fill lightly greased miniature muffin tins two-thirds full with batter. Bake 10 to 15 minutes or until a muffin springs back when pressed. Remove muffins from pans and cool on wire racks.

Split cooled muffins in half and fill each with a piece of turkey and a small amount of cranberry relish.
Yield: about 45 muffins

These tiny Bacon and Lettuce Stuffed Tomatoes were inspired by that all-American sandwich, the BLT.

KIELBASA PALMIERS

- 1 pound kielbasa sausage, finely chopped or ground, divided
- 1 package (17¹/4 ounces) frozen puff pastry dough, thawed and divided
- 1 cup hot and sweet mustard, divided

In a skillet, brown sausage over medium heat. Drain well. Unfold one sheet of pastry and spread with ¹/2 cup of mustard. Spread half of the sausage over the mustard. Roll each long end tightly and evenly to center of pastry. Repeat with remaining pastry sheet, mustard, and sausage. Wrap tightly in aluminum foil and refrigerate at least 1 hour.

Preheat oven to 450 degrees. Cut palmiers crosswise into ¹/2-inch-thick slices. Place on ungreased baking sheets. Bake 15 to 20 minutes or until pastry is puffed and golden. Serve warm or at room temperature.
Yield: about 40 palmiers

(Left) Your guests will come back for more of these scrumptious treats — and don't be surprised if Santa himself drops in for a bite: Miniature Corn Muffins with Turkey and Relish *(top)* are bite-size sandwiches with the taste of a traditional turkey dinner. Crispy Kielbasa Palmiers have a wonderful spicy-sweet flavor.

(Top right) Sweet orange marmalade paired with tangy Cheddar cheese makes our Marmalade Cheese Tarts an unusual (and delicious!) treat.

(Bottom right) To add pizzazz to your party tray, try our Marinated Olives, which are flavored with tarragon wine vinegar and herbs.

Made with canned artichokes and crabmeat that can be kept on hand in the pantry, Hot Seafood Dip *(left, on cracker)* is quick to fix for unexpected guests. Our sophisticated Spinach Puffs have gourmet flair, but they're actually simple to prepare using frozen convenience items.

HOT SEAFOOD DIP

2   cans (14 ounces each) artichoke
    hearts, drained and coarsely
    chopped
2¼ cups mayonnaise
2   cups grated Parmesan cheese
2   cans (6 ounces each) lump
    crabmeat, drained
⅓   cup seasoned bread crumbs
1½ teaspoons garlic salt
1   teaspoon lemon pepper

    Crackers to serve

Preheat oven to 325 degrees. In a medium mixing bowl, combine all ingredients, blending well. Pour into a greased 3-quart baking dish. Bake 20 to 25 minutes or until heated through. Serve warm or at room temperature with crackers.
Yield: about 6 cups of dip

SPINACH PUFFS

1   sheet (from a 17¼-ounce package)
    frozen puff pastry dough, thawed
1   package (12 ounces) frozen
    spinach soufflé, thawed
1   egg, lightly beaten
    Grated Parmesan cheese

Preheat oven to 350 degrees. Unfold puff pastry sheet and cut lengthwise into three equal rectangles. Cut each rectangle into four equal pieces. Place on an ungreased baking sheet and bake 20 to 25 minutes or until golden brown and puffed. Remove tops from puffs and pull out soft dough. Fill each rectangle with about 2 tablespoons of softened soufflé. Replace tops and brush with egg. Sprinkle with Parmesan cheese. Bake 20 minutes. Cut each puff in half diagonally. Serve warm.
Yield: 24 puffs

This attractive Fruit Wreath with Sweet Cheese Dip was inspired by a Della Robbia wreath. Served on your prettiest platter, the wreath is sure to gather compliments.

FRUIT WREATH WITH SWEET CHEESE DIP

A pretty tray of fruit and dip is really quick and easy party fare. The wreath may be prepared ahead of time, but keep the cut fruit fresh by sprinkling with lemon juice.

2   packages (8 ounces each)
      cream cheese, softened
1   jar (7 ounces) marshmallow
      creme

1/4   cup milk
1 1/2   teaspoons vanilla extract
1/2   teaspoon ground nutmeg

      Assorted fruits to serve

In a medium mixing bowl, combine cream cheese, marshmallow creme, milk, vanilla, and nutmeg, beating until smooth.

Place dip in a serving bowl. Arrange fruit around bowl.
Yield: about 3 1/2 cups of dip

(Left) Seasoned with garlic and herbs, Boursin Cheese Spread is a typical French treat. The creamy cheese is best if it's "aged" in the refrigerator overnight. *(Right)* A packaged dressing mix seasons our Salmon Mousse with a hint of bacon. Decorated with cherry tomato roses and fresh parsley, the mousse has an elegant look — without a lot of work!

BOURSIN CHEESE SPREAD

2 packages (8 ounces each)
    cream cheese, softened
1 cup butter, softened
2 cloves garlic, minced
1 teaspoon dried oregano leaves
1 teaspoon dried basil leaves
¼ teaspoon dried dill weed
¼ teaspoon dried marjoram leaves
¼ teaspoon dried thyme leaves
¼ teaspoon ground black pepper

    Crackers to serve

Combine all ingredients, blending until smooth. Cover and refrigerate overnight to allow flavors to blend. Serve at room temperature with crackers.
Yield: about 3 cups of spread

SALMON MOUSSE

We garnished this mousse with cherry tomato roses and leaves of parsley. To make a rose, thinly peel a tomato in a continuous strip. Roll up the strip and secure the base with a toothpick.

1 envelope unflavored gelatin
¼ cup chicken broth
2 cans (6 ounces each) pink
    salmon, drained
⅓ cup mayonnaise
¼ cup minced onion
1 package (1.2 ounces) ranch-
    style dressing mix with bacon
3 tablespoons sherry
3 tablespoons minced parsley
1 tablespoon Dijon-style mustard
2 cloves garlic, minced

1 teaspoon Worcestershire sauce
1 teaspoon lemon juice
    Salt and ground black pepper to taste

    Crackers to serve

In small saucepan, soften gelatin in chicken broth. Place pan over low heat and stir until gelatin dissolves.

In a large mixing bowl, combine gelatin mixture with remaining ingredients, blending well. Pour mixture into a well-greased 3-cup gelatin mold. Cover with plastic wrap and refrigerate until firm. Serve with crackers.
Yield: about 3 cups of spread

FRIED WON TONS

- 1 pound ground pork
- 8 canned water chestnuts, minced
- 2 cloves garlic, minced
- 2 green onions, finely chopped
- 1 teaspoon ground ginger
- 1/4 teaspoon ground black pepper
- 1/2 teaspoon garlic salt
- 1 package (16 ounces) won ton skins
- 1 egg, lightly beaten
  Vegetable oil

  Plum Dipping Sauce to serve (recipe follows)

Combine the pork, water chestnuts, garlic, onions, ginger, pepper, and garlic salt, mixing well. Unwrap won ton skins and cover with damp paper towels to keep skins from drying out. For each won ton, place one won ton skin on work surface with one point facing up. Place 1 heaping teaspoon of filling in center of skin. Bring bottom point up over filling; bring side points over center of filling. Seal seams with egg. Place won tons on a baking sheet; cover with damp paper towels.

In a Dutch oven, heat 3 inches of oil to 360 degrees over medium-high heat. Fry won tons, three or four at a time, until golden brown (about 2 to 2 1/2 minutes; do not fry too quickly or the pork centers will not be thoroughly cooked). Drain on paper towels. Serve warm or at room temperature with Plum Dipping Sauce.
Yield: about 50 won tons

PLUM DIPPING SAUCE

- 1 cup red plum jam
- 1 clove garlic, minced
- 3 tablespoons white wine
- 1 tablespoon Dijon-style mustard
- 1 1/2 teaspoons dry mustard

Combine all ingredients in a small saucepan over low heat. Stir just until jam is melted. Serve with Fried Won Tons.
Yield: about 1 cup of sauce

PARTY PIZZA

- 2 pita breads, split into round halves
- 1/4 cup grated Parmesan cheese
- 1 can (14 1/2 ounces) undrained whole, peeled tomatoes, chopped
- 1 can (6 ounces) tomato paste
- 1/2 cup chopped mushrooms
- 1 1/2 teaspoons Italian seasoning
- 1 teaspoon garlic salt
- 1/4 teaspoon minced dried garlic
- 1 pound spicy pork sausage, cooked and drained
- 4 cups shredded mozzarella cheese

Preheat oven to 400 degrees. Place pita bread halves on a large baking sheet. Sprinkle each half with 1 tablespoon Parmesan cheese. Bake 8 to 10 minutes or until lightly toasted.

In a medium saucepan, combine tomatoes, tomato paste, mushrooms, Italian seasoning, garlic salt, and garlic. Stir over medium heat until heated through. Generously spread sauce over bread halves. Top with sausage and mozzarella. Return to oven and bake 10 to 12 minutes or until cheese is bubbly and melted. Cut each pizza into 4 wedges to serve.
Yield: 16 servings

Crispy pork-filled Fried Won Tons (*left*) served with Plum Dipping Sauce make great party fare. A pita bread crust is a unique base for Party Pizza; spicy tomato sauce, chunks of sausage, and mozzarella cheese top it off.

Easy-to-make Puff Pastry Sticks *(clockwise from top)* combine buttery flavor and crisp texture. Skewers of Marinated Chicken Bites, alternated with chunks of bell pepper, make colorful, delicious hors d'oeuvres. A great make-ahead snack, the Bacon-Cheddar Cheese Ball is sure to be a favorite. Tangy Bacon-Apricot Twists are served with a dipping sauce.

MARINATED CHICKEN BITES

These moist chunks of chicken are perfect to make ahead. Just place the marinated meat and vegetables on the skewers, cover, and refrigerate until ready to broil. Inexpensive bamboo skewers are available in the party supplies section of most grocery stores.

1½ pounds boneless, skinless
      chicken breasts, cut into
      1-inch pieces
½ cup mango chutney
⅓ cup white wine
¼ cup olive oil
1 tablespoon raspberry vinegar
1 green pepper, cut into 1-inch pieces
1 sweet red pepper, cut into 1-inch
      pieces
½ cup red plum jam

In a large glass bowl, combine chicken, chutney, wine, olive oil, and vinegar. Cover and marinate in refrigerator overnight.

Drain chicken. On each 6-inch skewer, place 2 chicken pieces and 2 pepper pieces.

In a small saucepan, melt jam over low heat. Generously brush chicken and peppers with jam. Place on wire rack in baking pan. Brushing often with jam, broil 12 to 15 minutes or until chicken is thoroughly cooked.
Yield: about 24 skewers

PUFF PASTRY STICKS

Keep a package of frozen puff pastry dough in the freezer for easy last-minute snacks like these.

1 package (17¼ ounces) frozen
      puff pastry dough, thawed
1 cup grated Romano cheese
½ cup sesame seed

Preheat oven to 400 degrees. Unfold each puff pastry sheet and cut lengthwise into three equal rectangles. Cut each rectangle crosswise into ½-inch-wide strips. Sprinkle both sides of strips generously with cheese and sesame seed, gently pressing into dough. Place on an ungreased baking sheet and bake 8 to 10 minutes or until puffed and golden.
Yield: about 10 dozen sticks

BACON-APRICOT TWISTS

12 slices bacon, cut in half
24 dried apricot halves
½ cup red plum jam
¼ cup soy sauce

Preheat oven to 350 degrees. Wrap one half slice of bacon around an apricot half, securing with toothpick. Repeat with remaining bacon and apricots. Place on ungreased baking sheet and bake 20 to 25 minutes, turning once. Bacon should be brown and crisp.

While twists are baking, combine jam and soy sauce in a small saucepan. Cook over low heat just until jam melts; set aside.

Drain twists on paper towels. Serve warm or at room temperature with sauce.
Yield: 24 twists

BACON-CHEDDAR CHEESE BALL

A miniature cookie cutter is all you need to cut out simple garnishes. We cut the tiny stars on top of this zesty cheese ball from a sweet red pepper.

2 packages (8 ounces each)
      cream cheese, softened
½ pound sharp Cheddar cheese,
      shredded
½ cup chopped green onions
6 slices bacon, cooked and
      crumbled
1 clove garlic, minced
3 tablespoons diced pimiento
3 tablespoons minced fresh parsley

   Crackers to serve

Combine all ingredients, blending well. Form into a ball. Cover with plastic wrap. Refrigerate overnight to allow flavors to blend. Serve with crackers.
Yield: 1 cheese ball

BRIE EN CROÛTE

Keep these ingredients on hand for this quick-to-fix appetizer. You'll be amazed at how delicious something so easy to prepare can be!

1 package (17¼ ounces) frozen
      puff pastry dough, thawed and
      divided
2 packages (4¼ ounces each)
      whole round Brie cheese, divided
¼ cup apricot preserves, divided
¼ cup chopped pecans, toasted and
      divided
1 egg yolk, lightly beaten

Unfold one sheet of puff pastry and place one Brie in the center. Cover top of cheese with 2 tablespoons preserves and 2 tablespoons pecans. Gather the edges of the dough over the cheese to resemble a bag. Tie top of "bag" with cotton twine. Repeat with remaining sheet of pastry, cheese, preserves, and pecans. Place each bundle on a lightly greased baking sheet and chill 1 hour.

Preheat oven to 400 degrees. Brush the dough with egg yolk. Bake 25 to 30 minutes or until pastry is puffed and golden. (If pastry browns too quickly, reduce temperature to 350 degrees.) Cool slightly and cut into wedges. Serve warm or at room temperature.
Yield: 2 cheese bundles, 4 to 5 servings each

Brie en Croûte is made with soft cheese topped with apricot preserves and pecans, all tucked inside a bundle of puff pastry.

71

Layered Crab Taco Dip is a delectable mixture of crabmeat and vegetables marinated in citrus juices and nestled on a bed of cream cheese and avocado chunks.

LAYERED CRAB TACO DIP

2 cans (6 ounces each) lump
    crabmeat, drained
2 green onions, minced
1/2 cup diced cucumber
1/2 cup diced red onion
1 medium tomato, finely chopped
2 tablespoons minced fresh parsley
1/4 cup lime juice
1/4 cup lemon juice
1/4 cup orange juice
    Salt and ground black pepper

2 packages (8 ounces each)
    cream cheese, softened
1/4 cup mayonnaise
1 avocado, peeled, pitted, and
    diced

Tortilla chips to serve

In a glass bowl, combine crabmeat, green onions, cucumber, red onion, tomato, and parsley. In a small bowl, combine juices. Stir into crab mixture. Salt and pepper to taste. Cover and refrigerate at least 6 hours or overnight.

Combine cream cheese and mayonnaise, blending well. Spread mixture over the bottom of a serving platter. Place avocado pieces over cream cheese mixture. Drain crab mixture, pressing out as much moisture as possible. Spread mixture over avocado. Serve with tortilla chips.

Yield: about 5 3/4 cups of dip

CORNMEAL CHICKEN NUGGETS

    ½   cup cornmeal
    1   tablespoon chili powder
    2   teaspoons ground cumin
    4   boneless, skinless chicken
          breasts, cut into 1-inch cubes
    3   tablespoons vegetable oil

        Adobado Sauce to serve (recipe
          follows)

Combine cornmeal, chili powder, and cumin; mix well. Add chicken and toss to coat well with mixture. In a large skillet, heat oil over medium heat. Add chicken and cook, stirring frequently, 5 to 6 minutes or until chicken is browned on all sides and done in middle. Serve with Adobado Sauce.
Yield: about 36 nuggets

ADOBADO SAUCE

    2   cans (4 ounces each) chopped
          green chilies
    1   cup chicken broth
    3   tablespoons butter or margarine
    2   medium onions, diced
    2   tablespoons ground cumin
    2   teaspoons chili powder
    2   cloves garlic, minced
    ¼   cup firmly packed light brown
          sugar
    ¼   cup orange juice
    ¼   cup ketchup
    2   tablespoons lemon juice

In a blender or food processor, purée chilies. Combine purée with chicken broth and set aside.

In a large skillet, melt butter over medium heat. Add onions and cook 15 minutes, stirring frequently. Blend in cumin, chili powder, and garlic. Stir in chili purée mixture. Reduce heat to medium-low and cook 20 minutes, stirring frequently.

Combine brown sugar, orange juice, ketchup, and lemon juice. Stir into chili mixture. Continue cooking, stirring occasionally, about 15 minutes or until mixture is the consistency of thick purée. Cool slightly. Serve warm or at room temperature.
Yield: about 2¾ cups of sauce

Spicy Cornmeal Chicken Nuggets served with Adobado Sauce will bring Southwest flavor to your holiday gathering.

ORANGE CREAM

4 cups orange juice
3 cinnamon sticks
1 tablespoon vanilla extract
1 pint vanilla ice cream

Miniature marshmallows to serve

In a large saucepan, combine orange juice, cinnamon sticks, and vanilla over medium-high heat. Bring mixture to a boil and reduce to low heat. Simmer 10 minutes. Remove cinnamon sticks. Stir in ice cream. Cook over low heat, stirring constantly, until heated through. Do not allow mixture to boil. Serve with miniature marshmallows.
Yield: 4 to 6 servings

Luscious Orange Cream, a mixture of orange juice and vanilla ice cream, is flavored with a hint of cinnamon. Serve it warm for a special holiday beverage.

GOUGÈRE

½ cup butter or margarine
1¼ cups all-purpose flour
4 eggs
3 cups shredded sharp Cheddar cheese
1 cup shredded Swiss cheese
¼ cup chopped onion
½ teaspoon salt
2 jalapeño peppers, chopped
1 clove garlic, minced
¼ teaspoon ground black pepper
⅛ teaspoon cayenne pepper

Preheat oven to 375 degrees. In a medium saucepan, melt butter over medium heat. Add flour and stir until mixture forms a ball. Remove from heat and continue stirring until mixture cools.

Beat in eggs, one at a time, stirring until mixture is slightly glossy and smooth. Stir in remaining ingredients. Pour batter into a greased 10-inch iron skillet. Bake 40 to 45 minutes or until golden brown. Cut bread into slices to serve.
Yield: about 32 slices of bread

Gougère is a hearty bread flavored with Cheddar and Swiss cheeses and hot jalapeño peppers.

Little open-faced sandwiches make great finger foods: Mini Bagels with Dilled Shrimp Spread *(top)* are flavored with dill and garlic. Sun-Dried Tomato Spread is delicious on Melba toast with ricotta cheese.

MINI BAGELS WITH DILLED SHRIMP SPREAD

- ¹/₂ pound cooked shrimp, peeled, deveined, and finely chopped
- 1 package (8 ounces) cream cheese, softened
- 2 tablespoons mayonnaise
- 2 tablespoons sherry
- 1 tablespoon lemon juice
- 2 cloves garlic, minced
- ¹/₂ teaspoon salt
- ¹/₂ teaspoon lemon pepper
- ¹/₂ teaspoon dried dill weed

- 20 mini bagels, split, to serve

Combine all ingredients in a small bowl, blending well. Cover and chill at least 1 hour before serving with mini bagels.
Yield: about 2 cups of spread

SUN-DRIED TOMATO SPREAD

- 1 cup sun-dried tomatoes
  Boiling water
- 5 tablespoons olive oil
- 2 tablespoons red wine vinegar
- 1 tablespoon capers
- 2 cloves garlic, minced
- 2 teaspoons Italian seasoning
- 1 teaspoon salt

  Melba toast and ricotta cheese to serve

Place tomatoes in a small bowl and add boiling water to cover. Allow to sit 15 minutes; drain.

Place tomatoes in a food processor and purée. Add oil, vinegar, capers, garlic, Italian seasoning, and salt. Process until well blended and mixture is still slightly coarse. Adjust seasonings, if desired. Store in a jar in refrigerator until ready to serve.

To serve, spread Melba toast with ricotta cheese and top with sun-dried tomato spread.
Yield: about 1 cup of spread

CARNITAS

1 pound bulk pork sausage
1/2 cup diced onion
1/2 cup diced green pepper
3 tablespoons ketchup
2 teaspoons chili powder
1/2 teaspoon ground cumin
1/8 teaspoon ground cloves
24 miniature taco shells

Shredded Cheddar cheese and
shredded lettuce to serve

In a skillet over medium heat, cook
sausage with onion and green pepper;
drain well. Stir in ketchup, chili powder,
cumin, and cloves. Cook 3 minutes, stirring
constantly. Drain again. Serve mixture in
taco shells with cheese and lettuce.
Yield: 24 miniature tacos

MUSHROOM AND CHICKEN PASTRIES

2 cans (5 ounces each) chunk
white chicken, drained and
chopped
1 cup finely chopped fresh mushrooms
1/3 cup mayonnaise
1/4 cup minced onion
2 tablespoons Worcestershire sauce
2 tablespoons minced fresh parsley
1 teaspoon garlic salt
1 teaspoon lemon pepper
1/2 teaspoon grated lemon peel
1 package (17 1/4 ounces) frozen puff
pastry dough, thawed

Combine all ingredients except puff
pastry dough. Blend well, cover, and
refrigerate until ready to use.

Preheat oven to 350 degrees. Unfold puff
pastry dough. Using a 2-inch round cookie
cutter, cut out dough. Place circles on
lightly greased baking sheet and bake
15 to 20 minutes or until puffed and
golden. Cool slightly and use a sharp knife
to cut off tops of pastries; set aside.
Remove soft inner dough from pastries. Fill
with chicken mixture; replace tops.
Yield: about 40 pastries

MUSHROOM CROUSTADES

36 thin slices wheat bread, cut into
3-inch rounds
1/4 cup butter or margarine
1/3 cup finely chopped green onion
8 ounces fresh mushrooms, finely
chopped
2 tablespoons all-purpose flour
1 tablespoon minced fresh parsley
1/2 teaspoon salt
1/8 teaspoon cayenne pepper
1 pound bulk pork sausage,
cooked and drained
1 cup whipping cream
2 teaspoons lemon juice
3 tablespoons freshly grated
Parmesan cheese

Preheat oven to 400 degrees. Carefully fit
bread into lightly greased miniature muffin
tins, pressing gently into sides to form
cups. Bake 8 to 10 minutes or until firm
to touch.

In a large skillet, melt butter over
medium-high heat. Add green onion and
sauté 3 to 4 minutes. Stir in mushrooms
and cook, stirring constantly, 10 to
15 minutes or until most of liquid is
evaporated. Stir in flour, parsley, salt, and
cayenne until well blended. Stir in sausage
and whipping cream and bring to a low
boil. Reduce heat to medium-low and
simmer about 10 minutes or until mixture
thickens. Stir in lemon juice and remove
from heat. Let cool slightly.

Preheat oven to 350 degrees. Spoon
filling evenly into bread cups. Sprinkle
cheese over tops. Bake 8 to 10 minutes or
until cheese melts. Serve warm.
Yield: 36 croustades

These tiny tidbits are packed with flavor: Mushroom and Chicken Pastries
(*clockwise from left*) are easy to make with purchased puff pastry dough. Carnitas
are miniature tacos with a sausage filling. Mushroom Croustades offer a creamy
combination of sausage and mushrooms in a toasted bread cup.

76

CHICKEN FAJITAS

1 cup tequila
1/2 cup plus 3 tablespoons vegetable oil, divided
1/2 cup lime juice
1/4 cup tomato paste
2 cloves garlic, minced
1 whole jalapeño pepper
1/2 teaspoon salt
1/2 teaspoon chili powder
1/2 teaspoon ground cumin
1 1/2 pounds boneless, skinless chicken breasts, cut into strips
10 flour tortillas for fajitas

1 large green pepper, cut into strips
1 large onion, cut into strips

Guacamole, sour cream, salsa, and shredded Cheddar cheese to serve

In a glass bowl or baking dish, combine tequila, 1/2 cup oil, lime juice, tomato paste, garlic, jalapeño pepper, salt, chili powder, and cumin. Blend well. Add chicken, cover, and marinate in refrigerator at least 6 hours or overnight.

Preheat oven to 350 degrees. Wrap tortillas in aluminum foil. Bake 15 minutes while preparing fajitas.

Remove chicken from marinade. In a large heavy skillet over medium-high heat, heat remaining 3 tablespoons oil. Add chicken and cook, stirring constantly, 5 to 7 minutes or until chicken is done. Add green pepper and onion and cook 2 to 3 minutes more, just until vegetables are crisp-tender. Serve with tortillas, guacamole, sour cream, salsa, and cheese.
Yield: 10 fajitas

Take your party south of the border with quick-and-easy Chicken Fajitas. Marinate the chicken ahead of time in our special mixture of tequila and spices, then prepare these zesty morsels in minutes.

A zesty blend of crabmeat and shrimp, Hot Creole Seafood Dip will perk up your party.

HOT CREOLE SEAFOOD DIP

    2 tablespoons butter or margarine
 1/2 cup chopped green pepper
    1 green onion, chopped
    1 package (8 ounces) cream
      cheese
    1 tablespoon Worcestershire sauce
 1 1/2 teaspoons Creole seasoning
 1/2 teaspoon chili powder
 1/8 teaspoon cayenne pepper
    3 to 4 drops hot pepper sauce
    2 cans (6 1/2 ounces each) lump
      crabmeat, drained
    1 package (5 ounces) frozen small
      cooked shrimp, thawed

      Crackers to serve

In a small skillet, melt butter over medium-high heat. Add green pepper and green onion and sauté 3 minutes; set aside.

In a large saucepan, melt cream cheese over low heat. Add green pepper mixture, Worcestershire sauce, Creole seasoning, chili powder, cayenne pepper, and hot pepper sauce. Stir in crabmeat and shrimp, blending well. Cook until heated through. Serve warm with crackers. May be served in a chafing dish.

Yield: about 3 1/2 cups of dip

For a change of pace, serve Middle Eastern Sesame Spread with Toasted Pita Chips. It's delicious topped with coconut, chutney, almonds, or raisins!

SESAME SPREAD WITH TOASTED PITA CHIPS

- 1 can (15 ounces) garbanzo beans, drained
- 1/3 cup tahini (sesame seed paste)
- 1/3 cup lemon juice
- 1/4 cup chopped green onion
- 1 tablespoon minced fresh parsley
- 1 clove garlic, minced
- 1/4 teaspoon salt
- 1/4 teaspoon ground black pepper
  Pita bread

  Coconut, chutney, toasted slivered almonds, and golden raisins to serve

Combine first 8 ingredients in a blender or food processor and process until smooth. Spoon mixture into a small bowl; cover and refrigerate at least 1 hour before serving.

Preheat oven to 450 degrees. Separate pita rounds in half. Cut each circle into 8 wedges. Place on ungreased baking sheet. Bake 5 to 8 minutes or until lightly browned and crisp. Serve sesame spread on pita chips topped with coconut, chutney, almonds, or golden raisins.
Yield: about 1 1/2 cups of spread

LONDON BROIL

- 1/2 cup vegetable oil
- 1/4 cup lemon juice
- 2 tablespoons minced onion
- 1 1/2 teaspoons salt
- 1 teaspoon granulated sugar
- 1/2 teaspoon dry mustard
- 1/2 teaspoon Italian seasoning
- 1/2 teaspoon ground black pepper
- 1/4 teaspoon ground ginger
- 1 clove garlic, minced
- 1 flank steak (about 2 pounds)

  Purchased hors d'oeuvre-size buns, mustard, and mayonnaise to serve

Combine all ingredients except steak, blending well. Place steak in a glass or enamel baking dish. Cover with marinade mixture and refrigerate at least 6 hours or overnight, turning steak occasionally.

Preheat broiler. Remove steak from marinade and broil about 5 inches from heat for 5 to 6 minutes on each side. Meat should be rare. Cut steak diagonally across the grain in thin slices. Serve with buns, mustard, and mayonnaise.
Yield: about 36 servings

LAMB'S WOOL

- 3 apples, peeled, cored, and chopped
- 3 tablespoons butter or margarine
- 3 bottles (12 ounces each) dark beer
- 1/2 cup firmly packed brown sugar
- 1 teaspoon ground cinnamon
- 1 teaspoon ground ginger
- 1/2 teaspoon ground nutmeg

Preheat oven to 350 degrees. Place apples in baking dish; dot with butter. Bake 30 minutes.

In a large saucepan, combine apples, beer, brown sugar, and spices. Cook, stirring occasionally, over medium-low heat until heated through. Serve warm.
Yield: 6 to 8 servings

A hot spiced ale made with apples and dark beer, Lamb's Wool (*top*) is a perfect accompaniment to London Broil, a marinated rare steak served on a bun with mayonnaise and mustard.

Garnished with a wreath of broccoli flowerets and colorful peppers, this Fresh Vegetable Tart includes crunchy carrots, broccoli, and green onions in a creamy filling.

FRESH VEGETABLE TART

CRUST

- 1¼ cups all-purpose flour
- ¼ teaspoon salt
- 7 tablespoons butter or margarine, chilled and cut into pieces
- 3 tablespoons ice water

FILLING

- 12 ounces (one and one-half 8-ounce packages) cream cheese, softened
- ⅓ cup sour cream
- ¼ cup mayonnaise
- 1 package (1 ounce) ranch salad dressing mix
- ½ cup chopped fresh broccoli
- ½ cup chopped fresh carrot
- ¼ cup chopped green onion
- 2 cups broccoli flowerets
- 1 cup shredded sharp Cheddar cheese
- ¼ cup chopped green pepper
- ¼ cup chopped sweet red pepper

Preheat oven to 450 degrees. For crust, sift flour and salt into a small mixing bowl. Using a pastry blender or 2 knives, cut butter into flour mixture until mixture resembles coarse meal. Sprinkle ice water over dough and mix quickly just until dough forms a soft ball. On a lightly floured surface, use a floured rolling pin to roll out dough into a 12- to 13-inch circle. Press dough into an 11-inch tart pan with removable bottom. Prick bottom of crust with a fork. Trim edges of dough. Bake 10 to 12 minutes or until golden brown. Cool completely before removing crust from pan.

For filling, beat cream cheese in a large bowl until smooth. Add sour cream, mayonnaise, and dressing mix, beating until smooth. Stir in next 3 ingredients. Spread cream cheese mixture into crust. Refrigerate 8 hours or overnight.

Place broccoli flowerets along edge of crust. Sprinkle cheese and peppers over filling, leaving center ungarnished. Slice into wedges and serve chilled.
Yield: 10 to 12 servings

CAJUN CANAPÉS

- 2 cans (10 biscuits per can) refrigerated buttermilk biscuits
- ½ pound mild pork sausage, cooked and drained
- 1½ cups (6 ounces) shredded sharp Cheddar cheese
- ¼ cup chopped green pepper
- ¼ cup mayonnaise
- 2 green onions, chopped
- 2 teaspoons lemon juice
- ½ teaspoon salt

Cajun Canapés (*left*) are stuffed with zesty sausage and cheese. Showy yet simple to make, Cornucopia Appetizers have olives and cocktail onions tucked inside rolls of spicy salami and Havarti cheese.

- ½ teaspoon paprika
- ¼ teaspoon cayenne pepper
- ¼ teaspoon garlic powder
- ¼ teaspoon ground thyme

Place biscuits 1 inch apart on a greased baking sheet. Following baking time and temperature listed on package directions, bake biscuits, turning over halfway through baking time. Allow to cool. Using a melon ball cutter, scoop out center of each biscuit.

Preheat oven to 400 degrees. In a large bowl, mix together remaining ingredients. Spoon about 1 tablespoon of mixture into each hollowed biscuit. Place on baking sheet and bake 8 to 10 minutes or until heated through. Serve warm.
Yield: 20 canapés

Note: Filled biscuits may be refrigerated overnight before baking. If refrigerated, decrease oven temperature to 325 degrees and bake 12 to 15 minutes or until golden brown and cheese melts.

CORNUCOPIA APPETIZERS

- ½ pound Havarti cheese, sliced paper-thin
- ¼ pound Genoa salami, sliced paper-thin
- 24 cocktail onions
- 24 pimiento-stuffed green olives

Cut cheese slices slightly smaller than salami slices. For each appetizer, place 1 cheese slice on top of each salami slice. Roll into a cone shape. Place 1 onion and 1 olive inside and secure with a toothpick. Refrigerate 1 hour or until firm. Remove toothpicks before serving.
Yield: 24 appetizers

CHEESE BLOSSOMS

2 cups (8 ounces) shredded sharp
    Cheddar cheese
1 cup all-purpose flour
1/2 cup butter or margarine, softened
2 tablespoons sesame seed,
    toasted
1/2 teaspoon salt
1 package (3 ounces) cream
    cheese, softened
3 ounces (1/2 of 6-ounce package)
    pasteurized process cheese food
    with garlic

    Sliced pimiento-stuffed green
    olives for garnish

Preheat oven to 375 degrees. Combine
first 5 ingredients in a large bowl. Knead
with hands, shaping dough into a smooth
ball. Cover and refrigerate 1 hour. Shape
dough into 3/4-inch balls and place on
greased baking sheets. Bake 12 to
15 minutes or until light brown. Cool on
wire rack.

In a small bowl, blend cream cheese
and garlic cheese until smooth; refrigerate
1 hour. Spoon cheese mixture into a pastry
bag fitted with a small star tip. Pipe cheese
onto biscuits just before serving. Garnish
each cheese blossom with 1 slice of olive.
Yield: about 3 dozen cheese blossoms

Rich, buttery Cheese Blossoms look especially festive when garnished with
pimiento-stuffed olive slices.

Stuffed with slices of roast beef and a spicy sauce, Snow Peas with Curry Filling
make elegant hors d'oeuvres.

SNOW PEAS WITH CURRY FILLING

2 dozen fresh snow pea pods
1/8 pound deli roast beef, sliced
    paper-thin
4 ounces (1/2 of 8-ounce
    package) cream cheese,
    softened
1/4 cup sour cream
1 teaspoon curry powder
1/2 teaspoon garlic powder
1/4 teaspoon granulated sugar

Trim stem and remove strings from sides
of each pod. Blanch pea pods in lightly
salted boiling water 2 to 3 minutes. Drain
and rinse in cold water. Using a sharp
knife, slit each pea pod open along straight
edge. Cut twenty-four 2 x 3-inch pieces
from roast beef. In a small bowl, combine
remaining ingredients. Spread about
1 teaspoon of filling in each pea pod;
tightly roll a piece of roast beef and insert
into pod. Refrigerate 1 hour or until firm.
Yield: 2 dozen snow peas

PESTO VEGETABLE DIP

1½ cups chopped fresh parsley
¾ cup grated Parmesan cheese
¼ cup pine nuts
¼ cup olive oil
1 cup mayonnaise
1 cup sour cream
1 clove garlic
1 teaspoon seasoned salt
¼ teaspoon ground black pepper

Fresh vegetables to serve

Place first 4 ingredients in a blender or food processor fitted with a steel blade. Process until mixture resembles coarse meal. Add remaining ingredients and process until smooth. Serve with fresh vegetables.

Yield: about 3 cups of dip

POLYNESIAN MEATBALLS

MEATBALLS
1½ pounds ground pork
1¼ pounds ground round
2 cups crushed corn flake cereal
1 cup milk
2 eggs, beaten
3 tablespoons prepared horseradish
3 tablespoons Worcestershire sauce
2 teaspoons dry mustard
1 teaspoon salt
½ teaspoon ground black pepper

SAUCE
1 cup ketchup
½ cup firmly packed brown sugar
½ cup water
⅓ cup soy sauce
2 tablespoons honey
2 tablespoons apple cider vinegar
1 teaspoon dry mustard
1 can (8 ounces) crushed pineapple, drained

Preheat oven to 450 degrees. For meatballs, combine all ingredients in a large bowl, mixing well. Shape mixture into 1-inch balls. Place on a rack in a shallow baking pan. Bake 12 to 15 minutes or until brown.

For sauce, mix together all ingredients except pineapple in a large saucepan over medium-high heat. Bring to a boil; reduce heat to medium and simmer 10 minutes. Stir in pineapple. Spoon meatballs into sauce, stirring until well coated. Continue to cook 10 to 15 minutes or until heated through. Serve hot.

Yield: about 75 meatballs

Flavorful Pesto Vegetable Dip *(top)* is a variation of an Italian favorite. Crushed pineapple lends tropical appeal to Polynesian Meatballs.

Savory Mixed Grill includes morsels of marinated beef, chicken, and shrimp. Served with tangy Cherry Sauce, it satisfies the heartiest of appetites.

MIXED GRILL WITH CHERRY SAUCE

GRILLED MEAT
1 1/2 pounds filet mignon or rib eye steak
1 1/4 pounds boneless, skinless chicken breasts
1 pound fresh large shrimp
1 cup vegetable oil
1 cup sherry
1/2 cup soy sauce
3 tablespoons honey
3 cloves garlic, minced
1 teaspoon ground ginger
1/4 teaspoon ground black pepper

  Wooden skewers

CHERRY SAUCE
2/3 cup plum jam
1 teaspoon soy sauce
1/4 teaspoon dry mustard
1/4 teaspoon ground ginger

1 can (16 ounces) pitted dark sweet cherries, drained
2 tablespoons water
1 tablespoon cornstarch

For grilled meat, cut beef and chicken into 1/2-inch cubes. Peel and devein shrimp. Place chicken, beef, and shrimp in separate resealable plastic bags. Combine next 7 ingredients in a jar. Secure lid on jar and shake well to mix. Pour 1/3 of marinade into each bag and seal. Refrigerate overnight, turning occasionally. (To prevent skewers from burning during cooking, place skewers in a flat dish, cover with water, and soak overnight.)

For cherry sauce, place first 4 ingredients in a blender or food processor fitted with steel blade; process until smooth. Add

cherries and process briefly to chop. Refrigerate at least 2 hours to allow flavors to blend.

Preheat oven to 375 degrees. Place chicken, beef, and shrimp on soaked skewers. Place on a rack in a roasting pan, loosely cover with aluminum foil, and bake 25 to 30 minutes.

To serve, heat cherry sauce in a small saucepan over medium heat. Combine water and cornstarch in a small bowl and slowly stir into sauce. Cook 3 to 4 minutes or until sauce thickens, stirring frequently. Serve warm with meat.
Yield: about 25 skewers

NUTTY GARLIC CHEESE SPREAD

- 3 heads (about 30 cloves) garlic, peeled
- 2 tablespoons vegetable oil
- 2 teaspoons white wine vinegar
- 1½ teaspoons Worcestershire sauce
- 1 package (8 ounces) cream cheese, softened
- 1¼ cups slivered almonds, toasted and finely chopped
- 1 cup sour cream
- ¼ cup chopped fresh parsley
- ½ teaspoon dry mustard
- ½ teaspoon dried oregano leaves
- ½ teaspoon salt
- ¼ teaspoon ground white pepper

Crackers or bread to serve

Preheat oven to 300 degrees. Place garlic and oil in a shallow baking dish, stirring until well coated. Bake 30 minutes or until garlic is light brown. Drain garlic on paper towels and cool completely.

In a blender or food processor fitted with a steel blade, process garlic, vinegar, and Worcestershire sauce until garlic is finely chopped. In a medium bowl, beat cream cheese until smooth. Stir in garlic mixture and remaining ingredients until thoroughly blended. Cover and refrigerate 8 hours or overnight.

To serve, bring to room temperature and serve with crackers or bread.
Yield: about 3 cups of spread

The surprisingly mild flavor of Nutty Garlic Cheese Spread is enhanced with toasted almonds.

Hot Cranberry Punch *(from left)* is a delicious blend of cranberry and orange juices, lemonade, and spices. Smoked Oyster Spread has a rich, creamy flavor, and Spicy Pastrami Rolls are easy to create with refrigerated crescent rolls.

HOT CRANBERRY PUNCH

6   cups cranberry juice
4   cups orange juice
1   cup water
1   can (6 ounces) frozen lemonade
     concentrate, thawed
1/2 cup firmly packed brown sugar
3   teaspoons whole cloves
3   teaspoons ground allspice
1   whole nutmeg, crushed
4   3-inch-long cinnamon sticks, broken
     into pieces

In a large saucepan or Dutch oven, combine first 5 ingredients. Place spices in a piece of cheesecloth and tie with string; add to punch. Bring to a boil, stirring occasionally. Reduce to low heat, cover, and simmer 30 minutes. Serve hot.
Yield: about 3 quarts of punch

SMOKED OYSTER SPREAD

2   packages (8 ounces each)
     cream cheese, softened
1/4 cup chopped green onion
2   tablespoons mayonnaise
1   tablespoon lemon juice
2   teaspoons prepared horseradish
2   teaspoons Worcestershire sauce
1/2 teaspoon salt
1/4 teaspoon onion powder
1/4 teaspoon hot pepper sauce
2   cans (3.6 ounces each) smoked
     oysters, drained and chopped

     Crackers to serve

In a large mixing bowl, beat cream cheese until smooth. Add next 8 ingredients, mixing well. Stir in oysters. Cover and chill 8 hours or overnight. Serve with crackers.
Yield: about 3 cups of spread

SPICY PASTRAMI ROLLS

2   packages (8 ounces each)
     refrigerated crescent rolls
1/2 pound deli pastrami, sliced
     paper-thin
1/2 cup soft cream cheese with
     chives and onions
1/3 cup Dijon-style mustard

Preheat oven to 375 degrees. Separate crescent rolls into triangles. Cut triangles in half to make 2 smaller triangles. Cut pastrami into 1 x 2-inch strips. Spread 1 teaspoon cream cheese and 1/2 teaspoon mustard on each triangle, leaving about 1/4 inch of the pointed end uncovered. Stack 3 pieces of pastrami at wide end of the triangle. Beginning at the wide end, roll up triangle and place on an ungreased baking sheet with point side down. Bake 12 to 15 minutes or until golden brown. Serve warm.
Yield: 32 rolls

FLORENTINE DIP

- 1   package (10 ounces) frozen chopped spinach, thawed and squeezed dry
- 1   package (3 ounces) cream cheese, softened
- ¹/₂ cup sour cream
- 2   tablespoons minced green onion
- 2   teaspoons prepared horseradish
- 1   jalapeño pepper, seeded and chopped
- ¹/₂ teaspoon salt
- ¹/₄ teaspoon ground black pepper
- ¹/₂ cup shredded sharp Cheddar cheese, divided
- ¹/₂ cup shredded Monterey Jack cheese, divided
- 1   jar (6 ounces) marinated artichoke hearts, drained and chopped

  Tortilla Wedges to serve (recipe follows)

Preheat oven to 350 degrees. In a large mixing bowl, combine first 8 ingredients, blending until smooth. Stir in ¹/₄ cup Cheddar cheese and ¹/₄ cup Monterey Jack cheese. Spread mixture into a greased 9-inch pie plate. Arrange chopped artichoke hearts around edge of plate. Bake 15 to 20 minutes. Sprinkle remaining cheeses on top and bake 5 minutes longer or until bubbly. Serve warm with Tortilla Wedges.

Yield: about 3 cups of dip

TORTILLA WEDGES

- 12 large flour tortillas
     Vegetable oil

Cut each tortilla into 8 wedges. Pour oil into a 10-inch skillet to a depth of ¹/₂ inch and heat to 350 degrees. Fry tortilla wedges, 2 at a time, about 10 seconds on each side or until light brown. Drain on paper towels.

Yield: 96 tortilla wedges

Note: Tortilla wedges may be made 1 day in advance and stored in an airtight container.

Light, crispy Tortilla Wedges are the perfect accompaniment for Florentine Dip, a tasteful blend of spinach, cheese, and artichoke hearts.

FESTIVE FAMILY FEASTS

When the family is home for Christmas, it means lots of good food and fun. This year, serve a picture-perfect holiday dinner with our collection of all-time favorites! From succulent meats to side dishes, desserts, and more, you'll find six complete menus from which to choose. A couple of the menus even offer more than one entrée so that you can tailor your meal to your family's tastes. Most recipes are traditional, but we've also included some new offerings for those who'd like to try something a little different.

This Tenderloin of Beef in Pastry showcases a succulent beef fillet with mushrooms and green onions.

CHRISTMAS EVE DINNERS

*For your convenience, we've provided two complete menus for a special holiday dinner —
or you can create your own tasty combination from the many delicious offerings.*

Shrimp Mousse	*Smoked Parmesan Almonds*
Cider-Baked Ham	*Lobster Bisque*
Red and Green Vegetable Medley	*Tenderloin of Beef in Pastry*
Corn Bread Loaf	*Creamy Pesto Spinach*
Peachy Sweet Potatoes	*Onion Casserole*
Flaming Bread Pudding	*Festive Rice Cups*
	Raspberry Soufflé

TENDERLOIN OF BEEF IN PASTRY

- 3 to 4 pound beef tenderloin, trimmed of fat
- 1 teaspoon salt, divided
- 1 teaspoon ground black pepper, divided
- 1/2 cup butter or margarine
- 1 pound fresh mushrooms, chopped
- 4 green onions, finely chopped
- 1 sheet (from a 17 1/4-ounce package) frozen puff pastry, thawed
- 1 egg yolk
- 1 teaspoon water

Preheat oven to 400 degrees. Rub beef with 1/2 teaspoon salt and 1/2 teaspoon pepper. Cook beef in roasting pan 25 to 30 minutes or until a meat thermometer inserted in center of meat registers 120 degrees. Cover and chill. Reduce oven temperature to 350 degrees.

In a medium skillet, melt butter over medium-high heat. Stir in mushrooms, onions, and remaining salt and pepper. Sauté 2 to 3 minutes or until onions are soft.

On a lightly floured surface, use a floured rolling pin to roll out pastry to a 10 x 13-inch rectangle (or large enough to wrap completely around beef). Mix egg yolk and water in a small bowl. Spread mushroom mixture evenly over pastry to within 2 inches of each edge. Center beef on pastry. Fold pastry around beef and seal edges with egg yolk mixture. Place beef, seam side down, on a greased baking sheet. Brush top of pastry with egg yolk mixture. Using dough scraps or another sheet of pastry, cut shapes from dough for garnish. Arrange cutouts on top of pastry; brush with remaining egg yolk mixture. Bake 30 to 40 minutes or until meat thermometer registers 140 degrees. If pastry browns too quickly, cover with aluminum foil. Cool 15 minutes. Slice to serve.
Yield: about 10 servings

SHRIMP MOUSSE

- 12 ounces frozen cooked and peeled shrimp (about 2 cups), thawed and finely chopped
- 1/2 cup finely chopped celery
- 3 tablespoons lemon juice
- 2 tablespoons white wine vinegar
- 1 teaspoon prepared horseradish
- 1 teaspoon ground black pepper
- 1/2 teaspoon salt
- 1/4 cup water
- 1 envelope unflavored gelatin
- 1/2 cup whipping cream
- 4 ounces (1/2 of 8-ounce package) cream cheese, softened
- 1/3 cup mayonnaise

Avocado slices and crackers to serve

To marinate shrimp, combine shrimp, celery, lemon juice, vinegar, horseradish, pepper, and salt in a large bowl. Cover and refrigerate 8 hours or overnight.

In a small saucepan, soften gelatin in water. Place over low heat, stirring until gelatin is dissolved. Remove from heat; cool to room temperature.

In a large bowl, beat cream until stiff. Stir in gelatin mixture, cream cheese, mayonnaise, and shrimp mixture. Pour into a greased 8-inch-diameter ring mold. Stirring occasionally, chill until mixture begins to set; chill until firm.

To unmold, dip mold into hot water up to rim and invert onto a serving plate. Serve with avocado slices and crackers.
Yield: 10 to 12 servings

Chopped celery adds crunch to cool, refreshing Shrimp Mousse. We garnished it with fresh avocado slices and crispy crackers for serving.

Broccoli and cherry tomatoes seasoned with lemon and basil make up the Red and Green Vegetable Medley *(from left)*. Festive Rice Cups are mildly flavored with onion and sweet peppers, and our recipe for Peachy Sweet Potatoes is an innovative version of a holiday favorite.

RED AND GREEN VEGETABLE MEDLEY

1 large bunch fresh broccoli, cleaned and chopped
³/₄ cup water
¹/₄ cup butter or margarine
3 tablespoons lemon juice
¹/₂ teaspoon dried basil leaves
¹/₂ teaspoon salt
¹/₄ teaspoon ground black pepper
1 pint cherry tomatoes, halved

In a large saucepan, cook broccoli in water until tender. Rinse with cold water and drain well. In a large skillet, melt butter over medium-high heat. Stir in broccoli, lemon juice, basil, salt, and pepper. Cook over high heat 1 to 2 minutes, stirring constantly. Add tomatoes and toss. Serve immediately.
Yield: about 6 servings

FESTIVE RICE CUPS

3 tablespoons butter or margarine
3 tablespoons olive oil
1 cup chopped onion
5 cups chicken broth
2 cups uncooked brown rice
¹/₂ teaspoon salt
¹/₄ teaspoon ground turmeric
¹/₄ teaspoon ground black pepper
¹/₄ cup chopped sweet red pepper
¹/₄ cup chopped green pepper

In a large saucepan, melt butter with oil over medium-high heat. Add onion and sauté until golden brown. Add chicken broth, rice, salt, turmeric, and black pepper. Bring to a boil and reduce heat to low. Cover and simmer 50 to 60 minutes or until all liquid is absorbed. Stir in red and green peppers. For each serving, firmly press about ¹/₂ cup rice mixture into a 3-inch tart mold; invert onto plate. Serve immediately.
Yield: 8 to 10 servings

PEACHY SWEET POTATOES

2 large sweet potatoes, peeled and cut into pieces
6 cups water
2 tablespoons firmly packed brown sugar
2 tablespoons butter or margarine, softened
1 teaspoon lemon juice
¹/₄ teaspoon salt
¹/₄ teaspoon ground cloves
2 cans (29 ounces each) peach halves, drained

In a large saucepan, cook potatoes in boiling water 25 to 30 minutes or until tender; drain. Cool to room temperature. In a large bowl, mash potatoes. Mix in next 5 ingredients, beating until smooth.
Preheat oven to 400 degrees. Place peach halves in an ungreased 9 x 13-inch baking pan. Using a pastry bag fitted with a large star tip, pipe potato mixture into center of each peach half. Bake 15 minutes or until potato mixture is light brown. Serve immediately.
Yield: 12 to 14 servings

LOBSTER BISQUE

- 1 gallon water
- 4 lobster tails (about 4 pounds)
- 6 tablespoons butter or margarine, divided
- 1/3 cup cognac
- 1/2 cup plus 3 tablespoons chopped green onions, divided
- 2 1/2 cups dry white wine
- 4 cloves garlic, minced
- 3 tablespoons tomato paste
- 1 teaspoon dried tarragon leaves
- 1/2 teaspoon dried thyme leaves
- 1/4 teaspoon ground cayenne pepper
- 2 bay leaves
- 3 tablespoons all-purpose flour
- 2 1/2 cups milk
- 3/4 cup whipping cream
- 2 egg yolks
- 1 teaspoon salt
- 1/4 teaspoon ground black pepper

Whipping cream to garnish

In a Dutch oven, heat water to boiling. Add lobster tails, cover, and cook about 12 minutes or until lobster is pink. Remove lobster from water. Reserve 4 cups of water used in cooking lobster tails. When cool enough to handle, remove lobster meat from shells and finely dice; chill.

For stock, melt 3 tablespoons butter in Dutch oven over medium heat. Stir in cognac. Bring mixture to a boil and simmer 3 minutes. Stir in reserved 4 cups water, 1/2 cup green onions, and next 7 ingredients. Simmer 30 minutes longer. Strain into a large bowl.

In Dutch oven, melt remaining 3 tablespoons butter over medium-high heat. Add remaining 3 tablespoons green onions and sauté 2 minutes. Whisk flour into butter mixture and cook 1 minute longer, stirring constantly. Whisk in stock and next 5 ingredients until blended. Bring to a boil, reduce heat to medium-low, and simmer 5 minutes. Stir in lobster meat. Simmer 10 to 15 minutes longer or until heated through. Garnish each serving with about 1 tablespoon whipping cream and swirl with a knife. Serve immediately.
Yield: about 8 servings

Perfect for nibbling before dinner, Smoked Parmesan Almonds *(top)* have a crispy cheese coating. The creamy Lobster Bisque is flavored with a hint of cognac and elegantly garnished with a swirl of cream.

SMOKED PARMESAN ALMONDS

- 1 egg white
- 1 cup whole unsalted almonds
- 2 tablespoons butter or margarine
- 1/4 cup grated Parmesan cheese
- 2 teaspoons liquid smoke flavoring
- 1 teaspoon salt

Preheat oven to 350 degrees. In a small bowl, beat egg white until foamy. Stir in almonds, coating well.

In a small saucepan, melt butter over medium heat. Stir in remaining ingredients. Add almonds to butter mixture, stirring until well coated. Pour onto an ungreased baking sheet. Bake 25 to 30 minutes or until cheese is brown. Cool completely on pan. Store in an airtight container.
Yield: about 1 cup almonds

Basted and browned to perfection, juicy Cider-Baked Ham *(right)* is served with a tangy-sweet sauce. Slices of sage-flavored Corn Bread Loaf are a tasty variation of traditional dressing.

CIDER-BAKED HAM

    5 to 6 pound ham
    2 cups apple cider, divided
 1/2 cup soy sauce
    2 tablespoons cornstarch
    1 tablespoon water

Preheat oven to 450 degrees. Place ham in a large roasting pan. Bake 30 minutes or until outside is crisp. Remove from oven. Reduce oven temperature to 325 degrees.

In a large bowl, combine 1 1/2 cups cider and soy sauce; pour over ham. Basting ham frequently with cider mixture, cover and bake 2 to 3 hours or until meat thermometer inserted in center of ham registers 185 degrees.

For sauce, combine meat drippings and remaining 1/2 cup cider in a medium saucepan. In a small bowl, combine cornstarch and water to make a paste. Spoon into meat drippings, stirring until smooth. Cook over medium heat 10 to 15 minutes or until thick, stirring occasionally. Transfer ham to serving plate and serve with sauce.

Yield: 12 to 16 servings

CORN BREAD LOAF

    6 tablespoons butter or margarine
    1 cup chopped green onions
 3/4 cup chopped celery
    4 cups corn bread crumbs
    4 cups finely crumbled white bread
  10 slices bacon, cooked and crumbled
 1 1/2 teaspoons ground sage
 3/4 teaspoon salt
 1/2 teaspoon ground black pepper
    6 eggs, beaten
    1 cup chicken broth

Preheat oven to 350 degrees. In a large skillet, melt butter over medium-high heat. Stir in onions and celery; sauté 8 minutes or until soft. In a large bowl, combine bread crumbs. Stir in onion mixture and next 4 ingredients. Stir in eggs and chicken broth. Spoon evenly into a greased and floured 4 x 12-inch loaf pan. Bake 30 to 40 minutes or until top is brown. Unmold onto serving plate and slice. Serve immediately.

Yield: about 10 servings

(Left) This savory Onion Casserole combines red, yellow, and green onions in a sauce of Havarti and blue cheeses with white wine. *(Right)* Creamy Pesto Spinach is presented in tomato cups to create a festive color combination.

ONION CASSEROLE

- 2 large yellow onions, thinly sliced and separated into rings, divided
- 2 large red onions, thinly sliced and separated into rings, divided
- 12 green onions, chopped and divided
- 1 teaspoon ground black pepper, divided
- 10 ounces blue cheese, crumbled
- 10 ounces (about 2½ cups) shredded Havarti cheese
- 3 tablespoons butter or margarine, cut into small pieces
- ¾ cup dry white wine

Preheat oven to 350 degrees. In a greased 9 x 13-inch baking dish, layer half of yellow, red, and green onions. Sprinkle ½ teaspoon pepper over onions. Top with blue cheese. Layer remaining onions and sprinkle remaining pepper over top. Top with Havarti cheese. Place butter evenly over cheese. Pour wine over casserole. Bake 1 hour or until onions are tender. If cheese browns too quickly, cover with aluminum foil. Serve hot.

Yield: about 12 servings

Note: Casserole may be assembled 1 day in advance and refrigerated. If refrigerated, increase baking time to 1 hour 15 minutes

CREAMY PESTO SPINACH

- 3 medium tomatoes
- 1 tablespoon salt
- 2 packages (10 ounces each) frozen chopped spinach, thawed and squeezed dry
- ¼ cup purchased pesto sauce
- ½ cup whipping cream
- ⅔ cup grated Romano cheese
- 1 teaspoon ground black pepper
- 1 tablespoon grated Parmesan cheese

Cut tomatoes in half; remove seeds and pulp. Sprinkle salt inside tomato shells and turn upside down on a wire rack to drain 30 minutes. Use a paper towel to pat inside of each tomato dry.

Preheat oven to 400 degrees. In a medium skillet, cook spinach over medium heat 5 to 10 minutes or until heated through. Stir in pesto sauce; cook 2 to 3 minutes longer. Stir in cream; cook until mixture is thick (about 2 minutes). Stir in Romano cheese and pepper. Spoon about ½ cup spinach into each tomato shell. Sprinkle Parmesan cheese over top. Bake in a greased 8-inch square baking pan 10 minutes or until heated through. Serve immediately.

Yield: 6 servings

RASPBERRY SOUFFLÉ

SOUFFLÉ

- 8 eggs, separated
- 1 cup granulated sugar
- 1 cup puréed raspberries
- ¼ cup crème de cassis liqueur
- 2 envelopes unflavored gelatin
- ½ cup lemon juice
- 2 cups whipping cream

SAUCE

- 2 cups sliced fresh or frozen strawberries
- ½ cup granulated sugar
- 4 tablespoons orange-flavored liqueur

For soufflé, prepare a 2-quart soufflé dish with a waxed paper collar extending 2 to 3 inches above rim of dish. Tape in place. Grease dish, including collar. In a medium bowl, beat egg yolks and sugar until fluffy. Stir in raspberries and crème de cassis. In a medium saucepan, soften gelatin in lemon juice. Cook over low heat, stirring until gelatin is dissolved. Stir raspberry mixture into gelatin mixture, mixing well. Cook over medium-low heat until mixture coats the back of a spoon (about 5 minutes). Cool to room temperature. In a large bowl, beat egg whites until stiff. In a chilled large bowl, beat cream until stiff. Fold egg whites into raspberry mixture. Gently fold in whipped cream. Pour into soufflé dish and chill 8 hours or overnight. Remove paper collar before serving.

For sauce, combine strawberries and sugar in a medium saucepan over medium heat. Cook 2 to 3 minutes or until heated through. Remove from heat and stir in liqueur. Serve with soufflé.

Yield: 8 to 10 servings

FLAMING BREAD PUDDING

PUDDING
- 2 cups raisins
- 1 cup cooking sherry
- 1 cup butter or margarine, softened
- 1 cup granulated sugar
- 1 cup all-purpose flour
- 1 teaspoon baking soda
- ¹/₂ teaspoon salt
- 2 cups finely chopped dates
- 1¹/₂ cups grated carrots

- 1¹/₂ cups chopped pecans
- 1 cup fine plain bread crumbs
- 1 cup milk
- 4 eggs, beaten
- ¹/₄ cup molasses
- ¹/₄ cup cognac
- 1 tablespoon dried orange peel
- 1 tablespoon dried lemon peel
- 2 teaspoons ground cinnamon
- ¹/₂ teaspoon ground cloves
- ¹/₂ teaspoon ground nutmeg
- ¹/₄ teaspoon ground mace

SAUCE
- 3 eggs, separated
- 1 cup granulated sugar
- 2 tablespoons butter or margarine, softened
- 1 cup whipping cream, whipped until stiff
- 3 tablespoons brandy
- ¹/₄ cup cognac

For pudding, marinate raisins in sherry 8 hours or overnight. In a large bowl, cream butter and sugar until fluffy. In a small bowl, combine flour, baking soda, and salt. Stir dry ingredients into creamed mixture. Stir in raisins (including sherry) and remaining pudding ingredients, mixing well. Spoon into a greased 3-quart metal mold with lid. Cover loosely with lid. Place mold on a wire rack in a large stockpot. Fill pot with hot water to come halfway up sides of mold. Cover pot and steam pudding in simmering water over medium heat about 5 hours. Check water level occasionally; add hot water as needed. Remove mold from water, uncover, and cool 30 minutes. Invert onto a serving plate, leaving pudding in mold until completely cooled.

For sauce, beat egg yolks in a large bowl. Add sugar and butter; beat until thick. In a medium bowl, beat egg whites until stiff; fold into egg yolk mixture. Fold in whipped cream and brandy.

Heat cognac in a small saucepan over medium heat. Remove from heat and carefully ignite with a long kitchen match. Pour over pudding. When flames die, slice and serve with sauce.

Yield: 10 to 12 servings

(Left) A spirited sauce of strawberries and orange liqueur complements this elegant Raspberry Soufflé. *(Right)* Flaming Bread Pudding makes a grand finale to Christmas Eve dinner. Laden with fruits and nuts, the traditional steamed pudding is served with a creamy brandy sauce.

AMERICAN HERITAGE DINNER

Corn Chowder	Cabbage with Raisins
Compound Sallet	Baked Beans
Johnnycakes	Sack Posset
Roast Turkey	Sweet Potato Pudding
Corn Bread Dressing with Dried Fruit	Almond Flummery
Christmas Chicken Pie	Ginger Custard
Sweet Potatoes and Chestnuts	Plum Custard

A succulent Roast Turkey *(left)* accompanied by Corn Bread Dressing with Dried Fruit will be enjoyed by all. A traditional English dish, Christmas Chicken Pie is a delicious way to dress up everyday fare.

ROAST TURKEY

12 to 14 pound turkey
  Salt and ground black pepper
1/4 cup butter, softened
2 cups apple cider

Preheat oven to 350 degrees. Remove giblets from turkey and discard or reserve for another use. Rinse turkey and pat dry with paper towels. Liberally salt and pepper turkey inside and out. Tie ends of legs to tail with kitchen twine; lift wing tips up and over back so they are tucked under turkey. Place on rack in roasting pan with breast side up. Insert meat thermometer into thickest part of thigh without touching bone. Pour 1 cup water into pan. Spread butter over turkey. Baste with some of the apple cider. Loosely cover with aluminum foil and roast 2½ hours. Remove foil from turkey. Reduce heat to 325 degrees. Basting often with apple cider, roast uncovered 1 hour or until meat thermometer registers 180 degrees (juices should run clear when thickest part of thigh is pierced with a fork). Remove from oven and allow turkey to stand 20 minutes before carving.
Yield: 10 to 12 servings

CORN BREAD DRESSING WITH DRIED FRUIT

1½ cups dried mixed fruit bits
1/2 cup butter
1 medium onion, chopped
1 cup chopped celery
5 cups corn bread crumbs
2 cups white bread crumbs
1½ cups chicken broth
1½ teaspoons rubbed sage
1 teaspoon poultry seasoning
1 teaspoon salt
1/2 teaspoon ground black pepper
1 egg, lightly beaten

Place fruit in a bowl and add enough water to cover fruit. Cover and allow fruit to sit at room temperature overnight.

Preheat oven to 350 degrees. Melt butter in skillet. Add onion and celery and sauté until onion is transparent. Remove from heat and set aside.

Drain fruit. In a large mixing bowl, combine fruit, sautéed mixture, bread crumbs, chicken broth, sage, poultry seasoning, salt, and pepper, adjusting seasoning as desired. Stir in egg. Spoon dressing into a lightly greased 2-quart baking dish. Cover with aluminum foil and bake 25 to 30 minutes or until dressing is heated through.
Yield: about 10 servings

CHRISTMAS CHICKEN PIE

CRUST
3 cups all-purpose flour
1½ teaspoons salt
1 cup butter
1/4 cup ice water

FILLING
8 chicken breast halves
1/4 cup butter
1/4 cup all-purpose flour
2½ cups chicken broth
1½ teaspoons salt
1 teaspoon ground thyme
1 teaspoon dried marjoram flakes
1 teaspoon rubbed sage
1/2 teaspoon ground black pepper
1 pound pork sausage, browned
5 slices bacon, cooked and broken into 1-inch pieces
1 egg yolk
1 teaspoon water

For crust, sift flour and salt into a medium bowl. Using a pastry blender or two knives, cut butter into flour mixture until mixture resembles coarse meal. Sprinkle water over dough, mixing quickly just until dough forms a ball. Divide dough in half. Press half of dough into bottom and up sides of a lightly greased 2-quart round baking dish. Cover top with plastic wrap. Wrap remaining dough in plastic wrap; refrigerate baking dish and remaining dough until needed.

For filling, cook chicken breasts in salted boiling water in a large stockpot. Remove from water and cool. Remove meat from bone and tear into bite-sized pieces.

Melt butter in a large saucepan over medium heat. Stir in flour. Stirring constantly, cook until mixture thickens and bubbles. Gradually stir in chicken broth. Stir in salt, thyme, marjoram, sage, and pepper. Cook, stirring constantly, until mixture thickens (3 to 4 minutes).

Preheat oven to 325 degrees. On a lightly floured surface, use a floured rolling pin to roll out remaining dough. Layer half of chicken in bottom of dough-lined baking dish. Layer sausage and bacon over chicken. Top with remaining chicken. Pour sauce over meat. Top with remaining rolled dough. Trim dough and crimp edges of pie. Cut slits in top of pie for steam to escape. (If desired, roll out dough scraps and use a cookie cutter to cut out a decoration for top of pie. Apply cutout to pie with a small amount of egg yolk.) Bake 1½ hours. Combine egg yolk with water and brush over top of crust. Bake 5 minutes.
Yield: about 8 servings

Johnnycakes (also called Journey Cakes) were early American favorites.

JOHNNYCAKES

4 cups cornmeal
3 cups boiling water
2 eggs, lightly beaten
1/4 cup firmly packed brown sugar
2 tablespoons butter, softened
1 teaspoon salt

  Butter and maple syrup or molasses to serve

Preheat oven to 400 degrees. In a medium mixing bowl, combine cornmeal and water, stirring well by hand (mixture will be very thick). Stir in remaining ingredients. Using about 1/2 cup mixture for each cake, spread mixture into circles about 4 inches in diameter on greased baking sheets. Bake 20 to 25 minutes or until centers are set. Serve warm with butter and maple syrup or molasses.
Yield: 10 to 12 Johnnycakes

CORN CHOWDER

 1/4 pound salt pork, skin removed and
      thinly sliced
 1   medium onion, chopped
 2   large baking potatoes, peeled and
      chopped
 3   cups water, divided
 1   cup finely crushed cracker crumbs
 3   cups milk
 1   can (17 ounces) creamed corn
 1 1/2 teaspoons salt
 1   teaspoon ground nutmeg

In a large saucepan, fry salt pork with onion until pork is crisp and browned. Stir in potatoes and 2 cups water. Cook over medium heat until potatoes are tender. Combine cracker crumbs and milk; stir into potato mixture. Stir in corn, salt, nutmeg, and remaining 1 cup water. Reduce heat to medium-low and cook, stirring occasionally, 10 minutes or until heated through.
Yield: about 8 1/2 cups of chowder

Savory Corn Chowder makes a satisfying light meal or first course. We used a pumpkin and acorn squash halves for our soup tureen and bowls.

COMPOUND SALLET

DRESSING
 1   cup olive oil
 1/3 cup red wine vinegar
 2   tablespoons granulated sugar

SALAD
 2   bunches fresh spinach, rinsed and
      torn into pieces
 1   cup currants
 1   cup chopped canned red beets
 1   lemon, peeled, thinly sliced, and
      seeds removed
 1   cup toasted slivered almonds
 1/4 cup drained capers

For dressing, combine oil, vinegar, and sugar in a jar with a tight-fitting lid. Close jar and shake vigorously to blend.

For salad, combine spinach, currants, beets, lemon slices, almonds, and capers in a serving bowl.

To serve, pour dressing over salad and toss.
Yield: about 8 servings

Compound Sallet, a flavorful medley of fresh spinach, beets, lemons, and nuts is tossed with a vinaigrette dressing.

Apples and chestnuts complement a traditional holiday vegetable in Sweet Potatoes and Chestnuts *(from left)*. Once a favorite Colonial party beverage, Sack Posset is a warm custard drink with sherry. Buttery Sweet Potato Pudding is best served with lots of whipped cream.

SWEET POTATOES AND CHESTNUTS

    6   large sweet potatoes
    3   apples, peeled, cored, and sliced
    1   can (15.5 ounces) whole chestnuts
          packed in water, drained
  3/4   cup firmly packed brown sugar
    2   teaspoons ground nutmeg
  1/4   cup butter
    1   cup apple cider

In a large saucepan, boil whole, unpeeled sweet potatoes until tender (about 20 minutes). Remove from water and allow to cool.

Preheat oven to 350 degrees. Peel and slice sweet potatoes. In a lightly greased 13 x 9 x 2-inch baking pan, layer sweet potato slices, apples, and chestnuts. Sprinkle top with brown sugar and nutmeg; dot with butter. Pour apple cider over top. Bake 45 minutes or until mixture is bubbly.
Yield: 8 to 10 servings

SACK POSSET

    1   cup granulated sugar
    1   cup cream sherry
    1   whole nutmeg
    2   cups milk
    5   egg yolks, lightly beaten

In a medium saucepan, combine sugar, sherry, and nutmeg. Bring to a boil and cook until sugar dissolves; set aside.

In a large saucepan, scald milk. Beat about 1/2 cup milk into egg yolks; then beat in remaining milk. Return mixture to pan and cook, stirring constantly, over medium-low heat until mixture coats the back of a metal spoon. Gradually stir sherry mixture into milk mixture, blending well. Stirring occasionally, cook over low heat until heated through. Remove nutmeg; serve warm.
Yield: 4 to 6 servings

SWEET POTATO PUDDING

    1   pound sweet potatoes, peeled and
          cut into chunks
    6   eggs, lightly beaten
    3   cups confectioners sugar
 1 1/2   cups butter, softened
  1/2   cup brandy
    1   teaspoon ground cinnamon
    1   teaspoon ground nutmeg
  1/2   teaspoon grated lemon peel
  1/2   cup firmly packed brown sugar
    1   cup whipping cream
    2   tablespoons granulated sugar

In a large saucepan, boil sweet potatoes in water until tender. Drain potatoes and mash until smooth.

Preheat oven to 375 degrees. In a large mixing bowl, combine mashed potatoes, eggs, confectioners sugar, butter, brandy, cinnamon, nutmeg, and lemon peel; blend well. Pour mixture into a greased 13 x 9 x 2-inch baking pan. Bake 40 to 45 minutes or until top is set. Sprinkle brown sugar over top and bake 5 minutes.

In a medium bowl, beat cream with granulated sugar until stiff peaks form. Serve whipped cream with pudding.
Yield: about 12 servings

CABBAGE WITH RAISINS

    1 head (about 2 pounds) red
          cabbage, quartered
 ½ cup raisins
 ¼ cup butter
 ¼ cup apple cider vinegar
    2 tablespoons firmly packed brown
          sugar

Fill a large saucepan with salted water and bring to a boil. Add cabbage; cover and cook until tender. Remove from heat and drain. Using a large spoon, separate leaves of cabbage. Stir in remaining ingredients. Return saucepan to medium heat and cook 5 minutes.

Yield: 4 to 6 servings

ALMOND FLUMMERY

    3 egg yolks
    3 cups whipping cream, divided
 ¾ cup zwieback cracker crumbs
 ½ cup almond paste
    4 tablespoons granulated sugar,
          divided
    2 tablespoons rose flower water
          (available at gourmet specialty
          stores)
 ¼ teaspoon ground cinnamon
 ¼ teaspoon ground nutmeg
 ¾ cup golden raisins
 ¼ cup toasted slivered almonds

Preheat oven to 350 degrees. In a large mixing bowl, beat egg yolks with 2 cups cream until well blended. Stir in cracker crumbs and allow to sit 5 minutes to soften. Blend in almond paste, 2 tablespoons sugar, rose flower water, cinnamon, and nutmeg. Stir in raisins. Sprinkle almonds in bottom of a lightly greased 1-quart metal ring mold. Pour mixture into mold. Cover top of mold tightly with aluminum foil. Place mold in a larger pan and add hot water to larger pan to come halfway up sides of mold. Bake 1 hour. Remove from oven and allow to cool 15 minutes in water. Remove mold from water; remove foil. Allow to cool at room temperature 15 minutes. Unmold onto serving platter.

Beat remaining 1 cup cream and remaining 2 tablespoons sugar until stiff peaks form. Serve sweetened whipped cream with almond flummery.

Yield: 8 to 10 servings

The sweet-and-sour flavor of Cabbage with Raisins will be a welcome addition to the meal. It's especially colorful served in a hollowed-out pumpkin.

A traditional English steamed pudding served with sweetened whipped cream, Almond Flummery will delight you with its delicious blend of almonds and raisins.

PLUM CUSTARD

CRUST
  1½ cups all-purpose flour
  ½ teaspoon salt
  ½ cup butter

FILLING
  1 can (1 pound) whole, pitted plums
      in heavy syrup, drained
  ½ cup granulated sugar
  1 teaspoon ground cinnamon
  1½ cups half and half
  2 eggs, lightly beaten

Preheat oven to 350 degrees. For crust, sift flour and salt into a mixing bowl. Using a pastry blender or two knives, cut butter into flour until mixture resembles coarse meal. Using the back of a spoon, firmly press mixture into bottom and halfway up sides of a lightly greased 8-inch square baking pan.

For filling, layer plums over crust. Sprinkle sugar and cinnamon over plums. Bake 20 minutes. In a small bowl, combine half and half and eggs. Pour over plums. Bake 30 to 35 minutes or until custard is firm around edges but still slightly soft in center (custard will become firmer as it cools). Serve warm or chilled.
Yield: about 9 servings

Moist and fruity Ginger Custard *(left)* makes a wonderful, lightly sweet side dish. We garnished it with a barley sugar Indian. The hearty Baked Beans are laced with maple syrup and molasses.

GINGER CUSTARD

  5 cups torn white bread pieces
  2 cups buttermilk
  2 cups half and half
  6 apples, peeled, cored, and chopped
  ½ cup water
  ½ cup maple syrup
  ½ cup granulated sugar
  4 eggs, lightly beaten
  1 teaspoon ground ginger
  1 teaspoon ground cinnamon
  1 teaspoon ground nutmeg
  ¼ teaspoon ground cloves
  1 cup golden raisins

In a large mixing bowl, combine bread, buttermilk, and half and half; set aside. In a saucepan, combine apples and water over medium heat. Cover and cook until apples are tender; cool.

Preheat oven to 350 degrees. Stir syrup, sugar, eggs, and spices into bread mixture. Stir in apples. Pour mixture into a greased 13 x 9 x 2-inch baking pan. Sprinkle with raisins. Bake 50 to 60 minutes or until center is set.
Yield: 8 to 10 servings

BAKED BEANS

  2 cups dried navy beans
  4 cups water
  1 medium onion, chopped
  2 tablespoons butter
  ½ cup molasses
  ½ cup maple syrup
  2 teaspoons salt
  1 teaspoon dry mustard
  1 teaspoon ground ginger
  ½ teaspoon ground cinnamon

Cover beans with water and allow to soak overnight.

Drain beans and combine with 4 cups water in a 2-quart saucepan. Bring to a boil over high heat. Cover beans, reduce heat, and simmer 2 hours. Drain beans, reserving 2 cups liquid (add additional water to equal 2 cups if necessary).

In a small skillet, sauté onion in butter until onion is limp. Preheat oven to 350 degrees. In a lightly greased 2-quart baking dish, combine beans, sautéed onion, reserved liquid, molasses, syrup, salt, mustard, ginger, and cinnamon. Mix well. Cover and bake 2 hours, stirring occasionally. Add more water to dish if necessary. Uncover and bake 35 to 45 minutes or until top is browned.
Yield: about 8 servings

Featuring layers of tasty plums and egg custard on a pastry crust, Plum Custard is a dessert your family will love. We garnished ours with a maple leaf made of barley sugar.

KEEPING CHRISTMAS

<table>
<tr><td>Acorn Squash Soup</td><td>Roast Turkey Glazed with Honey</td></tr>
<tr><td>Peach Aspic with Cream Cheese Dressing</td><td>Corn Bread Dressing in Grape Leaves</td></tr>
<tr><td>Spinach Salad with Warm Dressing</td><td>Sour Cream Giblet Gravy</td></tr>
<tr><td>Candied Ginger Biscuits</td><td>Caramelized New Potatoes</td></tr>
<tr><td>Standing Rib Roast with
Madeira Mushroom Gravy</td><td>Corn-Stuffed Tomatoes</td></tr>
<tr><td></td><td>Green Beans with Dill Sauce</td></tr>
<tr><td>Yorkshire Pudding</td><td>Pumpkin-Apple Pie</td></tr>
</table>

Thin slices of Standing Rib Roast with Madeira Mushroom Gravy make an elegant serving. Individual Yorkshire Puddings are a unique accompaniment for this English entrée.

STANDING RIB ROAST WITH MADEIRA MUSHROOM GRAVY

ROAST
- 1 standing rib of beef
  (about 10 pounds or 4 ribs)
- 2 teaspoons salt
- 1 teaspoon ground black pepper
- 1 teaspoon ground thyme

GRAVY
- $2/3$ cup water
- $1/4$ cup plus 2 tablespoons butter or margarine, divided
- 2 tablespoons lemon juice
- $1/2$ pound fresh mushrooms, sliced
- $1/2$ cup finely chopped onion
- $1 1/2$ cups beef broth
- $1/2$ cup Madeira wine
- 2 tablespoons tomato paste
- 2 tablespoons all-purpose flour
  Salt and ground black pepper

For roast, sprinkle beef with salt, pepper, and thyme; rub into meat. Place on rack in roasting pan. Insert meat thermometer into thickest portion of meat without touching bone. Allow to stand at room temperature 30 minutes.

Preheat oven to 500 degrees. Roast meat 10 minutes. Reduce temperature to 350 degrees. Continue roasting 2 1/2 to 4 hours or until meat thermometer registers 140 degrees. Transfer roast to a serving platter.

For gravy, combine water, 2 tablespoons butter, and lemon juice in saucepan. Bring to a boil over medium-high heat. Reduce heat to low and add mushrooms. Cover and cook 5 minutes. Pour off fat from roasting pan, reserving 3/4 cup for Yorkshire Pudding (recipe follows), if desired. Add remaining 1/4 cup butter to roasting pan and place over medium-high heat, stirring to melt. Add onion and sauté until transparent. Drain mushroom liquid into roasting pan. Add beef broth, wine, and tomato paste; blend well. Stir in mushrooms and flour. Stirring constantly, cook until gravy is slightly thickened and mushrooms are heated through. Salt and pepper to taste. Serve with roast.

Yield: 8 to 10 servings

SPINACH SALAD WITH WARM DRESSING

DRESSING
- $1/2$ cup red wine vinegar
- $1/2$ cup olive oil
- $1/4$ cup water
- 2 teaspoons lemon juice
- 1 teaspoon Dijon-style mustard
- 1 teaspoon Worcestershire sauce
- 1 tablespoon granulated sugar
- $3/4$ teaspoon garlic salt
- $1/4$ teaspoon ground black pepper

SALAD
- 1 bunch fresh spinach, rinsed and torn into pieces
- 1 bunch red leaf lettuce, rinsed and torn into pieces
- $1/2$ pound fresh mushrooms, sliced
- $1/2$ cup slivered almonds, toasted
- 3 green onions, chopped
- 4 slices bacon, cooked and crumbled

For dressing combine all ingredients in a jar with a tight-fitting lid. Close jar and shake vigorously.

For salad, toss all ingredients together in serving bowl.

To serve, pour dressing into a non-aluminum saucepan and stir over medium heat until heated through. Serve warm dressing with salad.

Yield: 8 to 10 servings

YORKSHIRE PUDDING
- $3/4$ cup meat drippings from roast **or** melted margarine
- $1 1/2$ cups all-purpose flour
- 1 teaspoon salt
- $3/4$ cup milk at room temperature
- 3 eggs at room temperature
- $3/4$ cup water at room temperature

Preheat oven to 400 degrees. Spoon 1 tablespoon meat drippings or margarine into each cup of a 12-cup muffin pan. Place muffin pan in oven to heat drippings while preparing batter. In a medium mixing bowl, combine flour and salt. Make a well in center and stir in milk. Beat in eggs. Add water, beating until bubbly. Remove muffin pan from oven and immediately fill each cup slightly less than half full with batter. Bake 20 minutes. Reduce heat to 350 degrees; bake 15 minutes. Serve immediately.

Yield: 12 servings

Spinach Salad with Warm Dressing features fresh mushrooms, toasted almonds, and crisp bacon. Warming the dressing intensifies its spicy vinegar flavor.

CORN-STUFFED TOMATOES

5 medium tomatoes
2 tablespoons butter or margarine
2 tablespoons all-purpose flour
1 teaspoon salt
1/4 teaspoon ground black pepper
1 cup milk
3 cups frozen corn, cooked in salted water and drained
1/2 cup finely chopped green onion
5 slices bacon, cooked and crumbled
   Salt and ground black pepper

Cut tomatoes in half. Scoop out as much flesh as possible, invert on paper towels, and drain.

Preheat oven to 350 degrees. Melt butter in saucepan over medium-low heat. Stir in flour, 1 teaspoon salt, and 1/4 teaspoon pepper. Cook until mixture is smooth and bubbly. Slowly pour in milk, stirring constantly. Increase heat to medium and continue cooking and stirring until mixture thickens (about 1 minute). Remove from heat and stir in corn, green onion, and bacon. Salt and pepper to taste. Fill each tomato half with corn mixture and place on baking sheet. Cover with aluminum foil and bake 25 to 30 minutes or just until heated through.
Yield: 10 servings

CARAMELIZED NEW POTATOES

20 small new potatoes
1/2 cup butter or margarine
1/2 cup firmly packed brown sugar

Cook unpeeled potatoes in well-salted boiling water 15 to 20 minutes or until tender. Remove from heat, drain, and allow to cool slightly; peel.

Melt butter in a heavy large skillet over medium heat. Stir in brown sugar and cook, stirring constantly, until mixture bubbles and thickens slightly (about 5 minutes). Add potatoes and cook 2 to 3 minutes, stirring constantly until potatoes are thoroughly coated with caramel. Place in a heated serving dish and serve immediately.
Yield: 8 to 10 servings

Corn-Stuffed Tomatoes (*left*) bring exciting new flavor to the table, and Caramelized New Potatoes offer a taste of Olde World ingenuity.

Roast Turkey Glazed with Honey is a delicious main course. A distinctive touch is added when Corn Bread Dressing is nestled in grape leaves and served with Sour Cream Giblet Gravy.

ROAST TURKEY GLAZED WITH HONEY

12 to 14 pound turkey
   Salt and ground black pepper
1 cup water
1/4 cup butter or margarine, melted
1/2 cup honey

Preheat oven to 350 degrees. Remove giblet packet from turkey and reserve for Sour Cream Giblet Gravy (recipe follows). Rinse turkey and pat dry with paper towels. Liberally salt and pepper turkey inside and out. Tie ends of legs to tail with kitchen twine; lift wing tips up and over back so they are tucked under turkey. Place on rack in roasting pan with breast side up. Insert meat thermometer into thickest part of thigh without touching bone. Pour 1 cup water into pan. Brush turkey with butter. Loosely cover with aluminum foil and roast 2 1/2 hours. Remove foil from turkey. Reduce heat to 325 degrees. Basting often with honey, roast uncovered 1 hour or until meat thermometer registers 180 degrees (juices should run clear when thickest part of thigh is pierced with a fork). Remove from oven and allow turkey to stand 20 minutes before carving.
Yield: 10 to 12 servings

SOUR CREAM GIBLET GRAVY

   Neck and giblets from turkey
1 medium onion, chopped
3 tablespoons butter or margarine
4 1/2 cups water, divided
2 tablespoons chopped fresh parsley
1 teaspoon paprika
1/2 cup all-purpose flour
1/2 cup sour cream
   Salt and ground black pepper

Clean and wash neck and giblets; set aside. In large saucepan, sauté onion in butter until transparent. Add neck and giblets and 4 cups water. Simmer over medium heat until meat is tender (1 to 1 1/2 hours). Add parsley and paprika; simmer 10 minutes more. Remove neck and giblets from pan, reserving liquid and onion. Remove meat from neck; discard bone. Chop meat and giblets and return to saucepan with reserved liquid and onion. In small bowl, combine flour with remaining 1/2 cup reserved water. Beat in sour cream until smooth. Stir 1/2 cup reserved liquid from saucepan into sour cream mixture and stir sour cream mixture into giblets. Salt and pepper to taste. Cook over medium-low heat 15 to 20 minutes or until thickened and heated through.
Yield: about 4 1/2 cups gravy

CORN BREAD DRESSING IN GRAPE LEAVES

1/2 cup butter or margarine
1/2 cup chopped celery
1 small onion, coarsely chopped
2 tablespoons minced fresh parsley
5 cups corn bread crumbs
2 cups white bread crumbs
1 1/2 cups chicken broth
1 teaspoon ground sage
1 teaspoon salt
1/2 teaspoon poultry seasoning
1/2 teaspoon ground black pepper
1 egg, lightly beaten
14 grape leaves in brine, rinsed and separated

Preheat oven to 350 degrees. Melt butter in skillet. Stir in celery, onion, and parsley; sauté until onion is transparent. Remove from heat; pour into large mixing bowl. Stir in bread crumbs and chicken broth. Add sage, salt, poultry seasoning, and pepper, adjusting seasonings as desired. Stir in egg. Place about 1/2 cup dressing in center of each grape leaf; gently press sides of each leaf around dressing. Place stuffed leaves in a baking dish with sides touching. Cover and bake 25 to 30 minutes or until dressing is heated through.
Yield: 14 servings

(Left) Garnished with sage leaves and apple slices, Acorn Squash Soup makes an attractive first course for an elegant dinner. A subtle blend of apples and curry complements the squash and adds delicate flavor to this rich soup. *(Right)* Easy to prepare, Green Beans with Dill Sauce and Candied Ginger Biscuits are tasty additions to your holiday meal.

ACORN SQUASH SOUP

    4   cups water
    2   medium acorn squash, scrubbed,
            halved, and seeds removed
    1   large onion, sliced
    1   sweet yellow pepper, sliced
    3   tablespoons butter or margarine
    3   apples, peeled, cored, and diced
    3   cups chicken broth
    1   tablespoon Worcestershire sauce
    1   teaspoon curry powder
        Salt and ground black pepper
    2   cups half and half

In large saucepan, bring water to a boil. Add squash, cover, and boil 15 to 20 minutes or until tender. Remove squash and allow to cool; reserve liquid. When cool enough to handle, scoop out squash with a spoon and discard skin.

In a large saucepan, sauté onion and yellow pepper in butter until onion is transparent. Add squash, reserved liquid, apples, chicken broth, Worcestershire sauce, and curry. Salt and pepper to taste. Bring to a boil. Reduce heat to simmer. Partially cover and cook 15 minutes, stirring occasionally.

Place squash mixture in a blender or food processor and purée. Return to saucepan. Stir in half and half, adjust seasonings, and cook over medium heat just until heated through; do not allow to boil.
Yield: 8 to 10 servings

GREEN BEANS WITH DILL SAUCE

    1   cup sour cream at room temperature
    6   slices bacon, cooked and crumbled
    1   tablespoon chopped dried chives
  1 1/2 teaspoons lemon pepper
    1   teaspoon dried dill weed
        Salt
    2   packages (10 ounces each) frozen
            French-style green beans

Combine first 5 ingredients in small saucepan. Salt to taste and set aside (do not refrigerate). Cook green beans according to package directions. Warm sour cream mixture over low heat, stirring constantly. Drain green beans and place about 1/2 cup on each serving plate. Indent center of beans with the back of spoon. Place a heaping tablespoon of dill sauce in center of beans.
Yield: about 8 servings

CANDIED GINGER BISCUITS

    2   cups all-purpose flour
    1   tablespoon baking powder
    1   teaspoon salt
  1/3   cup vegetable shortening
  1/2   cup finely minced crystallized ginger
    2   tablespoons firmly packed brown
            sugar
    1   teaspoon ground ginger
  1/2   teaspoon ground cinnamon
    1   cup milk
    2   tablespoons butter, melted

Preheat oven to 450 degrees. In a large bowl, combine flour, baking powder, and salt. Cut in shortening with a pastry blender or two knives until mixture resembles coarse meal. Stir in crystallized ginger, brown sugar, ground ginger, and cinnamon. Add milk and stir just until blended. Turn dough onto a lightly floured surface and gently knead just until dough holds together. Pat out dough to about 1/2-inch thickness. Use a 2 1/2-inch biscuit cutter to cut out biscuits; place on an ungreased baking sheet. Bake 15 to 20 minutes or until golden brown. Remove from oven and brush with melted butter.
Yield: about 20 biscuits

PUMPKIN-APPLE PIE

- ¼ cup butter or margarine
- 3 medium apples, peeled, cored, and coarsely chopped
- 1½ teaspoons ground cinnamon, divided
- ½ teaspoon ground nutmeg, divided
- ¼ teaspoon ground allspice
- ¼ cup apple juice
- ⅓ cup plus 2 tablespoons granulated sugar, divided
- 1 tablespoon all-purpose flour
- 1 unbaked 9-inch pie shell
- 1 cup pumpkin
- 1 egg
- ¼ teaspoon ground cloves
- ½ cup half and half

Preheat oven to 425 degrees. Melt butter in a skillet over medium heat. Stir in apples, 1 teaspoon cinnamon, ¼ teaspoon nutmeg, and allspice; cook 5 minutes. Stir in apple juice, 2 tablespoons sugar, and flour. Cook 1 minute and pour into pie shell.

In a medium mixing bowl, combine pumpkin, remaining ⅓ cup sugar, egg, remaining ½ teaspoon cinnamon, remaining ¼ teaspoon nutmeg, and cloves. Beat until well blended. Stir in half and half. Carefully pour pumpkin mixture over apple mixture. Bake 15 minutes. Reduce heat to 350 degrees and bake 30 minutes more or until center is set.

Yield: about 8 servings

PEACH ASPIC WITH CREAM CHEESE DRESSING

ASPIC

- 2 packages (3 ounces each) peach gelatin
- 1½ cups boiling water
- 1 can (1 pound, 13 ounces) peaches in syrup, drained, puréed, and divided
- 1 cup orange juice
- 3 tablespoons lemon juice
- 2 tablespoons granulated sugar
- ½ teaspoon grated lemon peel

DRESSING

- 1 package (8 ounces) cream cheese, softened
- 3 tablespoons mayonnaise
- 1 tablespoon granulated sugar

For aspic, combine peach gelatin and boiling water in mixing bowl; stir until gelatin is dissolved. Stir in 1½ cups puréed peaches, orange juice, lemon juice, sugar, and lemon peel. Pour into lightly oiled 1½-quart ring mold and chill 4 to 6 hours or until set.

For dressing, combine cream cheese, mayonnaise, sugar, and remaining ½ cup puréed peaches in small mixing bowl. Beat until smooth. Remove aspic from mold to serving platter; serve with dressing.

Yield: 8 to 10 servings

(Left) Pumpkin-Apple Pie is a layered creation that combines two favorites in one delicious dessert. *(Right)* A ring mold brings holiday elegance to Peach Aspic with Cream Cheese Dressing.

SPECIAL FAMILY DINNER

Cream of Artichoke Soup	*Christmas Cauliflower*
Fresh Broccoli-Mandarin Salad	*Peas, Mushrooms, and Onions in Cream Sauce*
Tomato Mousse Salad	
Brioche Rolls	*Baby Carrots with Horseradish*
Crown Roast of Pork with Brown Rice	*Corn Pudding*
	Sweet Potato Pie with Rum Cream

Crown Roast of Pork with Brown Rice is as flavorful as it is elegant. Chopped apples and golden raisins add natural sweetness to the rice.

CROWN ROAST OF PORK WITH BROWN RICE

Salt and ground black pepper
5 to 7 pound crown roast of pork (12 to 14 ribs)
1 jar (10 ounces) apple jelly
1/2 cup brandy, divided
3 cups chicken broth
6 tablespoons butter or margarine
2 1/4 cups chopped apples
1 1/2 cups uncooked brown rice
3/4 cup golden raisins
3/4 cup chopped celery
1 1/2 tablespoons chopped fresh parsley

Preheat oven to 325 degrees. Salt and pepper roast inside and out. With bone ends up, place roast in a shallow roasting pan. Insert meat thermometer into roast without touching bone or fat. Cover tips of ribs with aluminum foil.

In a saucepan, heat apple jelly and 1/4 cup brandy. Brush roast with jelly mixture and continue to baste every 15 minutes while cooking. Bake 30 to 35 minutes per pound or until meat thermometer registers 170 degrees (2 1/2 to 3 1/2 hours).

After first 30 minutes of roasting, bring chicken broth and butter to a boil in a large saucepan. Add remaining ingredients, except remaining 1/4 cup brandy; cover.

Reduce heat to medium-low and cook without removing cover 1 1/2 hours or until rice is tender. Remove from heat and stir in remaining 1/4 cup brandy. About 30 minutes before roast is done, fill center of roast with a portion of rice mixture. Cover the rice loosely with aluminum foil and continue cooking. (**Note:** Remaining rice can be heated in a tightly covered baking dish. Place in oven 30 minutes before roast is done to heat through.) Remove foil from tips of ribs and place roast on serving platter with rice.
Yield: 10 to 12 servings

FRESH BROCCOLI-MANDARIN SALAD

1 egg plus 1 egg yolk, lightly beaten
1/2 cup granulated sugar
1 1/2 teaspoons cornstarch
1 teaspoon dry mustard
1/4 cup tarragon wine vinegar
1/4 cup water
1/2 cup mayonnaise
3 tablespoons butter or margarine, softened
4 cups fresh broccoli flowerets
2 cups sliced fresh mushrooms
1 can (11 ounces) mandarin oranges, drained
1/2 cup raisins
1/2 cup slivered almonds, toasted
1/2 large red onion, sliced
6 slices bacon, cooked and crumbled

In the top of a double boiler, whisk together egg, egg yolk, sugar, cornstarch, and dry mustard. Combine vinegar and water. Slowly pour into egg mixture, whisking constantly. Place over simmering water and cook, stirring constantly, until mixture thickens. Remove from heat; stir in mayonnaise and butter. Chill.

To serve, toss dressing with broccoli, mushrooms, oranges, raisins, almonds, onion, and bacon in a serving bowl.
Yield: 10 to 12 servings

Fresh Broccoli-Mandarin Salad is served with a tangy dressing.

Cream of Artichoke Soup has a spicy chicken broth base. Rich, buttery Brioche Rolls are an excellent accompaniment.

CREAM OF ARTICHOKE SOUP

$^1/_2$ cup chopped green onion
2 carrots, peeled and sliced
2 ribs celery, chopped
$^1/_2$ cup butter or margarine, divided
4 cups chicken broth
1 can (14 ounces) artichoke hearts, drained and sliced
1 can (4 ounces) sliced mushrooms, drained
1 bay leaf
$^1/_2$ teaspoon ground thyme
$^1/_2$ teaspoon ground oregano
$^1/_8$ teaspoon cayenne pepper
3 tablespoons all-purpose flour
1 cup whipping cream
Salt and ground black pepper

In large saucepan over medium heat, sauté onion, carrots, and celery in $^1/_4$ cup butter. Add chicken broth, artichokes, mushrooms, bay leaf, thyme, oregano, and cayenne. Simmer 15 to 20 minutes. In small skillet, melt remaining $^1/_4$ cup butter over low heat. Stir in flour and cook, stirring constantly, until mixture thickens. Stir into artichoke mixture. Slowly add cream. Salt and pepper to taste. Cook 3 to 5 minutes or until slightly thickened and heated through.
Yield: 4 to 6 servings

BRIOCHE ROLLS

2 packages dry yeast
$^1/_4$ cup warm water
$^1/_2$ cup butter or margarine, softened
$^1/_3$ cup granulated sugar
$^1/_2$ teaspoon salt
$^1/_2$ cup evaporated milk
$3^1/_2$ cups all-purpose flour, divided
4 eggs
1 tablespoon granulated sugar

Dissolve yeast in warm water. In a medium mixing bowl, cream butter, $^1/_3$ cup sugar, and salt until fluffy. Stir in milk and 1 cup flour. In another medium bowl, beat 3 eggs and 1 egg yolk (reserve egg white). Add yeast and eggs to creamed mixture, beating until well blended. Stir in remaining $2^1/_2$ cups flour. Turn out dough onto a lightly floured surface and knead 3 to 5 minutes or until dough holds together. Place in lightly greased bowl, turning to coat entire surface. Cover and let rise in a warm place 1 hour or until doubled in size.

Punch down dough. Divide dough into fourths. Reserving one fourth, pull remaining dough into 24 equal pieces. Roll pieces into balls and place in greased muffin pans or fluted tart pans. Pull reserved dough into 24 pieces and roll pieces into small balls. Make indentation with thumb in top of each larger roll and press smaller ball into each indentation. Cover and let rise 45 minutes or until doubled in size.

Preheat oven to 375 degrees. Lightly beat reserved egg white with 1 tablespoon sugar; brush on tops of rolls. Bake 20 to 25 minutes or until golden brown.
Yield: 2 dozen rolls

CHRISTMAS CAULIFLOWER

    2 packages (10 ounces each) frozen
         chopped broccoli
 1/2 cup whipping cream
 1/3 cup chicken broth
    7 tablespoons butter, melted
 1/4 cup sour cream
 1/4 teaspoon ground nutmeg
        Salt and ground black pepper
    1 large head cauliflower

   Cook broccoli according to package directions. Drain well. Place broccoli in blender or food processor. Add whipping cream, chicken broth, butter, sour cream, and nutmeg; purée until smooth. Salt and pepper to taste. Transfer to a saucepan over low heat.
   Steam whole cauliflower until tender. Place on a heated serving platter and spoon warm broccoli purée over top of cauliflower.
Yield: 6 to 8 servings

CORN PUDDING

 1/4 cup butter or margarine
 1/4 cup all-purpose flour
 1/4 cup finely chopped onion
    1 tablespoon granulated sugar
    1 teaspoon salt
 1 1/2 cups half and half
    4 cups drained canned corn
    3 eggs, lightly beaten
    6 slices bacon, cooked and crumbled
    1 tablespoon chopped fresh parsley
 1/4 teaspoon cayenne pepper

   Preheat oven to 350 degrees. Melt butter in large saucepan over medium heat. Stir in flour, onion, sugar, and salt. Increase heat to medium-high and cook, stirring constantly, until mixture bubbles. Continuing to stir constantly, add half and half and cook until mixture thickens. Remove from heat. Stir in corn, eggs, bacon, parsley, and cayenne. Pour into a lightly greased 2-quart baking dish. Bake 45 to 50 minutes or until knife inserted in center comes out clean.
Yield: 8 to 10 servings

   Christmas Cauliflower *(top)* and old-fashioned Corn Pudding will delight the vegetable lovers in your family.

PEAS, MUSHROOMS, AND ONIONS IN CREAM SAUCE

- 2 tablespoons butter or margarine
- 2 tablespoons all-purpose flour
- 1 can (12 ounces) evaporated milk
- 1 package (10 ounces) frozen green peas, thawed
- 1 jar (16 ounces) pearl onions, drained
- 1 jar (4 ounces) pimientos, drained
- 1 can (4 ounces) button mushrooms, drained
   Salt and ground black pepper

Preheat oven to 350 degrees. Melt butter in a large saucepan over medium heat. Stir in flour. Add evaporated milk, stirring constantly. Increase heat and cook until mixture thickens. Remove from heat. Stir in peas, onions, pimientos, and mushrooms. Salt and pepper to taste. Pour into a lightly greased 1 1/2-quart baking dish. Bake 20 to 25 minutes or until bubbly.
Yield: 6 to 8 servings

BABY CARROTS WITH HORSERADISH

- 1 package (10 ounces) frozen baby carrots
- 2 cups water
- 1 cup mayonnaise
- 2 tablespoons grated onion
- 2 tablespoons prepared horseradish
- 1/2 teaspoon salt
- 1/4 teaspoon ground black pepper
- 1/4 cup cracker crumbs
- 2 tablespoons butter, cut into small pieces
   Paprika

Cook carrots in water until tender. Drain carrots, reserving 1/4 cup liquid. Combine reserved liquid with next 5 ingredients.
Preheat oven to 375 degrees. Place carrots in lightly greased 8-inch square baking dish. Pour sauce over carrots. Sprinkle with cracker crumbs; dot with butter. Sprinkle with paprika. Bake 15 to 20 minutes or until heated through.
Yield: about 6 servings

Garden-fresh veggies add crunchy texture to this Tomato Mousse Salad.

Peas, Mushrooms, and Onions in Cream Sauce (*left*) and Baby Carrots with Horseradish bring color and great taste to the table.

Sweet Potato Pie with Rum Cream is a smooth and spicy dessert flavored with just a hint of rum.

TOMATO MOUSSE SALAD

- 2 envelopes unflavored gelatin
- 1/2 cup cold water
- 1 can (10³/4 ounces) condensed tomato soup, undiluted
- 1/2 cup mayonnaise
- 2 tablespoons chopped fresh parsley
- 1 tablespoon lemon juice
- 1 tablespoon dried dill weed
- 2 to 3 drops hot pepper sauce
- 1 cup sour cream
- 1 medium tomato, finely chopped
- 1/2 cup finely chopped green pepper
- 1/2 cup peeled chopped cucumber
- 1/4 cup finely chopped onion

  Avocado slices and sour cream for garnish

Soften gelatin in water. Heat soup in a medium saucepan and add softened gelatin. Whisk in mayonnaise, parsley, lemon juice, dill weed, and pepper sauce. Fold in 1 cup sour cream. Chill mixture until partially set.

Fold in tomato, green pepper, cucumber, and onion. Pour into a well-oiled 9-inch square pan. Chill 4 to 6 hours or until set. Garnish with avocado slices and sour cream.

Yield: 8 to 10 servings

SWEET POTATO PIE WITH RUM CREAM

- 1 can (16 ounces) sweet potatoes, drained and puréed
- 1/3 cup firmly packed brown sugar
- 3 eggs
- 1/4 teaspoon salt
- 1 cup half and half
- 1/4 cup molasses
- 1 teaspoon ground cinnamon
- 1/2 teaspoon ground ginger
  Pie Crust (recipe follows)
  Rum Cream (recipe follows)

Preheat oven to 425 degrees. In large mixing bowl, combine sweet potatoes, brown sugar, eggs, and salt; beat well. Stir in half and half, molasses, cinnamon, and ginger. Pour into prepared pie crust. Bake 10 minutes. Reduce heat and bake 30 minutes or until filling is set and puffy. Allow pie to cool completely. Spread Rum Cream on top of pie.

Yield: about 8 servings

PIE CRUST

- 1¹/2 cups all-purpose flour
- 1 teaspoon granulated sugar
- 6 tablespoons cold butter
- 3 to 4 tablespoons cold water

Combine flour and sugar in a mixing bowl. Using a pastry blender or two knives, cut butter into flour mixture until mixture resembles coarse meal. Stir in enough water to form a stiff dough. Wrap dough in plastic wrap and refrigerate at least 1 hour.

Remove dough from refrigerator and let stand at room temperature 15 minutes. On a lightly floured surface, use a floured rolling pin to roll out dough into a 13-inch circle. Drape dough over rolling pin and transfer to a 9-inch pie pan. Press dough into pan. Trim dough around edges of pan. If desired, use a small cookie cutter to cut shapes from pie dough scraps; place cutouts around edge of pie.

RUM CREAM

- 2/3 cup whipping cream
- 3 tablespoons confectioners sugar
- 1 teaspoon rum flavoring
- 1/8 teaspoon ground nutmeg

Combine all ingredients in a large mixing bowl. Beat at high speed until mixture holds its shape.

A FESTIVE FAMILY DINNER

Cream of Pumpkin Soup	*Gravy*
Rolled Herb Toast	*Almond Broccoli Ring*
Twin Herb Turkeys	*Ambrosia Sweet Potatoes*
Corn Bread Dressing	*English Trifle*

Prepared and seasoned the night before cooking, Twin Herb Turkeys will become a favorite of busy homemakers as well as guests. A traditional Corn Bread Dressing and a ladling of savory Gravy are perfect accompaniments to these tasty turkeys.

TWIN HERB TURKEYS

Our turkey platter is garnished with steamed fresh miniature corn and beets. We added some fresh herbs for a picture-perfect holiday dinner.

- 4 onions
- 2 green peppers
- 1 cup fresh parsley
- 8 cloves garlic
- 2 teaspoons ground black pepper
- 1 cup butter
- 2 turkeys, 9 to 10 pounds each (reserve neck and giblets from one turkey for gravy)
- 2 teaspoons salt

In a food processor, purée onions, green peppers, parsley, garlic, and black pepper. Sauté mixture in butter until vegetables are soft and mixture forms a paste. Rub turkeys with salt. Pierce skin of turkeys and coat with the herb paste. Cover and refrigerate overnight.

Preheat oven to 325 degrees. Insert meat thermometer into thickest part of one turkey thigh without touching bone. Roast, breast side down, 15 to 20 minutes per pound or until thermometer reaches 185 degrees. Turn breast side up and brown (10 to 15 minutes). Remove from oven and allow turkeys to stand 20 minutes before carving.
Yield: 14 to 16 servings

CORN BREAD DRESSING

CORN BREAD
- 2 cups cornmeal
- 1/2 cup all-purpose flour
- 3 teaspoons baking powder
- 1 1/4 teaspoons salt
- 1 teaspoon granulated sugar
- 1 cup milk
- 3 eggs
- 4 tablespoons butter, melted

Combine cornmeal, flour, baking powder, salt, and sugar. Beat in milk and eggs. Add butter and beat again. Pour mixture into a greased 9-inch baking pan or cast-iron skillet. Bake in a preheated 425-degree oven 30 to 35 minutes or until golden brown. Corn bread may be made ahead and frozen.

DRESSING
- 1/2 cup butter
- 1 1/2 cups chopped celery
- 1 cup chopped onion
- 1/3 cup turkey or chicken broth
  Corn Bread, crumbled
- 1/2 cup bread crumbs, toasted
- 1/2 cup crumbled saltine crackers
- 1 1/2 teaspoons ground marjoram

Ambrosia Sweet Potatoes bring delightful color and zest to the meal.

- 1/2 teaspoon ground thyme
- 6 eggs, beaten
  Salt and ground black pepper
  Turkey or chicken broth

In a saucepan, melt butter; add celery, onion, and 1/3 cup broth. Sauté over medium heat until vegetables are soft.

In a large bowl, combine corn bread, bread crumbs, cracker crumbs, and vegetables. Add marjoram and thyme; mix lightly. Stir eggs into dressing. Add salt and pepper to taste. Dressing mixture should be very moist; add more broth if necessary. Pour into a greased 9 x 13-inch baking pan. Bake in a preheated 350-degree oven 45 to 60 minutes.
Yield: 10 to 12 servings

GRAVY

- Neck and giblets from one turkey
- 4 to 5 cups water
- 2 celery ribs
- 1 small onion, halved
- 1 bay leaf
  Salt and ground black pepper
- 4 tablespoons butter, divided
- 3 tablespoons all-purpose flour
- 1/2 cup chopped onion
- 1/4 cup chopped celery
- 1/4 cup chopped fresh parsley
- 2 to 3 cups turkey broth
  Salt and ground black pepper

Simmer neck and giblets in water with celery, onion, and bay leaf. Add salt and pepper to taste. Cook until tender (about 1 hour). Drain, reserving broth. Discard celery, onion, and bay leaf.

For roux, melt 2 tablespoons butter in a heavy saucepan. Remove from heat; blend in flour and return to heat. Stirring slowly, cook over medium heat 2 minutes. Remove from heat; set aside.

Sauté chopped onion, celery, and parsley in remaining butter. Combine vegetables with roux. Blend in 2 to 3 cups broth and cook over medium heat, stirring constantly until gravy thickens. Chop giblets and meat from neck; add to gravy. Add salt and pepper to taste.
Yield: about 5 cups gravy

AMBROSIA SWEET POTATOES

- 6 cups cooked sliced sweet potatoes
- 1 orange, sliced
- 1 cup crushed pineapple with juice
- 1/2 cup firmly packed light brown sugar
- 1/2 cup butter, melted
- 1/2 teaspoon salt
- 1/2 cup sweetened shredded coconut

In a buttered 2-quart casserole, alternate layers of potato and orange slices. Mix pineapple, brown sugar, butter, and salt. Pour mixture over potato and orange slices. Sprinkle coconut on top. Bake in a preheated 350-degree oven 30 minutes.
Yield: 8 to 10 servings

(Left) Our spicy Cream of Pumpkin Soup is served with Rolled Herb Toast. *(Right)* Sautéed cherry tomatoes add a festive touch to this Almond Broccoli Ring, which features a delicate blend of flavors.

CREAM OF PUMPKIN SOUP

- 1 onion, thinly sliced
- 2 tablespoons butter
- 2 cups orange juice
- 2 cups cooked, mashed pumpkin
- 2 cups chicken broth
- 1/2 teaspoon ground mace
- 1/2 teaspoon salt
- 1/4 teaspoon ground white pepper
- 1/4 teaspoon ground nutmeg
- 1 cup half and half

  Half and half, toasted walnut halves,
  and sage leaves to garnish

In a large saucepan, sauté onion in butter until soft. Add orange juice, pumpkin, broth, and seasonings. Simmer 20 minutes. Purée mixture in a food processor or blender until smooth. Return to saucepan and stir in 1 cup half and half. Heat, being careful not to boil. Garnish each serving with a swirl of half and half, walnut halves, and sage leaves. Serve immediately.
Yield: about 8 servings

ROLLED HERB TOAST

- 1/2 cup butter, melted
- 1 package (1/2 ounce) herb salad dressing mix
- 1 teaspoon dried dill weed
- 1/4 teaspoon garlic salt
- 20 slices thin-sliced bread

Preheat oven to 300 degrees. Combine melted butter, dressing mix, dill weed, and garlic salt in a medium bowl. Trim crusts from bread; flatten each slice with a rolling pin and roll tightly. Coat each roll with butter mixture. Place rolls on an ungreased baking sheet and bake 15 to 20 minutes or until lightly browned, turning several times. Serve hot.

Toast may be frozen or stored in an airtight container. Reheat before serving.
Yield: 20 servings

ALMOND BROCCOLI RING

You will be proud to serve this beautiful vegetable ring on Christmas Day. The broccoli mixture may also be baked in individual custard cups.

- 1 package (10 ounces) frozen chopped broccoli
- 1 package (10 ounces) frozen broccoli spears
  Salt
- 5 tablespoons margarine, divided
- 1/2 cup minced green onions, including tops
- 3 tablespoons all-purpose flour
- 1/4 cup chicken broth
- 1 cup sour cream
- 3 eggs, lightly beaten
- 3/4 cup shredded Swiss cheese
- 1/2 cup slivered almonds, toasted
- 1 teaspoon salt
- 3/4 teaspoon freshly grated nutmeg
- 1/2 teaspoon ground black pepper
- 1 pint cherry tomatoes

Steam broccoli until tender; drain and lightly salt. Using a sharp knife, finely chop broccoli and set aside.

In a saucepan, melt 3 tablespoons margarine; add onions and sauté lightly. Remove from heat; blend in flour and return to heat. Stirring slowly, cook over medium heat 2 minutes. Remove from heat; add broth and stir. Return to heat and continue to stir as sauce thickens. Lower heat and cook 2 minutes more. Blend in sour cream and heat thoroughly. Stir a few tablespoons of sauce into beaten eggs; add egg mixture to remainder of sauce in pan and cook 1 minute, stirring constantly. Blend in cheese. Add broccoli, almonds, and seasonings. Spoon mixture into an oiled 1-quart ring mold or eight 5-ounce custard cups. Place in a large baking pan and add hot water to come halfway up sides of mold. Bake in a preheated 350-degree oven about 50 minutes for mold (30 minutes for custard cups) or until a knife inserted in center comes out clean. When ready to serve, invert onto a serving plate.

Sauté cherry tomatoes in remaining margarine about 5 to 6 minutes. Garnish with tomatoes and fresh herbs or parsley.
Yield: 8 to 10 servings

ENGLISH TRIFLE

This is a perfect holiday recipe — rich custard combined with brandy-laced almond macaroons. You can make it ahead of time and then sit down and enjoy this treat with the family on Christmas Day.

8	eggs
8	tablespoons granulated sugar, divided
5	teaspoons cornstarch
4	cups milk, scalded
1 1/2	teaspoons vanilla extract, divided
1/4	teaspoon freshly grated nutmeg
20	(2-inch) almond macaroons
1/3	cup brandy
1	jar (12 ounces) red raspberry jam
1	pound cake (12 ounces), cut into 1/4-inch-thick slices, divided
1/2	cup cream sherry, divided
4	packages (10 ounces each) frozen raspberries, thawed, drained, and divided
2	cups whipping cream
	Fresh strawberry to garnish

In a heavy saucepan or in the top of a double boiler, whisk eggs. Combine 6 tablespoons sugar and cornstarch; add to eggs, blending well. Pour scalded milk into mixture in a steady stream, stirring constantly. Cook mixture over medium heat, stirring until thickened (5 to 6 minutes).

This luscious English Trifle looks as though it were created by a master chef, but it's actually simple to make with layers of pound cake, custard, raspberries, and brandy-laced almond macaroons.

Remove from heat and add 1 teaspoon vanilla and nutmeg. Set aside to cool.

Brush macaroons with brandy. Line bottom of a 12-cup glass serving bowl with a single layer of cookies. Spread flat side of additional cookies with jam and arrange in one layer around the sides of bowl (jam side out). Coat all cookies with another generous layer of jam. Spoon a portion of custard over jam layer. Arrange one-half of cake slices over custard. Carefully brush cake with about 1/4 cup sherry. Spread jam over cake. Add a layer of raspberries.

Repeat layers of custard, cake slices, sherry, and jam. Cover with raspberries and top with remaining custard. Place remaining cookies in center of dessert, flat side down. Cover tightly and refrigerate overnight.

To serve, beat cream with remaining 2 tablespoons sugar and remaining 1/2 teaspoon vanilla until stiff peaks form. Spoon over cookies. Garnish with fresh strawberry.
Yield: 10 to 12 servings

DELIGHTFUL DESSERTS

The rich flavors of Christmas bring to mind images of Yuletide sweets drenched in decadent chocolate, laced with aromatic spices, and covered with dreamy caramel. Our selection of scrumptious holiday fare includes all these flavors and more! We have traditional favorites like pumpkin pie and pound cake, as well as new delights such as mint-chocolate torte and caramel soufflé. May your celebration be as sweet and wonderful as these luscious desserts.

Peanut Butter Fudge Pie will be a hit with kids of all ages! Chocolate chunks and swirls of peanut butter re-create the flavors of a favorite candy.

119

PEANUT BUTTER FUDGE PIE

CRUST
- 1 1/4 cups all-purpose flour
- 1/4 teaspoon salt
- 7 tablespoons butter, chilled and cut into pieces
- 3 tablespoons ice water

FILLING
- 4 ounces semisweet baking chocolate
- 3 tablespoons butter or margarine
- 1/3 cup plus 3 tablespoons peanut butter, divided
- 1 1/2 teaspoons vanilla extract
- 1/2 cup plus 2 tablespoons granulated sugar
- 3 eggs
- 1 cup dark corn syrup
- 1/2 cup milk
- 2/3 cup coarsely chopped roasted unsalted peanuts
- 4 ounces semisweet chocolate candy bar, broken into small pieces

Preheat oven to 325 degrees. For crust, sift flour and salt into a mixing bowl. Using a pastry blender or two knives, cut butter into flour until mixture resembles coarse meal. Sprinkle ice water over dough, mixing quickly just until dough forms a soft ball. On a lightly floured surface, use a floured rolling pin to roll out dough to 1/8-inch thickness. Place the dough in an ungreased 9-inch pie pan. Trim and crimp edges of dough.

For filling, melt baking chocolate with butter in the top of a double boiler over simmering water. In a large mixing bowl, beat 1/3 cup peanut butter, vanilla, sugar, and eggs until fluffy. Combine corn syrup and milk; gradually beat corn syrup mixture into peanut butter mixture. Stir in melted chocolate mixture and peanuts. Pour filling into crust and sprinkle chocolate pieces over filling. Dot with remaining 3 tablespoons peanut butter. Bake 50 to 60 minutes or just until the filling is set. Cool pie completely and refrigerate at least 2 hours before serving.

Yield: about 8 servings

RUM-RAISIN CHEESECAKE

- 1 1/4 cups raisins
- 1 cup dark rum
- 2 cups vanilla wafer cookie crumbs
- 1 1/2 cups plus 1 tablespoon granulated sugar, divided
- 2 tablespoons butter or margarine, melted
- 5 packages (8 ounces each) cream cheese, softened
- 1 tablespoon vanilla extract
- 6 eggs
- 4 egg yolks
- 1/3 cup whipping cream

In a small bowl, combine raisins with rum. Marinate at least 2 hours.

Combine cookie crumbs, 1 tablespoon sugar, and melted butter in a medium bowl. Line a 10-inch springform pan with aluminum foil; lightly grease foil. Press crust into the bottom of prepared pan.

Preheat oven to 350 degrees. For filling, beat cream cheese until smooth. Add 1 1/2 cups sugar and vanilla. Beat in eggs and yolks, one at a time, beating well after each addition. Drain raisins, reserving rum. Stir rum and whipping cream into cream cheese mixture. Stir in raisins. Pour filling over crust. Place springform pan in a larger pan and add hot water to larger pan to come halfway up sides of springform pan. Bake 1 1/2 hours or until center is set. Remove cheesecake from oven and pan of water and allow to cool completely. Cover and refrigerate overnight.

To serve, use a knife to loosen sides of cheesecake from pan; remove springform.

Yield: 12 to 14 servings

Raisins marinated in rum add festive spirit to our Rum-Raisin Cheesecake.

Southern Pecan Pie is a traditional favorite. Crunchy Pecan Nuggets *(top, in box)* flavored with brown sugar are great for snacking or entertaining.

SOUTHERN PECAN PIE

CRUST
- 1¼ cups all-purpose flour
- ¼ teaspoon salt
- 7 tablespoons butter, chilled and cut into pieces
- 3 tablespoons ice water

FILLING
- 4 eggs
- 1¼ cups granulated sugar
- ½ cup light corn syrup
- ¼ cup butter or margarine
- 1 cup pecan halves

Preheat oven to 350 degrees. For crust, sift flour and salt into a mixing bowl. Using a pastry blender or two knives, cut butter into flour until mixture resembles coarse meal. Sprinkle ice water over dough, mixing quickly just until a soft dough forms. On a lightly floured surface, use a floured rolling pin to roll out dough. Place the dough in an ungreased 9-inch pie pan. Trim and crimp edges of dough.

For filling, place eggs in a medium mixing bowl and beat well by hand. In a saucepan, combine sugar, corn syrup, and butter. Bring mixture to a boil. Beating constantly by hand, gradually add sugar mixture to eggs. Stir in pecan halves. Pour mixture into pie shell. Bake 40 to 45 minutes or until a knife inserted in the center comes out clean.
Yield: about 8 servings

PECAN NUGGETS

- 1 cup firmly packed brown sugar
- 2 tablespoons all-purpose flour
- 1 tablespoon cornstarch
- 1 tablespoon dark rum
- 1 egg white
- ⅛ teaspoon cream of tartar
- ⅛ teaspoon salt
- 2 cups pecan halves

Preheat oven to 300 degrees. In a medium mixing bowl, combine brown sugar, flour, cornstarch, and rum. In a separate bowl, beat egg white with cream of tartar and salt until stiff peaks form. Stir one-third of the egg white mixture into the rum mixture; fold in the remaining egg white mixture. Stir in pecans. Drop individual pecan halves coated with mixture 2 inches apart onto a lightly greased baking sheet. Bake 12 to 15 minutes or until puffed and golden brown. Remove from pan and cool on wire rack.
Yield: about 6 dozen nuggets

CREAMY PUMPKIN PIE

- 1 cup all-purpose flour
- 1/2 cup ground pecans
- 1/3 cup butter or margarine, softened
- 1/4 cup firmly packed brown sugar
- 1/4 teaspoon ground cinnamon
- 1 can (16 ounces) pumpkin
- 1 can (14 ounces) sweetened condensed milk
- 1 package (3 ounces) cream cheese, softened
- 1 egg
- 1 teaspoon pumpkin pie spice
- 1 teaspoon vanilla extract
- 1/2 teaspoon ground nutmeg
- 1/2 teaspoon salt
- 1 cup hot water

  Anise stars to garnish
  Whipping cream to serve

Preheat oven to 350 degrees. Combine flour, pecans, butter, brown sugar, and cinnamon. Press firmly into the bottom of a lightly greased 10-inch springform pan. Bake 20 minutes.

Combine pumpkin, sweetened condensed milk, cream cheese, egg, pumpkin pie spice, vanilla, nutmeg, and salt; beat until smooth. Stir in water. Pour into crust and bake 50 to 60 minutes or until set. Allow to cool.

To serve, use knife to loosen sides of pie from pan; remove springform. Garnish with anise stars. Serve with whipping cream.
Yield: 10 to 12 servings

(Top left) The cool, rich flavor of chocolate mint candy makes this Chocolate Mint Pie a frozen delight.

(Top right) Featuring a cinnamon-pecan crust, Creamy Pumpkin Pie is a flavorful new version of a traditional holiday dessert. Anise stars and a drizzling of heavy cream top it off.

(Bottom left) Packaged ladyfingers are the key to Easy and Elegant Cherry Cream Dessert. With its colorful topping of cherry pie filling, this dessert is extra festive.

(Bottom right) Our Brandy Alexander Pie has star quality, all the way down to its chocolate cookie crumb crust.

EASY AND ELEGANT CHERRY CREAM DESSERT

- 2 packages (3 ounces each) ladyfingers, divided
- 2 tablespoons amaretto liqueur
- 1 package (8 ounces) cream cheese, softened
- 2/3 cup granulated sugar
- 1 teaspoon almond extract, divided
- 2 cups whipping cream, whipped
- 1 can (21 ounces) cherry pie filling

Lightly grease the bottom of a 9-inch springform pan. Brush ladyfingers with amaretto. Line the sides of the pan with half of the ladyfingers, placing the rounded sides towards outside of pan. Beat cream cheese until smooth. Add sugar and 1/2 teaspoon almond extract; beat 1 minute. Fold whipped cream into the cream cheese mixture. Spread half of the mixture in bottom of pan. Place remaining ladyfingers over the mixture with rounded sides up. Top with remaining cream cheese mixture, spreading to smooth. Cover and refrigerate overnight.

Combine cherry pie filling with remaining 1/2 teaspoon almond extract. Refrigerate at least 2 hours before serving. To serve, remove springform and top dessert with cherry pie filling. Serve chilled.
Yield: 10 to 12 servings

CHOCOLATE MINT PIE

- 1 cup plus 2 tablespoons chocolate cookie crumbs, divided
- 1 cup butter or margarine, softened
- 2 cups sifted confectioners sugar
- 4 eggs
- 4 ounces semisweet baking chocolate, melted
- 2 teaspoons vanilla extract
- 1/2 teaspoon peppermint extract
- 3/4 cup coarsely chopped individually wrapped layered chocolate mints

  Sweetened Whipped Cream to serve (recipe on page 129)

Spread 1 cup cookie crumbs evenly in the bottom of a 10-inch springform pan. Cream butter and confectioners sugar. Add eggs, one at a time, beating well after each addition. Stir in chocolate and extracts. Fold in mints. Pour into prepared pan. Freeze until firm.

To serve, use knife to loosen sides of pie from pan; remove springform. Serve with Sweetened Whipped Cream. Garnish with remaining 2 tablespoons cookie crumbs.
Yield: 12 to 15 servings

BRANDY ALEXANDER PIE

For chocolate stars, spread 4 ounces of melted semisweet chocolate evenly on a waxed paper-lined cookie sheet. Refrigerate until firm. Use star-shaped cookie cutters to cut out shapes.

- 1 1/2 cups chocolate cookie crumbs
- 1/3 cup ground blanched almonds
- 6 tablespoons butter or margarine, melted
- 2 envelopes unflavored gelatin
- 1 1/2 cups cold water, divided
- 1 1/4 cups granulated sugar, divided
- 4 eggs, separated
- 1/8 teaspoon salt
- 11 ounces (one 8-ounce and one 3-ounce package) cream cheese, softened
- 1/3 cup crème de cacao liqueur
- 3 tablespoons brandy
- 1 cup whipping cream, whipped

Preheat oven to 375 degrees. Combine cookie crumbs, ground almonds, and butter. Press mixture into the bottom of a 10-inch springform pan. Bake 10 minutes.

In small saucepan, soften gelatin in 3/4 cup water 5 minutes. Place over low heat and stir until gelatin is dissolved. Add remaining water and remove from heat. Stir in 1 cup sugar, egg yolks, and salt; blend well. Return to heat and cook 5 minutes or until slightly thickened. Remove from heat.

Place cream cheese in a large mixing bowl and gradually beat in egg yolk mixture until smooth. Add crème de cacao and brandy. Chill until slightly thickened.

Beat egg whites with remaining 1/4 cup sugar until stiff. Alternately fold egg whites and whipped cream into cream cheese mixture. Pour into crust. Chill until firm.

To serve, use knife to loosen sides of cake from pan; remove springform.
Yield: 10 to 12 servings

RAISIN PECAN PIE

1½ cups all-purpose flour
1 teaspoon granulated sugar
6 tablespoons cold butter
3 to 4 tablespoons cold water
3 eggs, separated
1½ cups firmly packed brown sugar
2 tablespoons apple cider vinegar
1 tablespoon butter or margarine, softened
1½ teaspoons ground cinnamon
1 teaspoon vanilla extract
2 cups coarsely chopped raisins
1 cup chopped pecans

Combine flour and granulated sugar in a mixing bowl. Using a pastry blender or two knives, cut butter into flour until mixture resembles coarse meal. Stir in enough water to form a stiff dough. Wrap dough in plastic wrap and refrigerate at least 1 hour.

Remove dough from refrigerator and let stand at room temperature 15 minutes. On a lightly floured surface, use a floured rolling pin to roll out dough into a 13-inch circle. Drape dough over rolling pin and transfer to a 9-inch pie pan. Press dough into sides of pan. Trim dough around edges of pan. If desired, use a small cookie cutter to cut shapes from pie dough scraps; place cutouts around edge of pie shell.

Preheat oven to 450 degrees. Beat egg yolks until frothy. Stir in brown sugar, vinegar, butter, cinnamon, and vanilla. Beat egg whites until stiff; fold into egg yolk mixture. Gently fold in raisins and pecans. Pour into unbaked pie crust. Bake 10 minutes. Reduce temperature to 350 degrees and bake 30 minutes longer.
Yield: about 8 servings

FRUITED POUND CAKE

¾ cup butter or margarine, softened
1 cup granulated sugar
2 eggs
2 egg yolks
⅓ cup dark rum
1¼ cups all-purpose flour, divided
1 teaspoon baking powder
¾ cup golden raisins
½ cup coarsely chopped English walnuts
¾ cup halved red and green candied cherries

Preheat oven to 350 degrees. Cream butter and sugar until light and fluffy. Add eggs, egg yolks, and rum; beat until very light in color (about 5 minutes). Sift flour and baking powder. Sprinkle 2 tablespoons of flour mixture over raisins. Gently fold remaining flour mixture into creamed mixture. Fold in raisins and walnuts. Pour half of batter into a greased and floured 8½ x 4½ x 2¾-inch loaf pan. Spread cherries on top and add remaining batter. Bake about 1 hour or until top is golden brown and toothpick inserted in center comes out clean. Cool in pan 15 minutes. Remove cake from pan and cool on wire rack.
Yield: 8 to 10 servings

RAISIN BREAD PUDDING

2 tablespoons butter or margarine, softened
12 ounces (about 12 slices) raisin bread, torn into pieces
2 cups milk
1½ cups whipping cream
1 cup granulated sugar
3 eggs
2 egg yolks
3 tablespoons brandy
3 tablespoons dark rum
1 teaspoon ground nutmeg

Whipping cream to serve

Spread butter in a 13 x 9 x 2-inch glass baking dish. Place bread in a large bowl. Pour milk over bread and allow to soak 1 hour or until most of liquid is absorbed.

Preheat oven to 350 degrees. In large mixing bowl, beat next 7 ingredients until thick and smooth. Stir in bread mixture. Pour into prepared baking dish. Place dish in a larger baking pan. Add hot water to larger pan to come halfway up sides of baking dish. Bake 1 hour or until knife inserted in center comes out clean. Serve with whipping cream.
Yield: 10 to 12 servings

CARAMEL APPLE PIE

4 ounces cream cheese, softened
½ cup plus 5 tablespoons butter or margarine, softened and divided
1 cup all-purpose flour
¼ cup apple jelly, melted
2 pounds (about 4 large) baking apples, peeled, cored, and sliced
2 tablespoons plus ½ cup firmly packed brown sugar, divided
2 teaspoons vanilla extract, divided
⅓ cup golden raisins
⅔ cup whipping cream
2 cups sour cream
2 tablespoons granulated sugar
2 tablespoons chopped pecans for garnish

In large mixing bowl, beat cream cheese and ½ cup butter. Stir in flour. Wrap dough in plastic wrap and refrigerate 1 hour.

Preheat oven to 450 degrees. On a lightly floured surface, use a floured rolling pin to roll out dough into a 13-inch circle. Drape dough over rolling pin and transfer to an 11-inch tart pan. Press dough into sides of pan. Trim dough around edges of pan. Line inside of pastry shell with aluminum foil and fill with dried beans or pie weights. Bake 10 minutes. Remove weights and foil and brush inside of shell with melted jelly. Reduce heat to 350 degrees and bake 12 to 15 minutes longer or until shell is lightly browned.

Place remaining 5 tablespoons butter in a large skillet. Sauté apples in butter over medium-high heat 2 to 3 minutes. Add 2 tablespoons brown sugar, 1 teaspoon vanilla, and raisins. Cook until apples are tender. Pour apples evenly into prepared pastry. Scald whipping cream in a small saucepan. Place remaining ½ cup brown sugar in a skillet over medium-high heat and stir constantly with a wooden spoon until sugar begins to melt. Stir until sugar is smooth and remove from heat. Cool 2 to 3 minutes. Slowly stir the hot cream into the sugar. Return to heat and stir until smooth. Reserving ¼ cup, pour remaining caramel over apples.

Preheat oven to 350 degrees. Combine sour cream, granulated sugar, and remaining 1 teaspoon vanilla. Spread evenly over top of pie. Bake 8 to 10 minutes (do not allow sour cream to bubble). Cool to room temperature. Pour reserved caramel over top of pie. Cover with plastic wrap and refrigerate several hours before serving. Garnish with chopped pecans.
Yield: 10 to 12 servings

(Top left) Mouth-watering Caramel Apple Pie starts with a cream cheese pastry crust, then adds sautéed apples and a topping of sour cream, caramel, and pecans.

(Top right) Spicy Raisin Bread Pudding has an appealing holiday eggnog flavor.

(Bottom) Golden raisins, walnuts, and candied cherries fill this colorful Fruited Pound Cake *(left)*. The Raisin Pecan Pie has old-fashioned good taste.

CANDY CANE CHEESECAKE

1⅓ cups chocolate cookie crumbs
¼ cup butter or margarine, melted
½ cup plus 2 tablespoons granulated
    sugar, divided
1½ cups sour cream
3 eggs
1 tablespoon all-purpose flour
2 teaspoons vanilla extract
¼ teaspoon peppermint extract
3 packages (8 ounces each)
    cream cheese, softened
2 tablespoons butter, softened
⅔ cup crushed peppermint candy
    Sweetened Whipped Cream (recipe
    on page 129; make ½ recipe)

Preheat oven to 325 degrees. Combine cookie crumbs, melted butter, and 2 tablespoons sugar; press into bottom of a 9-inch springform pan. Set aside.

In blender or food processor, blend sour cream, remaining ½ cup sugar, eggs, flour, and extracts until smooth. Add cream cheese and 2 tablespoons butter, blending until completely smooth. Stir in crushed candy. Pour into crust. Bake on lowest rack of oven 50 to 60 minutes or until firm. Allow to cool (cheesecake may crack while cooling); refrigerate overnight.

To serve, use knife to loosen sides of cheesecake from pan; remove springform. Spread top of cheesecake with Sweetened Whipped Cream.
Yield: 10 to 12 servings

(Top) Crushed peppermint candy adds pizzazz to this festive Candy Cane Cheesecake.

(Bottom left) Devonshire cream and a spicy raisin-pecan filling make Pears in Puff Pastry irresistible.

(Bottom right) Once you've tasted this rich, custard-like Chocolate Crème Brûlée, you'll want to serve it at all your special dinners — and just for the family, too!

PEARS IN PUFF PASTRY

2 cups water
1 cup granulated sugar
2½ teaspoons vanilla extract
4 medium pears, peeled, halved,
    and cored
1 package (17¼ ounces) frozen
    puff pastry dough, thawed and
    divided
    Filling (recipe follows)
    Devonshire Cream (recipe follows)
    Whole cloves

Heat water, sugar, and vanilla in a large heavy saucepan over low heat, stirring occasionally, until sugar dissolves. Increase heat and boil 5 minutes; add pears. Cover pan and lower heat to simmer. Cook until pears are tender, turning occasionally (4 to 10 minutes, depending on ripeness of pears). Remove pears to paper towels and allow to drain.

Preheat oven to 375 degrees. Unfold one sheet of puff pastry. On a lightly floured surface, use a floured rolling pin to roll puff pastry into a 17-inch square. Cut pastry into four 8-inch squares; reserve trimmings. Pat pears with paper towels to remove any moisture. Spoon Filling into center of each pear half. Place one pear half, filling side down, on one side of each pastry square. Fold other side of pastry over pear. Pinch edges of pastry together and fold edges underneath pear to seal. Repeat with remaining pastry and pear halves to make eight pastry-covered pears. Place on baking sheet. Bake 30 to 35 minutes or until pastry is golden.

While pears are baking, cut sixteen 1½-inch-long leaves from pastry trimmings. Place on ungreased baking sheet. Five minutes before pears are done, place leaves in oven; bake about 5 minutes or until golden. Allow pears and leaves to cool slightly before serving.

To serve, place a spoonful of Devonshire Cream on each dessert plate. Place a pear on top of cream and arrange two leaves at top of pear. Insert a clove into bottom of pear.
Yield: 8 servings

FILLING

2 pears, peeled, cored, and finely
    chopped
3 tablespoons butter
⅓ cup chopped pecans
¼ cup golden raisins
3 tablespoons firmly packed brown
    sugar
1 teaspoon vanilla extract
1 teaspoon ground cinnamon
½ teaspoon ground nutmeg

Sauté pears in butter until soft. Add pecans, raisins, brown sugar, vanilla, cinnamon, and nutmeg; cook, stirring constantly, 5 minutes or until pears are soft. Remove from heat and allow to cool.

DEVONSHIRE CREAM

1 cup whipping cream
1 cup granulated sugar
½ cup sour cream
1 teaspoon vanilla extract

Whip cream with sugar until soft peaks form. Fold in sour cream and vanilla.

CHOCOLATE CRÈME BRÛLÉE

1 quart whipping cream
1 cup firmly packed brown sugar,
    divided
2 tablespoons granulated sugar
8 ounces premium-quality milk
    chocolate, chopped
7 egg yolks
1 teaspoon vanilla extract

    Sweetened Whipped Cream to serve
    (recipe on page 129)

Preheat oven to 350 degrees. In a heavy saucepan over medium-high heat, bring cream, ½ cup brown sugar, and granulated sugar to a boil. Add chocolate and remove from heat; stir until chocolate is melted. Allow to cool slightly.

In a medium mixing bowl, whisk egg yolks and vanilla until blended. Whisk ¼ cup chocolate mixture into eggs. Pour in remaining chocolate mixture and whisk until blended. Pour mixture through a strainer into a 13 x 9 x 2-inch glass baking dish. Place dish in a larger baking pan. Add hot water to larger pan to come halfway up sides of baking dish. Bake 1 to 1½ hours or until knife inserted in center comes out clean. Cool to room temperature. Cover with plastic wrap and refrigerate 6 to 8 hours.

Set oven on broil. Pat top of dessert with paper towel to remove excess moisture. Cover top evenly with remaining ½ cup brown sugar. Place dessert under broiler just until sugar begins to melt, about 5 minutes. (Watch dessert carefully; sugar will melt very quickly.) Serve warm or chilled with Sweetened Whipped Cream.
Yield: 12 to 15 servings

RASPBERRY ELEGANCE

3 packages (10 ounces each) frozen
    raspberries in syrup, thawed
1 envelope unflavored gelatin
1/4 cup cold water
11 ounces (one 8-ounce and one
    3-ounce package) cream cheese,
    softened
1/2 cup sour cream
1/2 cup granulated sugar
3 tablespoons lemon juice
1 cup whipping cream, whipped
    Sweetened Whipped Cream (recipe
    follows)
    Raspberry Sauce (recipe follows)

Line an 8 1/2 x 4 1/2 x 2 3/4-inch loaf pan with aluminum foil. Drain berries, reserving 1/4 cup syrup. Place berries in a blender or food processor and purée. To remove seeds, place puréed berries in a fine strainer and push the berries through the strainer with the back of a spoon. Discard seeds.

In a small bowl, sprinkle gelatin over cold water. Let stand 5 minutes.

In a large mixing bowl, beat cream cheese with sour cream until smooth. Add sugar, lemon juice, and puréed berries, beating until well blended.

Place the bowl of gelatin in a pan of warm water. Let stand until gelatin is dissolved. Remove from water. Stir in reserved raspberry syrup. With mixer at medium speed, beat gelatin mixture into the raspberry mixture until smooth. Refrigerate 15 minutes or until mixture is slightly thickened.

Gently fold the whipped cream into the berry mixture just until blended. Pour into prepared pan. Cover pan with aluminum foil. Refrigerate overnight.

Uncover and invert pan onto serving platter; remove foil. Allow dessert to sit at room temperature 15 minutes to soften slightly. Cut into slices and top with Sweetened Whipped Cream and Raspberry Sauce.
Yield: 8 to 10 servings

(Top left) Tart, frozen Raspberry Elegance is served in grand style with a topping of raspberry sauce and sweetened whipped cream.

(Top right) Paired with fresh fruit slices or cookies, this Almond Dessert Spread is a treat you'll be proud to bring out when company comes.

(Bottom) Apricot Brandy Cake tastes great fresh from the oven, but it's even better when you wait for the flavors to blend.

SWEETENED WHIPPED CREAM

1 cup whipping cream
1/2 cup granulated sugar
1 1/2 teaspoons vanilla extract

Place all ingredients in a large mixing bowl. Beat at high speed until soft peaks form.

RASPBERRY SAUCE

1 package (10 ounces) frozen
    raspberries in syrup, thawed
1 teaspoon lemon juice
2 tablespoons sifted confectioners
    sugar

Drain berries, reserving half of the liquid. Place berries in a blender or food processor and purée. To remove seeds, place puréed berries in a fine strainer and push the berries through the strainer with the back of a spoon. Discard seeds. Stir in lemon juice, confectioners sugar, and reserved liquid.

ALMOND DESSERT SPREAD

1 can (8 ounces) almond paste
1/4 cup plus 1 tablespoon butter,
    softened and divided
1 package (3 ounces) cream cheese,
    softened
2 tablespoons sifted confectioners
    sugar
2 tablespoons amaretto liqueur, divided
4 ounces semisweet baking chocolate
2 tablespoons whipping cream
2 tablespoons sliced or slivered
    almonds

    Purchased shortbread cookies,
    apples, or pears to serve

Combine almond paste, 1/4 cup butter, cream cheese, confectioners sugar, and 1 tablespoon amaretto; beat until smooth.

Melt chocolate in the top of a double boiler over simmering water. Add cream, remaining 1 tablespoon butter, and remaining 1 tablespoon amaretto. Stir until smooth. Reserve 2 tablespoons chocolate mixture. Spoon one-third of the almond mixture into a 2-cup glass soufflé dish. Cover with half of the chocolate mixture. Repeat layers and top with an additional layer of almond mixture. Drizzle with reserved chocolate and sprinkle with almonds. Cover with plastic wrap and refrigerate 6 to 8 hours before serving.

Serve with purchased shortbread cookies, apples, or pears.
Yield: about 1 3/4 cups of spread

APRICOT BRANDY CAKE

1 cup butter or margarine, softened
3 cups granulated sugar
6 eggs
1 teaspoon orange extract
1 teaspoon almond extract
1/2 teaspoon lemon extract
3 cups all-purpose flour
1/2 teaspoon salt
1/4 teaspoon baking soda
1 cup sour cream
1/2 cup apricot brandy
    Glaze (recipe follows)
    Apricot Topping (recipe follows)

Preheat oven to 325 degrees. Cream butter and sugar. Add eggs, one at a time, blending well after each addition. Stir in extracts. In a small bowl, combine flour, salt, and baking soda. Add dry ingredients to creamed mixture, alternating with sour cream and brandy. Bake in a greased 10-inch fluted tube pan 1 hour 10 minutes or until toothpick inserted in cake comes out clean. Remove from pan and pour warm Glaze over cake. Cool cake completely.

Spoon Apricot Topping over top of cake and serve with additional topping.
Yield: 10 to 12 servings

GLAZE
1 cup granulated sugar
1/2 cup water
2 tablespoons apricot brandy

Combine sugar and water in a small saucepan. Bring to a boil and stir until slightly thickened. Remove from heat and stir in apricot brandy.

APRICOT TOPPING
2 cans (16 ounces each) apricots,
    drained and chopped
2 tablespoons apricot brandy
1 tablespoon cornstarch

Heat apricots in a small saucepan. Combine apricot brandy and cornstarch. Stir into apricots and cook until thickened.

CHOCOLATE TORTE WITH CRANBERRIES

1 cup strongly brewed coffee
³/₄ cup cocoa
¹/₂ cup butter or margarine
2 cups all-purpose flour
2 cups granulated sugar
1¹/₂ teaspoons baking soda
¹/₂ teaspoon salt
¹/₂ cup buttermilk
2 eggs, lightly beaten
2 teaspoons vanilla extract
1¹/₂ cups coarsely chopped cranberries
1¹/₂ cups whipping cream
³/₄ cup sifted confectioners sugar
Cranberry Filling and Garnish
  (recipe follows)
Chocolate Glaze (recipe follows)

Preheat oven to 375 degrees. In a small saucepan over medium-high heat, stir together coffee, cocoa, and butter until butter is melted. Pour chocolate mixture into medium mixing bowl; set aside. Sift together flour, granulated sugar, baking soda, and salt. Gradually add dry ingredients to chocolate mixture, alternating with the buttermilk. Beat in eggs and vanilla until well blended. Fold in the cranberries. Pour mixture evenly into two greased and floured 9-inch round cake pans. Bake 25 to 30 minutes or until toothpick inserted in center of cake comes out clean. Cool cakes in the pans 10 minutes. Remove cakes from pans and transfer to wire racks to cool completely. Wrap cakes in plastic wrap and freeze at least 1 hour.

To assemble torte, unwrap cakes and use a serrated knife to split each cake into two layers. Whip cream with confectioners sugar until stiff peaks form (reserve ¹/₂ cup for garnish). Spread the tops of three layers with a layer of Cranberry Filling and a layer of whipped cream; stack layers. Center remaining layer on top. Pour Chocolate Glaze over top of torte and use spatula to spread glaze onto sides. Garnish top of torte with reserved whipped cream and sugared cranberries.
Yield: 10 to 12 servings

CRANBERRY FILLING AND GARNISH

12 ounces frozen cranberries
1 cup granulated sugar
3 tablespoons water
1 tablespoon lemon juice
Granulated sugar

Combine first 4 ingredients in a heavy saucepan and bring to a boil. Reduce heat and simmer 3 minutes. Remove 14 cranberries and set aside. Continue simmering mixture 5 minutes or until thick. Remove from heat and cool completely.

Roll reserved cranberries in sugar; allow to dry. Use sugared cranberries for garnish.

CHOCOLATE GLAZE

1 package (12 ounces) semisweet chocolate chips
1 cup whipping cream

In a microwave or in the top of a double boiler, melt chocolate chips over simmering water. Remove from heat and stir in cream. Cool until slightly thickened.

Sugared cranberries make a colorful showing atop this heavenly Chocolate Torte with Cranberries. Inside the glazed dessert are layers of chocolate cake, whipped cream, and sweet cranberry filling.

(Left) A chocolate cookie crumb crust is a delicious base for Peppermint Pie; the filling has a texture similar to frozen custard. The candy ladybugs are a sweet garnish. *(Right)* European-style Vienna Torte is a light chocolate cake with a crème de menthe filling.

PEPPERMINT PIE

CRUST
- 2 cups chocolate cookie crumbs
- 1/2 cup granulated sugar
- 1/3 cup butter, melted

FILLING
- 24 large marshmallows
- 10 ounces white chocolate
- 1/2 cup milk
- 1 teaspoon peppermint extract
- 1 cup whipping cream, whipped

For crust, combine all ingredients and press into bottom of an ungreased 9-inch springform pan.

For filling, combine marshmallows, white chocolate, and milk in the top of a double boiler over simmering water. Stir constantly until mixture melts and is smooth. Remove from heat. Cool to room temperature. Fold peppermint extract and whipped cream into white chocolate mixture. Pour mixture into crust. Cover and freeze overnight.

Yield: 8 to 10 servings

VIENNA TORTE

CAKE
- 2 cups granulated sugar
- 2 cups all-purpose flour
- 1 teaspoon baking soda
- 1 cup butter or margarine
- 1 cup water
- 1/2 cup cocoa
- 1/2 cup buttermilk
- 2 eggs, lightly beaten
- 2 teaspoons vanilla extract

FROSTING
- 2 cups whipping cream
- 1 1/2 cups sifted confectioners sugar
- 3 tablespoons green crème de menthe liqueur
- 2 tablespoons white crème de cacao liqueur

Preheat oven to 400 degrees. For cake, combine sugar, flour, and baking soda in a large mixing bowl; set aside. In a saucepan, combine butter, water, and cocoa; bring to a boil. Add the chocolate mixture to the flour mixture and stir until well blended. Beat in buttermilk, eggs, and vanilla. Pour into a greased and floured 15 x 10 x 1-inch jellyroll pan. Bake 20 to 25 minutes or until cake springs back when touched in center. Allow cake to cool in pan.

For frosting, combine whipping cream, confectioners sugar, and liqueurs; beat until stiff peaks form.

Invert cake onto the back of another jellyroll pan. Cut cake crosswise into four equal sections. Placing layers on a serving plate, spread frosting evenly between layers and on top of cake; do not frost sides. Chill torte until ready to serve.

Yield: 10 to 12 servings

A caramel surprise is hidden beneath traditional egg custard in our Caramel Cream dessert.

Children will love a menagerie of Gingerbread Cutouts, especially when these moist, spicy treats are served with ice cream.

CARAMEL CREAM

1½ cups granulated sugar, divided
2 tablespoons water
2 eggs
3 egg yolks
1 tablespoon vanilla extract
2 cups milk

Preheat oven to 350 degrees. Combine 1 cup sugar with water in a heavy saucepan over medium heat. Swirl pan occasionally until sugar begins to melt and turns golden (do not stir mixture and do not increase temperature). Pour caramel into eight warmed custard cups. Tilt the cups to coat bottoms and sides; set aside.

Beat eggs, yolks, remaining ½ cup sugar, and vanilla until well blended. Slowly beat milk into egg mixture. Pour mixture into caramel-lined cups. Place cups in a 13 x 9 x 2-inch baking pan and add hot water to baking pan to come halfway up the sides of the cups. Bake 45 minutes or until custard is set in center. Serve warm or chilled.

Yield: 8 servings

GINGERBREAD CUTOUTS

½ cup vegetable shortening
2 tablespoons granulated sugar
1 egg
1 cup dark molasses
1 cup boiling water
2¼ cups all-purpose flour
1 teaspoon baking soda
½ teaspoon salt
1½ teaspoons ground ginger
1 teaspoon ground cinnamon
½ teaspoon ground cloves

Ice cream to serve

Preheat oven to 325 degrees. In a large mixing bowl, cream shortening, sugar, and egg. Blend in molasses and water. Combine flour, baking soda, salt, ginger, cinnamon, and cloves; add to molasses mixture. Beat until smooth. Pour into a 15 x 10 x 1-inch waxed paper-lined jellyroll pan. Bake 30 to 35 minutes or until cake springs back when touched in center. Cool cake in pan. Cut out shapes using desired cookie cutters (smaller shapes were cut from scraps using 1-inch-long cookie cutters). Serve with ice cream.

Yield: about 3 dozen 3-inch cutouts

Reminiscent of old-fashioned jam cake, the Christmas Keeping Cake gets more flavorful with each passing day.

CHRISTMAS KEEPING CAKE

1 cup butter or margarine, softened
2 cups granulated sugar
3 eggs, separated
1 teaspoon baking soda
½ cup buttermilk
3 cups all-purpose flour, divided
1½ teaspoons ground cinnamon
½ teaspoon ground nutmeg
½ teaspoon ground cloves
1 cup red plum jam
1 cup coarsely chopped pecans
1 cup golden raisins
1 cup quartered dates
1 cup brandy, bourbon, or sherry

Preheat oven to 300 degrees. Cream butter and sugar. Beat in egg yolks until fluffy. Dissolve baking soda in buttermilk. Beat buttermilk into butter mixture. Combine 2½ cups flour with spices. Add to creamed mixture alternately with jam. Beat egg whites until stiff; fold into batter. Combine remaining ½ cup flour with pecans, raisins, and dates. Fold into batter. Pour into a well-greased and floured 10-inch tube pan. Bake 3 to 3½ hours or until a toothpick inserted in center of cake comes out clean. Place pan on wire rack to cool. When completely cool, cut a piece of cheesecloth large enough to wrap around cake. Soak cheesecloth in liquor. Remove cake from pan and wrap cheesecloth around cake. Wrap cheesecloth-covered cake tightly with aluminum foil. Allow to age 4 to 6 weeks before serving.

Yield: 12 to 14 servings

BAKED FUDGE DESSERT WITH KAHLÚA CREAM

BAKED FUDGE
    2   cups granulated sugar
   3/4 cup cocoa
   1/2 cup all-purpose flour
    5   eggs, beaten
    1   cup plus 2 tablespoons butter or
          margarine, melted
    2   teaspoons vanilla extract
  1 1/2 cups chopped pecans

KAHLÚA CREAM
    1   cup whipping cream
   1/2 cup sifted confectioners sugar
    3   tablespoons Kahlúa liqueur

Preheat oven to 300 degrees. For baked fudge, combine sugar, cocoa, and flour in a medium mixing bowl. Add eggs and beat until smooth. Combine butter and vanilla. Beat into cocoa mixture. Stir in pecans. Pour into eight individual custard cups. Place cups in a 13 x 9 x 2-inch baking pan and add hot water to come halfway up the sides of the custard cups. Bake 40 to 45 minutes or until tops are crusty.

For Kahlúa cream, combine all ingredients and beat until soft peaks form. Serve cream with warm baked fudge.
Yield: 8 servings

(Top) Baked Fudge Dessert with Kahlúa Cream (left) is a moist brownie-like treat that's served warm with a topping of sweet liqueur-flavored whipped cream. Amaretto-Peach Cheesecake gets its delicious flavor combination from dried peaches marinated in amaretto.

(Bottom) Macadamia nuts, toasted coconut, and fresh bananas give this Safari Pie tropical appeal.

AMARETTO-PEACH CHEESECAKE

    1   cup diced dried peaches
    1   cup amaretto liqueur
    2   cups vanilla wafer cookie crumbs
  1 1/2 cups plus 1 tablespoon granulated
          sugar, divided
   1/2 cup almond paste, divided
    2   tablespoons butter, melted
    5   packages (8 ounces each)
          cream cheese, softened
    1   teaspoon almond extract
    6   eggs
    4   egg yolks
        Additional amaretto liqueur
   1/3 cup whipping cream

In a small bowl, combine peaches with 1 cup amaretto. Marinate at least 2 hours.

Combine cookie crumbs, 1 tablespoon sugar, 1/4 cup almond paste, and melted butter in a medium bowl. Press into the bottom of a lightly greased 10-inch springform pan.

Preheat oven to 350 degrees. For filling, beat cream cheese until smooth. Add remaining 1/4 cup almond paste, remaining 1 1/2 cups sugar, and almond extract. Beat in eggs and yolks, one at a time, beating well after each addition. Drain marinated peaches, reserving amaretto. Add additional amaretto to reserved amaretto to make 1 cup of liquid. Stir amaretto and cream into cream cheese mixture. Stir in marinated peaches. Pour filling over crust. Place springform pan in a larger pan and add hot water to larger pan to come halfway up sides of springform pan. Bake 1 1/2 hours or until center is set. Remove cheesecake from oven and pan of water; allow to cool completely. Cover and refrigerate overnight.

To serve, use a knife to loosen sides of cheesecake from pan; remove springform.
Yield: 12 to 14 servings

SAFARI PIE

CRUST
  1 1/4 cups all-purpose flour
   1/4 teaspoon salt
    7   tablespoons butter, chilled and cut
          into pieces
    3   tablespoons ice water

FILLING
  2 1/2 cups milk
   1/2 cup banana-flavored liqueur
    2   tablespoons vanilla extract
   1/2 teaspoon coconut extract
    4   egg yolks
   2/3 cup granulated sugar
   1/2 cup all-purpose flour
    2   bananas, cut into 1/4-inch slices,
          divided
    1   cup chopped macadamia nuts,
          divided
    1   cup toasted coconut,
          divided

MERINGUE
    4   egg whites
   1/8 teaspoon salt
   1/4 cup granulated sugar
    1   tablespoon toasted coconut

Preheat oven to 400 degrees. For crust, sift flour and salt into a mixing bowl. Using a pastry blender or two knives, cut butter into flour mixture until mixture resembles coarse meal. Sprinkle ice water over dough, mixing quickly just until dough forms a ball (dough will be soft). On a lightly floured surface, use a floured rolling pin to roll out dough. Place the dough in an ungreased 9-inch pie pan. Trim and crimp edges of pie, and prick bottom of shell with a fork. Bake 15 to 20 minutes or until lightly browned.

For filling, combine milk, liqueur, and extracts in a medium saucepan; bring to a boil. Cover and remove from heat. In a medium bowl, beat egg yolks with sugar until thickened and pale yellow. Add flour and beat until well blended. Gradually whisk milk mixture into egg yolk mixture. Return mixture to saucepan and bring to a boil over medium heat, whisking constantly. Continue cooking and whisking until mixture is thickened and smooth. Remove from heat.

Layer half of banana slices, 1/2 cup nuts, and 1/2 cup coconut in bottom of pie shell. Pour half of custard over bananas. Layer remaining bananas, nuts, and coconut over custard and top with remaining custard. Cover and refrigerate at least 2 hours or until custard is set.

Preheat oven to 350 degrees. For meringue, beat egg whites with salt until soft peaks form. Gradually beat in sugar until stiff peaks form. Spoon meringue on top of pie, sealing edges. Sprinkle top of meringue with coconut. Bake 12 to 15 minutes or until meringue is lightly browned. Serve warm or chilled. Store in refrigerator.
Yield: about 8 servings

CARAMEL SOUFFLÉ WITH CRÈME ANGLAISE

SOUFFLÉ
- 2½ cups granulated sugar, divided
- 8 egg whites
- ½ teaspoon cream of tartar
- ⅛ teaspoon salt

CRÈME ANGLAISE
- 1 cup whipping cream
- 3 egg yolks, lightly beaten
- ¼ cup granulated sugar
- 1 teaspoon vanilla extract

Preheat oven to 300 degrees. For soufflé, place 1¼ cups sugar in a heavy skillet over medium-low heat. Cook, stirring occasionally, until sugar liquefies and turns caramel in color (about 5 minutes). Pour half of the caramel into a 2-quart soufflé dish. Tilt dish to coat bottom and sides with caramel; cool.

Beat egg whites with cream of tartar and salt until soft peaks form. Gradually beat in remaining 1¼ cups sugar until stiff peaks form. Return skillet to medium-low heat to remelt remaining caramel. Gradually beat caramel into egg white mixture; beat 5 minutes. Pour mixture into soufflé dish. Place soufflé dish in a larger baking pan and add hot water to larger pan to come halfway up the sides of the soufflé dish. Bake 1 hour or until top is firm. (Soufflé may be served warm or at room temperature without falling.)

For crème anglaise, heat cream in a heavy saucepan just until cream begins to steam. Whisk about ¼ cup of cream into yolks. Whisk egg yolk mixture, sugar, and vanilla into remaining cream in saucepan. Return to heat and cook, stirring constantly, until mixture thickens (about 3 to 5 minutes). Remove from heat and strain sauce. Cool completely. Serve with soufflé.
Yield: 8 to 10 servings

(Top) Our Caramel Soufflé has a chewy upper crust, a fluffy filling, and a lining of caramelized sugar that liquefies during baking. Drizzled with Crème Anglaise, it's the next best thing to heaven!

(Bottom left) Cranberry Tarts with Orange and Port are a wonderful blend of tangy, spirited flavors. The pecan crust adds a pleasingly nutty taste and texture.

(Bottom right) For an alternative to old-fashioned fruitcake, try sweet, biscuit-like Fruitcake Scones with Devon Cream. They're filled with dried fruit bits and crunchy pecans.

CRANBERRY TARTS WITH ORANGE AND PORT

CRUST
- 1½ cups all-purpose flour
- ¾ cup ground toasted pecans
- ⅓ cup granulated sugar
- ½ cup butter, chilled and cut into pieces
- 3 tablespoons ice water

FILLING
- 4 cups fresh cranberries
- 2 cups granulated sugar
- 1 cup port wine
- 1 cup water
- 2 tablespoons orange juice concentrate
- 1 teaspoon grated orange peel

    Sweetened Whipped Cream to serve (recipe on page 129)

For crust, combine flour, pecans, and sugar in a mixing bowl. Using a pastry blender or two knives, cut butter into pecan mixture until mixture resembles coarse meal. Sprinkle water over dough, mixing quickly just until dough forms a ball. Wrap dough in plastic wrap and refrigerate 1 hour.

Preheat oven to 400 degrees. On a lightly floured surface, use a floured rolling pin to roll out dough to ⅛-inch thickness. Cut the dough into six 5½-inch circles. Place circles of dough in six 4½-inch round tart pans with removable bottoms. Trim edges of dough and prick bottoms of crusts with a fork. Place pans on a baking sheet and bake 12 to 15 minutes or until crusts are lightly browned. Cool completely before filling.

For filling, combine all ingredients in a large saucepan. Bring to a boil over medium-high heat. Reduce heat to simmer and cook, stirring occasionally, until mixture thickens (about 10 minutes). Cool completely.

Just before serving, fill tart shells with cranberry filling. Top with Sweetened Whipped Cream.
Yield: 6 tarts

FRUITCAKE SCONES WITH DEVON CREAM

DEVON CREAM
- 1 cup whipping cream, divided
- ¼ cup butter
- 1 tablespoon honey
- ½ teaspoon vanilla extract

SCONES
- ¼ cup butter or margarine, softened
- ½ cup granulated sugar
- 2 eggs
- 1½ cups all-purpose flour
- 1½ teaspoons baking powder
- ½ teaspoon baking soda
- ⅛ teaspoon salt
- ½ cup ricotta cheese
- 1 cup dried mixed fruit bits
- ½ cup coarsely chopped pecans
- ¼ cup water
- 1 teaspoon vanilla extract
- 1 teaspoon grated orange peel
- 2 tablespoons brandy

For Devon cream, combine ¼ cup cream and butter in a small saucepan. Place pan over low heat, stirring constantly, until butter is melted. Remove pan from heat and stir in honey and vanilla; cool to room temperature.

In a mixing bowl, beat remaining ¾ cup cream until soft peaks form. Gradually beat in butter mixture. Beat 5 minutes at high speed of electric mixer (mixture will appear to be thin). Refrigerate 3 hours.

Skim thickened cream from top of mixture and place in serving bowl. Discard remaining liquid in bottom of bowl. (Devon cream may separate slightly at room temperature, but stirring will correct this. Devon cream will keep in refrigerator 24 hours.)

Preheat oven to 350 degrees. For scones, cream butter and sugar in a large mixing bowl. Beat in eggs, one at a time, beating well after each addition. In a separate bowl, combine flour, baking powder, baking soda, and salt. Stir dry ingredients into butter mixture alternately with ricotta cheese. Stir in fruit, pecans, water, vanilla, and orange peel. Drop about ⅓ cup of dough for each scone onto a lightly greased baking sheet. Bake 12 to 15 minutes or until tops are golden brown and a toothpick inserted into a scone comes out clean. Sprinkle warm scones with brandy. Serve scones warm or at room temperature with Devon cream.
Yield: about 8 scones

PUMPKIN ICE CREAM

2 cups whipping cream
2 cups milk
1 cup granulated sugar
4 egg yolks, lightly beaten
1 cup canned pumpkin
1 teaspoon ground cinnamon
$^1/_2$ teaspoon ground ginger
$^1/_4$ teaspoon ground cloves

In a heavy saucepan, combine cream, milk, and sugar over medium heat. Cook just until mixture begins to steam; remove from heat. Whisk about $^1/_4$ cup of cream mixture into egg yolks. Whisk yolk mixture into cream mixture in pan. Return to heat and cook, stirring constantly, until mixture coats the back of a metal spoon. Remove from heat and cool completely. Stir in remaining ingredients. Freeze mixture in an ice cream freezer following manufacturer's instructions.
Yield: about 5$^1/_2$ cups of ice cream

Cinnamon, ginger, and cloves add spice to the mellow goodness of Pumpkin Ice Cream.

MACADAMIA NUT FUDGE TART

CRUST
1$^3/_4$ cups all-purpose flour
$^1/_3$ cup cocoa
$^1/_4$ cup granulated sugar
$^1/_8$ teaspoon salt
$^3/_4$ cup butter or margarine, chilled and cut into pieces
$^1/_2$ cup strongly brewed coffee, chilled

FILLING
1 package (6 ounces) semisweet chocolate chips, melted
$^2/_3$ cup granulated sugar
2 tablespoons butter or margarine, melted
2 tablespoons milk
2 teaspoons coffee-flavored liqueur
2 eggs, beaten
$^1/_2$ cup chopped macadamia nuts

For crust, combine first 4 ingredients in a large bowl. Using a pastry blender or two knives, cut butter into dry ingredients until mixture resembles coarse meal. Add coffee and knead until a soft dough forms. Cover and chill 8 hours or overnight.

On a lightly floured surface, use a floured rolling pin to roll out dough to an 11-inch circle. Press into a greased 9-inch tart pan. Chill at least 1 hour.

Preheat oven to 350 degrees. For filling, combine first 5 ingredients in a large bowl. Add eggs, beating until smooth. Fold in nuts. Pour batter into tart shell. Bake 30 to 40 minutes or until top is dry and firm (inside will be soft). Cool completely in pan.
Yield: about 16 servings

Nestled in a cocoa-mocha crust, Macadamia Nut Fudge Tart is a chocolate lover's delight!

POTS DE CRÈME

POTS DE CRÈME
    12 ounces semisweet baking chocolate
    2 cups whipping cream
    6 egg yolks
    2 tablespoons granulated sugar

SWEETENED WHIPPED CREAM
    1 cup whipping cream
    1/4 cup granulated sugar
    1 teaspoon vanilla extract

Preheat oven to 350 degrees. In the top of a double boiler over simmering water, melt chocolate with cream, stirring occasionally. In a large bowl, beat egg yolks with sugar. Gradually beat one-fourth of chocolate mixture into egg mixture until well blended. Beat in remaining chocolate mixture. Pour into small custard or oven-proof demitasse cups to within 1/2 inch of tops. Place cups in a baking pan and fill pan with hot water to come halfway up the sides of the cups. Bake 30 minutes or until set around edges but still soft in centers; cool. Cover and refrigerate overnight.

For sweetened whipped cream, beat all ingredients until stiff peaks form. Serve with Pots de Crème.

Yield: about 6 Pots de Crème

Chocolate lovers will rejoice in the creamy delights of Pots de Crème, a dense dessert topped with sweetened whipped cream.

Melted caramel and a hint of nutmeg add a sweet touch to a traditional treat. Crowned with dollops of whipped cream, Caramel Baked Apples are sure to please!

CARAMEL BAKED APPLES

    6 tablespoons butter or margarine, softened
    2 teaspoons ground nutmeg
    6 red baking apples, cored
    1/4 cup plus 2 tablespoons water, divided
    1 package (10 ounces) caramels
    1/2 cup whipping cream

    Sweetened Whipped Cream to serve (recipe on this page)

Preheat oven to 350 degrees. In a small bowl, combine butter and nutmeg. Using 1 tablespoon for each apple, fill centers of apples with butter mixture. Place apples in a baking pan and add 1/4 cup water to pan. Bake 30 to 35 minutes.

In a heavy saucepan over low heat, melt caramels with 2 tablespoons water, stirring occasionally. Remove from heat and stir in cream. To serve, pour caramel mixture over baked apples. Top with Sweetened Whipped Cream.

Yield: 6 apples

DATE MUFFINS

MUFFINS
1¼ cups chopped toasted pecans
1 package (8 ounces) chopped dates
1 cup granulated sugar
3 eggs, beaten
½ cup all-purpose flour
½ teaspoon salt
½ teaspoon ground cinnamon
¼ teaspoon ground nutmeg

HARD SAUCE
2 cups sifted confectioners sugar
½ cup butter, softened
1 teaspoon vanilla extract

Preheat oven to 350 degrees. For muffins, combine all ingredients in a large mixing bowl. Stir just until all ingredients are moistened. Fill lightly greased miniature muffin tins two-thirds full with batter. Bake 15 minutes or until tops are very lightly browned and a muffin springs back when lightly pressed. Remove from tins and cool on wire racks.

For hard sauce, combine all ingredients in a medium bowl and beat until smooth. Spread hard sauce on tops of muffins.
Yield: about 4 dozen muffins

Packed with pecans, chewy Date Muffins are moist, spicy treats. Top them with a hard sauce and gumdrop holly berries for a delectable difference.

IRISH CREAM DESSERT

3 tablespoons cold water
1 envelope unflavored gelatin
2 cups whipping cream
½ cup Irish cream liqueur
½ cup granulated sugar
½ cup finely chopped semisweet or bittersweet chocolate, reserving 2 tablespoons for garnish

In a small heatproof bowl, combine water and gelatin. Allow to sit 5 minutes to soften gelatin. Place bowl in a saucepan of water over low heat and stir until gelatin is dissolved. Remove from heat and cool to room temperature.

In a large mixing bowl, whip cream until soft peaks form. Gradually beat gelatin mixture into cream until stiff peaks form. Blend in liqueur and sugar. Fold in chocolate. Spoon into individual glasses and chill at least 1 hour. Before serving, sprinkle reserved chocolate over tops of desserts.
Yield: about 8 servings

Light and fluffy, this sumptuous Irish Cream Dessert is kissed with the flavor of a favorite liqueur. It's a cool way to warm up on a frosty night.

WHITE CHOCOLATE CHEESECAKE

*To make leaves for garnish, stir
2 tablespoons light corn syrup into
6 ounces melted green candy coating
wafers. Wrap mixture in plastic wrap and
allow to sit overnight at room temperature.
Knead mixture and roll out between two
sheets of waxed paper. Use a leaf-shaped
cookie cutter to cut out leaves. Arrange
leaves on cake and garnish with cranberries.*

CHEESECAKE
- 2 packages (8 ounces each) cream cheese, softened
- 1/3 cup granulated sugar
- 6 egg yolks
- 2 cups sour cream
- 1 tablespoon vanilla extract
- 1/2 teaspoon salt
- 12 ounces white chocolate, melted

FROSTING
- 1 package (8 ounces) cream cheese, softened
- 1/3 cup butter, softened
- 1 teaspoon vanilla extract
- 8 ounces white chocolate, melted

Preheat oven to 350 degrees. For cheesecake, beat cream cheese and sugar in a large mixing bowl until smooth. Beat in egg yolks, one at a time, beating well after each addition. Beat in sour cream, vanilla, and salt. Blend in white chocolate. Line an 8-inch springform pan with aluminum foil; lightly grease foil. Pour batter into prepared pan. Place springform pan in a larger pan and add hot water to come halfway up sides of springform pan. Bake 45 minutes. Turn off oven and allow cake to cool in oven 1 hour without opening door. Remove cheesecake from oven and pan of water and allow to cool completely. Cover and refrigerate overnight.

For frosting, beat cream cheese, butter, and vanilla in a medium mixing bowl until smooth. Gradually beat in white chocolate. Remove cheesecake from springform pan. Spread frosting over top and sides of cheesecake. Chill at least 1 hour before serving.

Yield: 10 to 12 servings

Covered with a luscious white chocolate buttercream frosting, this rich White Chocolate Cheesecake can be made ahead of time and frozen for up to a week.

each addition. Beat in vanilla. Spread filling in crust. Arrange pear halves over the filling. Bake 40 minutes or until filling is golden and set. Sprinkle tart with sugar and broil until bubbly and browned (watch closely; this happens very quickly). Brush with preserves while tart is still warm. Cool completely before cutting.
Yield: 10 to 12 servings

CHOCOLATE SPLURGE

- $1/2$ cup butter or margarine, softened
- $3/4$ cup sifted confectioners sugar
- 1 egg
- $1/2$ cup cocoa
- 3 ounces semisweet baking chocolate, melted
- 2 tablespoons crème de menthe liqueur
- 4 cups (about 14 ounces) chocolate mint-flavored cookies, broken into small pieces

  Sweetened Whipped Cream to serve (recipe on page 129)

In a medium mixing bowl, beat butter, confectioners sugar, and egg until creamy. Blend in cocoa, chocolate, and liqueur. Stir in cookie pieces. Turn mixture into a plastic wrap-lined 8-inch round pan. Cover and chill until firm (1 to 2 hours). Serve with Sweetened Whipped Cream.
Yield: 8 to 10 servings

VANILLA PASTRIES WITH CHERRY SAUCE

PASTRY
- 1 sheet (from a $17^{1}/4$-ounce package) frozen puff pastry dough, thawed
- 1 egg yolk
- 1 teaspoon water
- 1 tablespoon granulated sugar

CUSTARD
- 1 cup plus 2 tablespoons milk, divided
- 2 eggs, separated
- 2 tablespoons cornstarch
- 2 tablespoons granulated sugar
- 2 teaspoons vanilla extract
- $3/4$ cup sifted confectioners sugar

ICING
- 1 cup sifted confectioners sugar
- 3 tablespoons lemon juice

CHERRY SAUCE
- 1 can ($16^{1}/2$ ounces) pitted dark sweet cherries, drained
- $1/3$ cup firmly packed brown sugar
- 2 tablespoons lemon juice

This trio of elegant desserts is ideal for special occasions: A sweet almond flavor highlights the delightfully simple European-style Pear and Almond Tart *(clockwise from top left)*. Chocolate Splurge is both smooth and crunchy; chocolate mint cookies and crème de menthe liqueur add coolness to this frozen delight. Rich Vanilla Pastries with Cherry Sauce make a luscious ending to a holiday party.

PEAR AND ALMOND TART

CRUST
- $1^{1}/4$ cups all-purpose flour
- $1/3$ cup granulated sugar
- $1/4$ teaspoon salt
- 7 tablespoons butter, chilled and cut into pieces
- 3 tablespoons ice water

FILLING
- 1 cup almond paste
- $1/2$ cup butter or margarine, softened
- 2 eggs
- 1 teaspoon vanilla extract
- 1 can (29 ounces) pear halves, drained
- 1 tablespoon granulated sugar
- 3 tablespoons peach preserves

Preheat oven to 350 degrees. For crust, sift flour, sugar, and salt together in a medium mixing bowl. Using a pastry blender or two knives, cut butter into flour until mixture resembles coarse meal. Sprinkle ice water over dough, mixing quickly just until dough forms a soft ball. On a lightly floured surface, use a floured rolling pin to roll out dough to $1/8$-inch thickness. Place the dough in an ungreased $10^{1}/2$-inch tart pan with removable bottom. Trim edges of dough.

For filling, beat almond paste and butter in a medium mixing bowl until fluffy. Beat in the eggs, one at a time, beating well after

142

Preheat oven to 400 degrees. For pastry, cut puff pastry sheet in half lengthwise. Place pastry halves on a lightly greased baking sheet and prick each half several times with a fork. Combine egg yolk with water and brush over pastry halves. Sprinkle each half with sugar. Bake 15 to 20 minutes or until golden brown. Cool completely before removing from pan.

For custard, combine 2 tablespoons milk, egg yolks, cornstarch, granulated sugar, and vanilla in a mixing bowl, blending well. In a large heavy saucepan, bring remaining 1 cup milk to a boil. Whisk about half of hot milk into egg mixture. Whisk egg mixture into remaining milk in pan. Cook over medium heat, stirring constantly until mixture is very thick (about 2 to 3 minutes). Remove from heat. In a large mixing bowl, beat egg whites with confectioners sugar until stiff and shiny. Fold egg white mixture into warm mixture in pan. Cool completely, cover, and refrigerate 1 hour.

For icing, combine confectioners sugar and lemon juice in a small bowl, blending until smooth. Spread custard over one pastry piece. Top with remaining pastry piece and spread icing over top. Chill at least 1 hour. Use a serrated knife to cut pastry into slices.

For cherry sauce, purée cherries with brown sugar and lemon juice in a blender or food processor. Allow to stand at room temperature 15 minutes. To serve, place cherry sauce on a dessert plate and top with a pastry slice.
Yield: about 8 pastries

RAISIN-WALNUT PINWHEELS

1	sheet (from a 17¼-ounce package) frozen puff pastry dough, thawed
⅓	cup granulated sugar
1	tablespoon ground cinnamon
¼	cup butter or margarine
½	cup raisins
½	cup finely chopped walnuts
1	egg yolk, beaten

Preheat oven to 350 degrees. On a lightly floured surface, use a floured rolling pin to roll out pastry to an 8 x 12-inch rectangle. In a small bowl, combine sugar and cinnamon and set aside. In a small saucepan, melt butter. Add raisins and walnuts, stirring until well coated. Spread raisin mixture evenly over pastry. Sprinkle sugar mixture evenly over raisin mixture. Beginning at 1 long edge, roll up pastry. Brush egg yolk on long edge to seal. Place on a greased baking sheet. Bake 20 to 25 minutes or until golden brown. Cool completely. Cut into 1-inch slices.
Yield: about 12 pinwheels

Warm and creamy with a hint of coconut, Hot Cappuccino Punch *(left)* is laced with rum and brandy. It's a perfect complement to flaky Raisin-Walnut Pinwheels.

HOT CAPPUCCINO PUNCH

3	cups brewed coffee, room temperature
3	cups half and half
½	cup cream of coconut
½	cup rum
½	cup brandy

Combine all ingredients in a large saucepan. Cook over medium heat until mixture begins to boil. Remove from heat. Serve immediately.
Yield: about ten 6-ounce servings

MOCHA MINI PIES

CRUST
- 20 chocolate wafer cookies (2³/₄-inch diameter)
- 3 tablespoons butter or margarine, cut into pieces

FILLING
- 1 cup milk
- ³/₄ cup granulated sugar
- 3 tablespoons instant coffee granules
- ³/₄ cup marshmallow creme
- 2 egg yolks
- 2 cups whipping cream

Preheat oven to 375 degrees. For crust, process chocolate wafers in a blender or food processor fitted with a steel blade until finely crumbled. Add butter and process until mixture resembles coarse meal. Press crumbs into the bottoms of 18 paper-lined muffin tins. Bake 8 to 10 minutes. Cool completely.

For filling, combine milk, sugar, and coffee in a medium saucepan. Cook over medium heat, stirring constantly, until sugar and coffee are dissolved. Add marshmallow creme, stirring until melted. In a small bowl, beat egg yolks until foamy. Add 3 tablespoons marshmallow mixture to yolks and stir. Add yolks to marshmallow mixture and stir until well blended. Pour into a 3-quart bowl and chill until thick but not set (about 45 minutes).

In a medium chilled bowl, whip cream until stiff peaks form; fold into marshmallow mixture, mixing just until filling has a swirled appearance. Pour about ¹/₄ cup filling over each crust. Freeze until firm. Serve frozen.

Yield: 1¹/₂ dozen mini pies

PUMPKIN PIE SQUARES

CRUST
- 1³/₄ cups all-purpose flour
- 1¹/₄ cups granulated sugar
- 2 teaspoons baking powder
- ¹/₂ teaspoon salt
- ¹/₂ cup plus 2 tablespoons butter or margarine, chilled and cut into pieces
- 2 eggs, beaten

FILLING
- 2 eggs
- ¹/₄ cup firmly packed brown sugar
- 1 can (30 ounces) pumpkin pie mix
- ²/₃ cup milk
- 1 tablespoon pumpkin pie spice
- 1 teaspoon ground cinnamon
- 1 teaspoon ground nutmeg

FROSTING
- 1 cup butter or margarine
- 1 cup firmly packed brown sugar
- ¹/₂ teaspoon ground cinnamon
- 1¹/₂ cups chopped walnuts

Preheat oven to 350 degrees. For crust, sift together first 4 ingredients in a large bowl. Using a pastry blender or 2 knives, cut butter into flour until mixture resembles coarse meal. Add eggs, stirring until a soft dough forms. Press into bottom of a greased 9 x 13-inch baking pan. Bake 15 to 20 minutes or until golden brown.

For filling, beat eggs in a large bowl until foamy. Add brown sugar, beating until smooth. Stir in remaining ingredients, mixing well. Pour filling over crust. Bake 30 to 40 minutes or until center is set.

For frosting, combine first 3 ingredients in a medium saucepan over medium heat. Stir constantly 3 to 5 minutes or until syrup thickens. Stir in walnuts. Pour frosting evenly over warm filling. Cool completely. Cut into approximately 2-inch squares.

Yield: about 2 dozen squares

Pumpkin Pie Squares *(left)* are little bites of cake topped with a layer of creamy pumpkin and a luscious praline and walnut frosting. Light and fluffy, frozen Mocha Mini Pies have chocolate cookie crumb crusts.

This smooth Irish Cream Cheesecake is flavored with chocolate and the popular liqueur. A crown of chocolate curls makes a majestic finish.

IRISH CREAM CHEESECAKE

CRUST
- 2 cups finely ground chocolate wafer cookie crumbs (about thirty-six 2³/₄-inch diameter cookies)
- ¹/₄ cup granulated sugar
- 6 tablespoons butter or margarine, melted

FILLING
- 36 ounces (four and one-half 8-ounce packages) cream cheese, softened
- 1²/₃ cups granulated sugar
- 5 eggs
- 1¹/₂ cups Irish cream liqueur
- 1 tablespoon vanilla extract
- 1 cup (6 ounces) semisweet chocolate chips

TOPPING
- 1 cup whipping cream
- 2 tablespoons granulated sugar
- ¹/₂ cup (3 ounces) semisweet chocolate chips, melted

CHOCOLATE CURLS
- 2 cups (12 ounces) semisweet chocolate chips

Preheat oven to 325 degrees. For crust, combine crumbs and sugar in a large bowl. Add butter, stirring until mixture resembles coarse meal. Press into bottom and 1 inch up sides of a greased 9-inch springform pan. Bake 7 to 10 minutes.

For filling, beat cream cheese until smooth. Add sugar and eggs, beating until fluffy. Add liqueur and vanilla, mixing well.

Sprinkle chocolate chips over crust. Spoon filling over chocolate chips. Bake 1 hour 20 minutes to 1 hour 30 minutes or until center is set. Cool completely in pan. Remove sides of pan.

For topping, beat cream and sugar in a large chilled bowl until stiff. Continue to beat while slowly adding chocolate. Spread mixture over cooled cake.

For chocolate curls, melt chocolate in a small saucepan over low heat. Pour onto a baking sheet. Let stand at room temperature until set but not firm. To make curls, pull a cheese plane across surface of chocolate (curls will break if chocolate is too firm). Remelt and cool chocolate as necessary to form desired number of curls. Arrange on cake. Refrigerate until ready to serve.
Yield: about 16 servings

An incredible date and pecan frosting makes this three-layer Chocolate-Date Nut Cake *(left)* extra special. Chocolate Mocha Brownies are studded with chunks of white and semisweet chocolate.

CHOCOLATE-DATE NUT CAKE

CAKE
1 cup butter or margarine, softened
2 cups granulated sugar
3 eggs
$^1/_2$ cup cocoa
$^1/_2$ cup hot water
1 cup hot brewed coffee
1 teaspoon vanilla extract
3 cups all-purpose flour
1 teaspoon baking soda
$^1/_2$ teaspoon salt
1 cup finely chopped pecans

FROSTING
3 cups granulated sugar
1 can (14 ounces) sweetened condensed milk
$^1/_2$ cup water
2 cups chopped dates (about 1 pound)
1 cup finely chopped pecans

Preheat oven to 350 degrees. For cake, cream butter and sugar in a large bowl until fluffy. Add eggs and beat until smooth. In a small bowl, dissolve cocoa in hot water. Add cocoa, coffee, and vanilla to creamed mixture and mix well. In a large bowl, sift together next 3 ingredients. Add dry ingredients to creamed mixture, beating until smooth. Fold in pecans. Pour batter into 3 greased and floured 9-inch round cake pans. Bake 25 to 30 minutes or until a toothpick inserted in center of cake comes out clean. Cool in pans 10 minutes. Turn onto a wire rack to cool.

For frosting, combine sugar, sweetened condensed milk, and water in a medium saucepan. Bring to a boil over medium-high heat. Reduce heat to medium and cook 5 to 8 minutes, stirring constantly, until frosting thickens. Stir in dates and pecans. Frost between layers, on sides, and on top of cake.
Yield: about 20 servings

CHOCOLATE MOCHA BROWNIES

1 cup firmly packed brown sugar
$^3/_4$ cup butter or margarine
2 tablespoons instant coffee granules
1 tablespoon hot water
2 eggs
2 tablespoons vanilla extract
2 cups all-purpose flour
2 teaspoons baking powder
$^1/_2$ teaspoon salt
4 ounces semisweet baking chocolate, broken into small pieces
4 ounces white chocolate, broken into small pieces

In a medium saucepan, melt sugar and butter over medium-low heat. Dissolve coffee in hot water and stir into butter mixture. Cool to room temperature.

Preheat oven to 350 degrees. Beat eggs and vanilla into butter mixture. In a large bowl, sift together next 3 ingredients. Stir butter mixture into dry ingredients. Fold in chocolate pieces. Pour batter into a greased 8 x 11-inch baking pan. Bake 25 to 30 minutes or until light brown. Cool in pan. Cut into $1^1/_2$-inch squares.
Yield: about 3 dozen brownies

146

GINGER POUND CAKE

CAKE

- 1½ cups butter or margarine, softened
- 2¼ cups firmly packed brown sugar
- ½ cup granulated sugar
- 5 eggs
- 2 teaspoons vanilla extract
- 3 cups all-purpose flour
- 1 tablespoon ground ginger
- ½ teaspoon baking powder
- ¼ teaspoon salt
- 1 cup milk
- 1 cup chopped walnuts

GLAZE

- 16 marshmallows
- ⅔ cup apple jelly
- ¼ cup lemon juice
- ¼ cup butter or margarine, cut into pieces

  Walnut halves to garnish

Preheat oven to 350 degrees. For cake, cream butter and sugars in a large bowl until fluffy. Add eggs, one at a time, beating well after each addition. Beat in vanilla. In another large bowl, sift together next 4 ingredients. Add milk and dry ingredients alternately to creamed mixture. Fold in walnuts. Pour batter into a greased and floured 10-inch tube pan. Bake 1 hour 10 minutes to 1 hour 20 minutes or until a toothpick inserted in center of cake comes out clean. Cool in pan 15 minutes. Turn onto a wire rack to cool completely.

For glaze, combine marshmallows, jelly, and lemon juice in a medium saucepan over low heat, stirring until glaze is smooth. Add butter, 1 piece at a time, whisking until melted. Drizzle glaze over top of cake and garnish with walnut halves.
Yield: about 20 servings

EGGNOG MOUSSE

- 1 teaspoon unflavored gelatin
- 1 tablespoon cold water
- 1 cup prepared eggnog
- 1 tablespoon butter or margarine
- 1 tablespoon rum
- 1 teaspoon vanilla extract
- 1 cup whipping cream

  Ground nutmeg to garnish

In a small bowl, soften gelatin in water. In a small saucepan, combine eggnog and butter over low heat. Stirring constantly, cook until butter is melted. Add gelatin and continue to stir until gelatin is dissolved. Remove from heat and stir in rum and

Mild, nutty Ginger Pound Cake *(left)* is enhanced with a tangy apple-lemon glaze. Creamy Eggnog Mousse is a new way to enjoy a favorite holiday flavor.

vanilla. Cool to room temperature.

In a large chilled bowl, beat cream until stiff. Fold eggnog mixture into cream. Pour into individual bowls and chill until set. Garnish with nutmeg.
Yield: about 4 servings

GIFTS OF GOOD TASTE

Made with care and given with love, homemade goodies are ideal for spreading holiday cheer. Friends, family, and neighbors are sure to appreciate a basket or tin filled with a special treat, like a delicious hot drink mix, a fresh loaf of bread, or candy — and you'll love the feeling that comes with giving something from your heart. This assortment includes lots of great gift-giving ideas to brighten the Yuletide season!

Any of these flavorful condiments will make a tasty gift: Garlic and Horseradish Jellies *(top basket)* are delicious with meats or cream cheese and crackers. Christmas Antipasto *(top left)*, Marinated Vegetables *(top right)*, and Candied Baby Dills *(bottom left)* make zesty additions to a relish tray. Our gourmet mustards *(center and bottom baskets)* — Garlic, Horseradish, Peppercorn, and Curried — are easily made from purchased mustards. Painted wooden hearts make great labels and gift tags.

CHRISTMAS ANTIPASTO

    1   cup vegetable oil
    1   cup olive oil
    1/3 cup garlic wine vinegar
    2   tablespoons lemon juice
    1   teaspoon dry mustard
    1   teaspoon paprika
    1   teaspoon dried oregano leaves
    1   teaspoon salt
    1/2 teaspoon ground black pepper
    1/2 teaspoon dried basil leaves
    1/2 teaspoon green peppercorns
    1/4 teaspoon cayenne pepper
    2   cans (14 ounces each) artichoke
        hearts, drained
    1   jar (7 ounces) roasted peppers,
        drained

For dressing, combine oils, vinegar, lemon juice, dry mustard, paprika, oregano, salt, black pepper, basil, peppercorns, and cayenne until well blended. Place artichoke hearts and peppers in a jar with a tight-fitting lid. Pour dressing over vegetables; shake to blend. Allow mixture to marinate overnight at room temperature.
Yield: about 3 1/2 cups of antipasto

MARINATED VEGETABLES

    1 1/2 cups vegetable oil
    1/2   cup sherry wine vinegar
    1/2   cup olive oil
    1 1/2 teaspoons dry mustard
    1   teaspoon salt
    1   teaspoon dried tarragon leaves
    1/2   teaspoon dried lemon peel
    1 1/2 cups pickled okra, drained
    1 1/2 cups baby corn, drained
    8 to 10 cherry peppers

For dressing, combine vegetable oil, vinegar, olive oil, dry mustard, salt, tarragon, and lemon peel until well blended. Place okra, baby corn, and cherry peppers in a jar with a tight-fitting lid. Pour dressing over vegetables; shake to blend. Allow mixture to marinate overnight at room temperature.
Yield: about 4 1/2 cups of vegetables

GARLIC JELLY

    2   tablespoons butter or margarine
    1   head garlic, cloves separated,
        peeled, and minced
    3   cups granulated sugar
    3/4 cup apple cider vinegar
    3/4 cup water
    1   pouch (3 ounces) liquid fruit pectin

In a large saucepan, combine butter and garlic over medium heat. Cook, stirring constantly, until garlic is light golden brown (3 to 4 minutes). Add sugar, vinegar, and water. Cook, stirring constantly, until sugar dissolves and mixture comes to a rolling boil. Stir in pectin. Stirring constantly, bring to a rolling boil again and boil 1 minute. Remove from heat. Skim foam from top of jelly. Pour into heat-resistant jars with lids. Store in refrigerator.
Yield: about 3 cups of jelly

HORSERADISH JELLY

    3   cups granulated sugar
    3/4 cup apple cider vinegar
    1/2 cup prepared horseradish
    1/4 cup water
    1   pouch (3 ounces) liquid fruit pectin

In a large saucepan, combine sugar, vinegar, horseradish, and water over medium heat. Cook, stirring constantly, until sugar dissolves and mixture comes to a rolling boil. Stir in pectin. Stirring constantly, bring to a rolling boil again and boil 1 minute. Remove from heat. Skim foam from top of jelly. Pour into heat-resistant jars with lids. Store in refrigerator.
Yield: about 3 cups of jelly

GARLIC MUSTARD

    8   garlic cloves, peeled
    1   tablespoon olive oil
    1   jar (8 ounces) Dijon-style mustard
    1/2 teaspoon dried basil leaves
    1/4 teaspoon dried oregano leaves

Preheat oven to 325 degrees. Place garlic in a small baking dish and drizzle with oil. Roast garlic 20 to 30 minutes, stirring frequently, until garlic is soft. Mash garlic, removing any tough pieces. Combine mashed garlic with remaining ingredients; cover and refrigerate overnight to allow flavors to blend.
Yield: about 1 cup of mustard

HORSERADISH MUSTARD

    1   jar (8 ounces) sweet, hot mustard
    2   tablespoons prepared horseradish
    1/4 teaspoon garlic salt
    1/4 teaspoon ground allspice
    1/4 teaspoon cayenne pepper

Combine all ingredients; cover and refrigerate overnight to allow flavors to blend.
Yield: about 1 cup of mustard

CURRIED BROWN MUSTARD

    1   jar (8 ounces) spicy brown mustard
    1 1/2 teaspoons lemon pepper
    1   teaspoon curry powder
    1/2 teaspoon dried lemon peel

Combine all ingredients; cover and refrigerate overnight to allow flavors to blend.
Yield: about 1 cup of mustard

PEPPERCORN MUSTARD

    1   jar (8 ounces) Dijon-style mustard
    1   tablespoon crushed green
        peppercorns
    1/2 teaspoon dried tarragon leaves
    1/4 teaspoon ground allspice
    1/4 teaspoon salt

Combine all ingredients; cover and refrigerate overnight to allow flavors to blend.
Yield: about 1 cup of mustard

CANDIED BABY DILLS

    1   quart miniature dill pickles
    2   cups granulated sugar
    1/2 cup apple cider vinegar
    1   tablespoon fancy pickling spice
    1/2 teaspoon garlic salt

Drain pickles in colander; rinse. Combine remaining ingredients in a large saucepan and bring to a boil. Remove from heat and cool. Pack pickles into heat-resistant jars with lids and pour syrup over pickles. Refrigerate overnight to allow flavors to blend. Store in refrigerator.
Yield: 2 pints of pickles

LEMON NUT BREAD

1 cup butter, softened
1 1/2 cups granulated sugar
4 eggs, separated
3 1/2 tablespoons grated lemon peel
3 cups cake flour, sifted
2 1/2 teaspoons baking powder
1 teaspoon salt
1 1/2 cups finely chopped walnuts
1 cup milk
1 tablespoon lemon juice
   Citrus Glaze (recipe follows)

Cream butter and sugar, beating until fluffy. Add egg yolks, one at a time, beating well after each addition. Stir in lemon peel. Combine flour, baking powder, salt, and walnuts. Stir flour mixture into butter mixture. Stir in milk and lemon juice. Beat egg whites until stiff; fold one-half of whipped egg whites at a time into butter mixture. Spoon mixture into two greased and floured 9 x 5-inch pans. Bake in a preheated 350-degree oven 40 to 45 minutes or until a toothpick inserted in center comes out clean. Cool in pans 10 minutes. Remove bread from pans and cool on wire racks. Glaze if desired.
Yield: 2 loaves of bread

CITRUS GLAZE
1/4 cup **each** lemon juice, orange juice, and pineapple juice
2 tablespoons butter
2 1/2 cups confectioners sugar

Heat juices and butter. Stir in confectioners sugar; blend until smooth. Spoon glaze over bread.

MINCED PUMPKIN BREAD

This spicy, moist bread is excellent sliced and served with whipped cream cheese.

1 cup vegetable oil
3 cups granulated sugar
4 eggs
2 1/2 cups cooked pumpkin
1 1/2 cups chopped pecans
1 1/4 cups mincemeat
3 1/4 cups all-purpose flour
2 teaspoons baking soda
1 1/2 teaspoons salt
1 1/2 teaspoons ground nutmeg
1 teaspoon ground cinnamon
1 teaspoon baking powder

Blend oil and sugar. Add eggs, pumpkin, pecans, and mincemeat. Combine dry ingredients; stir into sugar mixture until well blended. Spoon mixture into three greased and floured 9 x 5-inch pans. Bake in a preheated 350-degree oven 50 minutes or until a toothpick inserted in center comes out clean. Cool in pans 30 minutes. (Freezes well.)
Yield: 3 loaves of bread

CRUSTY NUTMEG BREAD

Freshly grated nutmeg gives this butter-flavored bread a true holiday taste.

3 cups all-purpose flour, sifted and divided
2 1/4 cups firmly packed light brown sugar, divided
3/4 cup butter, softened and divided
3/4 cup chopped pecans, divided
2 eggs
1 teaspoon freshly grated nutmeg
1 teaspoon vanilla extract
1 cup sour cream
1 1/2 teaspoons baking soda

For topping, combine 1/4 cup each of flour, brown sugar, butter, and pecans. Set aside.
Cream remaining butter and brown sugar, beating until light and fluffy. Beat in eggs, nutmeg, and vanilla. Combine sour cream and baking soda in a separate bowl; stir into butter mixture. Stir in remaining flour and pecans. Spoon mixture into two greased and floured 9 x 5-inch pans. Sprinkle with reserved topping. Bake in a preheated 350-degree oven 45 to 50 minutes or until a toothpick inserted in center comes out clean. Cool in pans 10 minutes. Remove bread from pans and cool on wire racks.
Yield: 2 loaves of bread

Gifts from the kitchen are always appreciated, especially at Christmastime — and especially when those gifts are home-baked breads. Crusty Nutmeg Bread *(from left)*, Lemon Nut Bread *(shown with and without glaze)*, and Minced Pumpkin Bread are quick because they have no yeast and therefore require no rising time. We baked our breads in cans and mini loaf pans to make gift-giving fun and different.

HERB BREAD

3 tablespoons granulated sugar
1 package dry yeast
¼ cup warm water
6 cups all-purpose flour, divided
2 tablespoons dried basil leaves
1 tablespoon dried parsley flakes
2 teaspoons salt
4 eggs
1¼ cups warm milk
2 tablespoons vegetable oil
   Basil Butter to serve (recipe follows)

Stir sugar and yeast into warm water; let stand 5 minutes. In large mixing bowl, combine 4 cups flour, basil, parsley, and salt. Separate 1 egg (reserve egg yolk). Add remaining 3 eggs to egg white and beat with fork until frothy. Stir in yeast mixture, milk, and oil. Stir liquid mixture into flour mixture and beat until smooth. Stir in remaining 2 cups flour to make a stiff dough. Turn dough onto a lightly floured surface and knead 8 to 10 minutes or until smooth and elastic. Place in greased bowl, turning once to grease top. Cover and let rise until doubled in size (about 1 hour). Punch down dough and let rise until doubled again (about 1 hour).

Divide dough into three equal parts; roll each part into a rope about 18 inches long. Braid ropes and place on greased baking sheet. Press each end firmly together; tuck ends under loaf to seal. Cover and let rise until doubled in size (about 1 hour).

Beat reserved egg yolk with fork and brush over braid. Bake in a preheated 375-degree oven 40 to 45 minutes or until light golden brown. Remove from baking sheet and cool on wire rack. Serve with Basil Butter.

Yield: 1 braided loaf

BASIL BUTTER

1 cup butter, softened
3 tablespoons dried basil leaves

In mixing bowl, combine butter and basil. Chill before serving.

A loaf of homemade bread is a special way to say you care during this season of sharing. Braided Herb Bread, accompanied by a crock of Basil Butter, is a truly impressive gift.

152

'Tis the season to be baking. But if time is scarce, packaged breads and crackers can help you create "homemade" snacks. Savory Breadsticks *(left)* are rolled in butter and seasonings, then baked for ten minutes. Dilly Oyster Crackers are simply seasoned and require no baking.

DILLY OYSTER CRACKERS

1 package (1.6 ounces) ranch-style salad dressing mix
1 tablespoon dried dill weed
1/2 teaspoon garlic powder
1 box (16 ounces) unseasoned oyster crackers
1 cup vegetable oil

In a large bowl, combine dressing mix, dill weed, and garlic powder. Add crackers and blend thoroughly. Pour oil over mixture and stir thoroughly; allow crackers to absorb oil and seasonings. Store in an airtight container.
Yield: about 8 cups

SAVORY BREADSTICKS

3/4 cup butter or margarine
1/2 tablespoon instant beef bouillon granules
1 tablespoon dried parsley flakes
1/8 teaspoon dried marjoram leaves
2 packages (4 1/2 ounces each) prepared breadsticks
2 tablespoons grated Parmesan cheese

Melt butter in a jellyroll pan. Stir in bouillon, parsley, and marjoram. Roll breadsticks in butter mixture and sprinkle with cheese. Bake in a preheated 300-degree oven 10 minutes. Store in an airtight container.
Yield: 30 breadsticks

FUZZY NAVEL CAKES

- 1 package (18.25 ounces) yellow cake mix
- 4 eggs
- ³/₄ cup peach schnapps
- 1 package (6 ounces) instant vanilla pudding mix
- ¹/₂ cup vegetable oil
- ¹/₂ cup orange juice
- ¹/₂ teaspoon orange extract
- 1 cup peach schnapps
- 2 tablespoons orange juice
- 3 cups confectioners sugar, sifted

Preheat oven to 350 degrees. Combine first 7 ingredients in mixing bowl and blend well. Pour into 10 greased and lightly floured 1-cup metal gelatin molds, filling half full. Bake 25 to 30 minutes or until cake springs back when lightly touched. Combine 1 cup peach schnapps, 2 tablespoons orange juice, and confectioners sugar. While cakes are still warm in molds, poke holes in cakes; pour liqueur mixture over. Allow cakes to cool in molds at least 2 hours before removing.
Yield: 10 small cakes

CHOCOLATE-KAHLÚA CAKE

- 1 package (18.25 ounces) chocolate cake mix
- 4 eggs
- ³/₄ cup Kahlúa liqueur
- 1 package (6 ounces) instant chocolate pudding mix
- ¹/₂ cup vegetable oil
- ¹/₂ cup water
- 6 tablespoons Kahlúa liqueur
- 1 cup confectioners sugar, sifted

Preheat oven to 350 degrees. Combine first 6 ingredients in mixing bowl and blend well. Pour into greased and lightly floured 10-inch fluted tube pan. Bake 45 to 50 minutes or until cake springs back when lightly touched. Combine 6 tablespoons Kahlúa and confectioners sugar. While cake is still warm in pan, poke holes in cake; pour liqueur mixture over. Allow cake to cool in pan at least 2 hours before removing.
Yield: 1 cake

GOLDEN AMARETTO CAKES

- 1 package (18.25 ounces) yellow cake mix
- 4 eggs
- ³/₄ cup amaretto
- 1 package (6 ounces) instant vanilla pudding mix
- ¹/₂ cup vegetable oil
- ¹/₂ cup water
- ¹/₄ teaspoon almond extract
- 6 tablespoons amaretto
- 1 cup confectioners sugar, sifted

Preheat oven to 350 degrees. Combine first 7 ingredients in mixing bowl and blend well. Pour into 2 greased and lightly floured 6-cup metal gelatin molds. Bake 40 to 45 minutes or until cake springs back when lightly touched. Combine 6 tablespoons amaretto and confectioners sugar. While cakes are still warm in molds, poke holes in cakes; pour liqueur mixture over. Allow cakes to cool in molds at least 2 hours before removing.
Yield: 2 cakes

Spirited gift cakes are a delicious way to spread holiday cheer. Despite their expensive taste, Fuzzy Navel Cakes *(from left)*, Chocolate-Kahlúa Cake, and Golden Amaretto Cakes all have a surprisingly modest and easy start — store-bought cake and pudding mixes. Flavored with liqueurs, they make delightful gifts.

Your friends will love these tastes from the British Isles: Named for that lovable character created by Charles Dickens, Oliver Twists *(left)* are perfect for dunking in a hot drink. The Irish Cream Cakes, loaded with chocolate chips and rich liqueur flavor, are so wonderful that everyone will want you to give them year after year — and you won't mind when you see how easy they are to make! Baking these treats in miniature shapes adds a festive touch.

OLIVER TWISTS

        2 jars (2 ounces each) crystallized
             ginger
    ¹/₂ cup butter or margarine, softened
    ¹/₄ cup honey
        1 cup granulated sugar
        2 eggs
    3¹/₄ cups all-purpose flour
    1¹/₂ teaspoons baking powder
    ¹/₂ teaspoon salt
           Granulated sugar

In a blender or food processor, process ginger until very finely chopped; set aside.

In a large mixing bowl, cream butter, honey, and sugar until light and fluffy. Beat in eggs until smooth. Stir in ginger. In a medium bowl, combine flour, baking powder, and salt. Stir flour mixture into creamed mixture. Wrap dough in plastic wrap and refrigerate overnight.

Preheat oven to 325 degrees. Roll small amounts of dough into ¹/₄ x 10-inch ropes; form into pretzel shapes. Transfer cookies to lightly greased baking sheets and sprinkle cookies with sugar. Bake 20 to 25 minutes or until lightly browned. (Cookies will be slightly firm to touch and will become crisper as they cool.) Remove cookies from pans and cool on wire racks. Store in an airtight container.
Yield: about 3 dozen cookies

IRISH CREAM CAKES

CAKES
        1 package (18.25 ounces) white cake
             mix
    1¹/₂ cups Irish cream liqueur
        1 cup miniature semisweet chocolate
             chips
        4 eggs
        1 package (6 ounces) instant vanilla
             pudding mix
    ¹/₂ cup vegetable oil

GLAZE
        3 cups confectioners sugar
        1 cup Irish cream liqueur

Preheat oven to 350 degrees. For cakes, combine cake mix, liqueur, chocolate chips, eggs, pudding mix, and oil in a large mixing bowl; blend well. Pour into 10 greased and floured 1-cup metal gelatin or cake molds. Bake 25 to 30 minutes or until cake springs back when lightly touched.

For glaze, combine confectioners sugar and liqueur in a small bowl; blend well. While cakes are still warm in molds, poke holes in cakes; pour glaze over. Allow cakes to cool in molds at least 2 hours before removing.
Yield: 10 miniature cakes

GIANT PEANUT BUTTER CUPS

    ½ cup butter or margarine, softened
    2 cups confectioners sugar
    1 cup chunky peanut butter
    ½ cup ground pecans
    ½ teaspoon vanilla extract
    1 package (6 ounces) semisweet
       chocolate chips
    6 ounces chocolate-flavored candy
       coating

In a large mixing bowl, combine butter, confectioners sugar, peanut butter, pecans, and vanilla; mix well. Melt chocolate chips and candy coating in the top of a double boiler over simmering water. Lightly grease four 4½-inch or two 8-inch tart pans with removable bottoms. Spread a thin layer of melted chocolate mixture on bottom and sides of each pan. Refrigerate 5 minutes or until chocolate is set. Spread another thin layer of chocolate mixture over first layer; refrigerate to set.

Divide peanut mixture evenly between pans; level tops. Spread a layer of chocolate mixture over peanut layer in each pan, sealing edges. Refrigerate until set.

To remove peanut butter cups from pans, remove sides of pans. Insert the edge of a sharp knife between the bottom of each pan and the chocolate; remove pans.
Yield: four 4½-inch or two 8-inch peanut butter cups

Choose, from this treasure chest, homemade candies to make and give to the fortunate ones on your Christmas list: Microwave Peanut Brittle (*clockwise from top left*), quick and easy to make, has a taste that's good as gold. Millionaire Fudge strikes it rich with caramel and pecans. Pecan Logs have a wealth of caramel and nuts covering a creamy marshmallow center. Giant Peanut Butter Cups have a hidden treasure of golden chunky peanut butter filling, and Christmas Bonbons are delicious gems of coconut, cherries, and almonds.

MICROWAVE PEANUT BRITTLE

    1 cup granulated sugar
    ½ cup light corn syrup
    1 cup dry-roasted peanuts
    1 teaspoon butter or margarine
    1 teaspoon vanilla extract
    ½ teaspoon salt
    1½ teaspoons baking soda

In a 2-quart microwave-safe dish, combine sugar and corn syrup. Microwave on high power 4 minutes. Stir in peanuts. Microwave on high power 3 to 5 minutes or until light golden brown. Stir in butter, vanilla, and salt. Microwave on high power 1 to 2 minutes. Stir in baking soda until mixture foams. Quickly pour onto a greased baking sheet. Cool and break into pieces. Store in an airtight container.
Yield: about 3 cups of candy

CHRISTMAS BONBONS

    ½ cup butter or margarine, softened
    1 can (14½ ounces) sweetened
       condensed milk
    7 cups confectioners sugar
    3 cups shredded coconut
    1 cup chopped toasted almonds
    ½ cup chopped maraschino cherries,
       drained
    1 tablespoon vanilla extract
    30 ounces vanilla- **or** chocolate-flavored
       candy coating

Beat butter and sweetened condensed milk until smooth. Stir in confectioners sugar, coconut, almonds, cherries, and vanilla. Cover and chill until firm (about 1 hour). Shape into 1-inch balls; chill 30 minutes.

Melt desired candy coating in the top of a double boiler over simmering water. Insert a toothpick into each ball and dip into candy coating; place on waxed paper-lined baking sheet to harden.
Yield: about 9½ dozen candies

Variation: To dip 12 candies, place 2 cups melted vanilla-flavored candy coating in a small bowl. Drizzle 2 tablespoons melted chocolate-flavored candy coating onto vanilla coating. Use the tip of a knife to gently swirl candy coatings together (do not overmix). Dip candies as directed.

PECAN LOGS

    4 cups confectioners sugar, sifted
    1½ jars (7 ounces each) marshmallow
       creme (3 cups)
    1½ teaspoons vanilla extract
    1 package (14 ounces) caramels
    1 teaspoon water
    6 cups finely chopped pecans

In a large bowl, stir together confectioners sugar, marshmallow creme, and vanilla. Knead until all the sugar is incorporated. Divide into 6 pieces and shape into 8-inch-long logs. Place in freezer while preparing caramel.

In the top of a double boiler over simmering water or in a microwave, melt caramels with water; stir until smooth. Dip each log into caramel, then roll in chopped pecans. Refrigerate until set. Wrap each log in plastic wrap; store in an airtight container in a cool, dry place.
Yield: 6 pecan logs

MILLIONAIRE FUDGE

    2 cups granulated sugar
    12 regular marshmallows
    ⅔ cup evaporated milk
    ½ cup butter or margarine
    ⅛ teaspoon salt
    1 package (6 ounces) semisweet
       chocolate chips
    1 teaspoon vanilla extract
    1½ packages (14 ounces each)
       caramels
    2 teaspoons water
    1½ cups pecan halves

In a heavy 2-quart saucepan, combine sugar, marshmallows, evaporated milk, butter, and salt. Cook over medium heat, stirring constantly, until mixture comes to a boil. Continue cooking and stirring 5 minutes. Remove from heat. Add chocolate chips and vanilla; stir until chocolate melts. Pour mixture into a buttered 8 x 11½ x 2-inch pan; cool.

In the top of a double boiler over simmering water or in a microwave, melt caramels with water; stir until smooth. Spread over fudge. Press pecans into caramel. Allow caramel to set before cutting into pieces.
Yield: about 4 dozen pieces of fudge

Variation: In the top of a double boiler over simmering water or in a microwave, melt 1 cup semisweet chocolate chips. Drizzle melted chocolate over fudge. Allow to set before cutting into pieces.

Here's an all-star team of tasty snack packs that are perfect for friends who'll be spending the holidays watching all the big football games on TV. Made with packaged munchies, Mexican Cheese Crackers *(from left)*, Seasoned Pretzels, and Italian Cracker Snacks are quick to fix — just season and bake. Colorful tins, buckets, and baskets make festive containers for giving and serving the snacks.

MEXICAN CHEESE CRACKERS

1 package (14¹/₂ ounces) cheese
  crackers
¹/₂ cup butter or margarine, melted
1 package taco seasoning mix
1 tablespoon Worcestershire sauce
¹/₂ teaspoon seasoned salt

Preheat oven to 250 degrees. Place crackers in a large shallow baking pan. In a small bowl, combine butter, taco seasoning mix, Worcestershire sauce, and salt. Pour butter mixture over crackers; stir well. Bake 1 hour, stirring every 15 minutes. Pour onto waxed paper to cool. Store in an airtight container.
Yield: about 6 cups of snack mix

SEASONED PRETZELS

6 cups pretzels (mix shapes if desired)
¹/₂ cup butter or margarine, melted
1 package (1 ounce) ranch-style
  party dip mix
1 tablespoon Worcestershire sauce
¹/₂ teaspoon seasoned salt

Preheat oven to 250 degrees. Place pretzels in a large shallow baking pan. In a small bowl, combine butter, dip mix, Worcestershire sauce, and salt. Pour butter mixture over pretzels; stir well. Bake 1 hour, stirring every 15 minutes. Pour onto waxed paper to cool. Store in an airtight container.
Yield: 6 cups of snack mix

ITALIAN CRACKER SNACKS

1 package (9 ounces) small butter-
  flavored crackers
¹/₄ cup butter or margarine, melted
1 package zesty Italian salad dressing
  mix
1 tablespoon Worcestershire sauce
¹/₄ teaspoon seasoned salt

Preheat oven to 250 degrees. Place crackers in a large shallow baking pan. In a small bowl, combine butter, salad dressing mix, Worcestershire sauce, and salt. Pour butter mixture over crackers; stir well. Bake 1 hour, stirring every 15 minutes. Pour onto waxed paper to cool. Store in an airtight container.
Yield: about 4 cups of snack mix

WINE MULLS

For a non-alcoholic drink, use 3 cups of apple cider in place of the red wine.

- 1 medium orange
- ½ cup firmly packed light brown sugar
- 2 teaspoons ground allspice
- ½ teaspoon ground nutmeg
- 2 2-inch-long cinnamon sticks
  Whole cloves

Preheat oven to 200 degrees. Cut orange in half and scoop out pulp. Place a ball of aluminum foil inside each orange half. Place orange halves on a baking sheet and dry in oven 4 to 5 hours. Remove foil and dry an additional 15 minutes.

In a small bowl, combine brown sugar, allspice, and nutmeg. Pack mixture into each orange half. Decorate tops with cinnamon sticks and cloves. Wrap each mull in plastic wrap and include recipe for Mulled Wine (recipe follows).
Yield: 2 wine mulls

MULLED WINE

- 1 wine mull
- 1 bottle (750 ml) red wine

Place mull and wine in large saucepan. Simmer over low heat 20 minutes. Serve hot.
Yield: about six 4-ounce servings

INSTANT CHOCOLATE MOUSSE MIX

- 1 package (6 ounces) instant chocolate pudding mix
- 1 package (1¼ ounces) whipped dessert topping mix

  2⅓ cups milk to serve

Combine pudding mix and topping mix in a small bowl. Place mousse mix in a resealable plastic bag.

To serve, combine mousse mix and 2⅓ cups milk in a large mixing bowl. Beat with electric mixer at high speed until fluffy. Serve immediately or chill until ready to serve.
Yield: 6 to 8 servings

Variations: For Mocha Mousse, add 2 teaspoons instant coffee granules to dry mix. For Mint Mousse, add ¼ teaspoon peppermint extract to dry mix.

Sipping something warm and spicy on a cold winter's night is always a treat, especially when that "something" is hot Mulled Wine. These Wine Mulls — made by packing scooped-out orange halves with brown sugar, allspice, and nutmeg — make excellent gifts. When dropped into simmering wine, the mulls release their flavors for a festive drink your friends can relax and enjoy.

Instant Chocolate Mousse Mix will delight the chocolate lovers on your gift list. All they have to do to enjoy this creamy treat is add milk and beat until fluffy.

Your friends will be glad they don't have to wait until Christmas to open these gifts! Sweet and crunchy, Caramel Crackers *(from left)*, Cinnamon-Apple Popcorn, and Caramel Corn Puffs are delicious, easy-to-make snacks — and they're fun to eat, too! Purchased Christmas tins keep them fresh and ready to munch.

CARAMEL CRACKERS

    2   packages (9 ounces each) small
          butter-flavored crackers
    1   cup dry-roasted peanuts
    1   cup granulated sugar
  1/2   cup butter or margarine
  1/2   cup light corn syrup
    1   teaspoon vanilla extract
    1   teaspoon baking soda

Preheat oven to 250 degrees. Combine crackers and peanuts in a greased large shallow baking pan. In a saucepan, bring sugar, butter, and corn syrup to a boil and cook 5 minutes. Remove from heat; add vanilla and baking soda. Pour caramel mixture over crackers and peanuts; stir well. Bake 1 hour, stirring every 15 minutes. Pour onto waxed paper and break apart; allow to cool. Store in an airtight container.
Yield: about 9 cups of snack mix

CINNAMON-APPLE POPCORN

    2   cups chopped dried apples
   10   cups popped popcorn
    2   cups pecan halves
    4   tablespoons butter, melted
    2   tablespoons firmly packed brown
          sugar
    1   teaspoon ground cinnamon
  1/4   teaspoon ground nutmeg
  1/4   teaspoon vanilla extract

Preheat oven to 250 degrees. Place apples in a large shallow baking pan. Bake 20 minutes. Remove pan from oven and stir in popcorn and pecans. In a small bowl, combine remaining ingredients. Drizzle butter mixture over popcorn mixture, stirring well. Bake 30 minutes, stirring every 10 minutes. Pour onto waxed paper to cool. Store in an airtight container.
Yield: about 14 cups of snack mix

CARAMEL CORN PUFFS

    1   package (10.9 ounces) puffed corn
          cereal
    1   cup pecan halves
    1   cup granulated sugar
  1/2   cup butter or margarine
  1/2   cup light corn syrup
    1   teaspoon vanilla extract
    1   teaspoon baking soda

Preheat oven to 250 degrees. Combine cereal and pecans in a greased large shallow baking pan. In a saucepan, bring sugar, butter, and corn syrup to a boil and cook 5 minutes. Remove from heat; add vanilla and baking soda. Pour caramel mixture over cereal and pecans; stir well. Bake 1 hour, stirring every 15 minutes. Pour onto waxed paper and break apart; allow to cool. Store in an airtight container.
Yield: about 10 cups of snack mix

A box of fresh Soft Pretzels, paired with a jar of homemade Hot and Sweet Mustard or Cheddar Cheese Spread, gives Christmas gift-giving a new twist. Fringed muslin squares make cute jar lid toppers for the spread; a permanent felt-tip pen with a fine point is all you need to "stitch" the border and greeting. For a tasty addition to this scrumptious gift package, tuck in a sausage stick or two.

SOFT PRETZELS

1 1/2 cups warm water
1 package dry yeast
1 tablespoon granulated sugar
4 1/2 cups all-purpose flour
1 1/2 teaspoons salt
1 egg, lightly beaten
    Coarsely ground kosher or sea salt

Combine water, yeast, and sugar in a mixing bowl. Allow to stand until yeast is dissolved and begins to foam (about 5 minutes). Stir in flour and 1 1/2 teaspoons salt. Turn out onto lightly floured surface and knead 8 to 10 minutes or until dough is smooth and elastic. Separate dough into 16 equal pieces. Roll each piece into a 20-inch-long rope and form into a pretzel shape. Place on a lightly greased baking sheet. Cover and let rise 20 minutes.

Preheat oven to 425 degrees. Brush pretzels with egg and sprinkle with coarsely ground salt. Bake 15 minutes or until golden brown. Remove pretzels from baking sheet and cool on wire rack.
Yield: 16 pretzels

CHEDDAR CHEESE SPREAD

2 cups shredded Cheddar cheese
1 package (8 ounces) cream cheese, softened
1 tablespoon prepared horseradish
2 to 3 drops hot pepper sauce
6 slices bacon, cooked and crumbled

Combine Cheddar cheese, cream cheese, horseradish, and pepper sauce in the top of a double boiler over simmering water. Stir constantly until cheeses are melted and mixture is smooth. Remove from heat and stir in bacon. Cool and store in an airtight container in refrigerator.
Yield: about 3 cups of spread

HOT AND SWEET MUSTARD

1 cup apple cider vinegar
4 eggs, lightly beaten
1/2 cup granulated sugar
1/2 cup butter or margarine, melted
1 can (2 ounces) dry mustard
1 1/2 teaspoons cayenne pepper
1 teaspoon salt

Combine vinegar, eggs, sugar, butter, dry mustard, cayenne, and salt in the top of a double boiler over simmering water. Whisking constantly, cook until thickened (about 10 minutes). Cool and store in an airtight container in refrigerator.
Yield: about 2 cups of mustard

These flavorful condiments are sure to trigger smiles on the faces of those who receive them! Easy to prepare, the tasty relishes and seasonings make delicious and thoughtful Christmas gifts. Bell peppers, hot peppers, and golden raisins make this Sweet Pepper Jelly *(from left)* the best thing this side of the Rio Grande. The Barbeque Sauce, loaded with spices and red wine vinegar, gives a hearty flavor to hamburgers, steaks, and chicken. Crunchy Candied Pickles begin with a jar of store-bought hamburger dills — all you have to do is candy them.

BARBEQUE SAUCE

- 1 cup ketchup
- ¹/₂ cup red wine vinegar
- ¹/₄ cup water
- ¹/₄ cup vegetable oil
- 2 tablespoons firmly packed brown sugar
- 2 tablespoons Worcestershire sauce
- 1 tablespoon prepared mustard
- 1 tablespoon lemon juice
- 1 tablespoon chili powder
- 1¹/₂ teaspoons salt
- 1 teaspoon liquid smoke
- 1 teaspoon celery seed
- ¹/₂ teaspoon ground black pepper
- ¹/₄ teaspoon cayenne pepper
- ¹/₄ teaspoon garlic powder
- 2 to 3 drops hot pepper sauce

Combine all ingredients in a large saucepan. Simmer uncovered over low heat 20 minutes. Remove from heat. Cool and store in an airtight container in refrigerator.
Yield: about 2¹/₄ cups of sauce

SWEET PEPPER JELLY

- 3¹/₂ cups granulated sugar
- 1¹/₄ cups finely chopped green peppers
- ³/₄ cup finely chopped hot peppers
- ³/₄ cup apple cider vinegar
- 2 pouches (3 ounces each) liquid fruit pectin
- ¹/₂ cup golden raisins
  Yellow liquid food coloring

Combine sugar, peppers, and vinegar in a large saucepan; bring to a boil. Boil 5 minutes. Stir in liquid pectin. Stirring constantly, bring to a rolling boil again and boil 1 minute. Remove from heat and skim off foam. Stir in raisins and a few drops of food coloring. Pour into heat-resistant jars with lids. Allow to cool; store in refrigerator.
Yield: about 6 half-pint jars of jelly

CRUNCHY CANDIED PICKLES

- 1 quart hamburger dill pickle slices
- 2 cups granulated sugar
- ¹/₂ cup tarragon wine vinegar
- 1 teaspoon celery seed
- 1 teaspoon dry mustard
- ¹/₂ teaspoon crushed dried red pepper flakes
- ¹/₈ teaspoon garlic salt

Drain pickles in colander; rinse. Combine remaining ingredients in saucepan and bring to a boil. Remove from heat and cool. Pack pickles into two pint jars with lids and pour syrup over pickles. Cover jars and refrigerate at least 6 to 8 hours to allow flavors to blend. Store in refrigerator.
Yield: 2 pints of pickles

Give a taste of New Orleans this Christmas with our spicy Red Beans and Rice Dinner. This traditional Cajun meal will satisfy the heartiest appetite! To present the dinner, tuck a jar of dried red beans, a bundle of special seasoning mix, and a bag of rice inside a small crate. We used a calligraphy pen to label the ingredients and to add a humorous message. Don't forget to include the recipe!

RED BEANS AND RICE DINNER

1 tablespoon dried sweet pepper flakes
1 tablespoon dried minced onion
2 teaspoons seasoned salt
1 teaspoon granulated sugar
1 teaspoon ground cumin
½ teaspoon dried minced garlic
½ teaspoon celery seed
¼ teaspoon cayenne pepper
¼ teaspoon crushed red pepper flakes
1 bay leaf
2 cups (about 1 pound) dried red beans
1 cup uncooked long grain white rice

In a small bowl, combine first 10 ingredients for seasoning mixture. Place in a small, resealable plastic bag.

Fill a pint canning jar with red beans. Fill a resealable plastic bag with rice. Include recipe for Red Beans and Rice (recipe follows).

RED BEANS AND RICE
2 cups dried red beans
1 ham bone
  Seasoning mixture
2 cups water
1 cup uncooked long grain white rice
1 teaspoon salt
1 pound spicy smoked sausage, sliced
  Salt and ground black pepper to taste

Wash beans. Place beans in a Dutch oven; cover with water and soak overnight.

The following day, add ham bone and seasoning mixture to beans. If necessary, add additional water to cover beans. Cook, partially covered, over medium-low heat 3 to 4 hours. About 30 minutes before serving, combine 2 cups water, rice, and 1 teaspoon salt in a saucepan and bring to a boil. Reduce heat to low. Cover pan and cook 30 minutes without lifting lid. About 20 minutes before serving, add sausage to beans; salt and pepper to taste. Serve over rice.
Yield: 4 to 6 servings

DANISH PASTRIES

CAKE
- 1½ cups butter, softened and divided
- 3 cups all-purpose flour, divided
- ⅛ teaspoon salt
- ¼ cup cold water
- 1 cup milk
- ¼ cup granulated sugar
- 1 teaspoon almond extract
- 3 eggs

GLAZE
- 1½ cups confectioners sugar
- 2 tablespoons butter, softened
- 1 tablespoon milk
- 2 teaspoons vanilla extract

TOPPING
- 1 cup sliced almonds, toasted
- 2 tablespoons confectioners sugar

For cake, use a pastry blender or two knives to cut 1 cup butter into 2 cups flour in a medium mixing bowl until mixture resembles coarse meal. Stir in salt and water to make a dough. Divide dough into eight equal portions. Pat out each portion of dough into a 3 x 4-inch oval on an ungreased baking sheet. Refrigerate until ready to use.

Preheat oven to 350 degrees. In a large heavy saucepan, combine remaining ½ cup butter and milk over medium heat. Bring to a boil. Add remaining 1 cup flour, sugar, and almond extract. Quickly stir until mixture forms a ball; remove from heat. By hand, beat in eggs, one at a time, until well blended. Spread a thick, even layer of dough over chilled ovals. Bake 40 to 45 minutes or until puffy and golden.

For glaze, combine confectioners sugar with butter in a small bowl; stir until well blended. Stir in milk and vanilla until mixture is smooth.

For topping, combine almonds and confectioners sugar in a small bowl.

Spread glaze evenly over warm pastries. Sprinkle each pastry with topping. Serve warm or at room temperature.
Yield: 8 pastries

These coffee cakes are delectable ways to spread Christmas cheer: The Poppy Seed Cake *(clockwise from top)* has a light lemony glaze that complements its buttery flavor, and extra-moist Cranberry Coffee Cake has a filling of tangy cranberry sauce. A Christmas bread cloth makes a pretty wrapper for almond-topped Danish Pastries; the delicate, flaky layers give them bakery-fresh flavor.

POPPY SEED CAKE

CAKE
- ½ cup poppy seed
- ⅓ cup milk
- 1 cup butter or margarine, softened
- 1½ cups granulated sugar
- 2 teaspoons grated lemon peel
- 1½ teaspoons lemon extract
- 1 teaspoon vanilla extract
- 4 eggs
- 2¼ cups all-purpose flour
- 1½ teaspoons baking powder
- ½ teaspoon salt
- ½ cup sour cream

GLAZE
- ½ cup confectioners sugar
- ¼ cup lemon juice

Soak poppy seed in milk 1 hour.
Preheat oven to 350 degrees. For cake, cream butter, sugar, lemon peel, and extracts in a large mixing bowl. Beat in eggs, one at a time, beating well after each addition. Drain poppy seed; stir poppy seed into mixture. In a medium bowl, combine flour, baking powder, and salt. Stir flour mixture into creamed mixture, alternating with sour cream. Pour into a greased and floured 9¼ x 5¼ x 2½-inch loaf pan. Bake 45 to 50 minutes or until a toothpick inserted in center of cake comes out clean.

For glaze, combine confectioners sugar and lemon juice, blending until smooth. Pour over warm cake in pan. Allow cake to cool completely before removing from pan.
Yield: 10 to 12 servings

CRANBERRY COFFEE CAKE

CAKE
- ½ cup butter or margarine, softened
- 1½ cups granulated sugar
- 2 eggs
- 1½ teaspoons almond extract
- 1 teaspoon vanilla extract
- 2 cups all-purpose flour
- 1 teaspoon baking powder
- 1 teaspoon baking soda
- 1 teaspoon salt
- 1 cup sour cream
- 1 cup whole berry cranberry sauce

GLAZE
- 1 cup confectioners sugar
- 3 tablespoons milk
- ½ teaspoon almond extract

Preheat oven to 350 degrees. For cake, cream butter and sugar in a large bowl. Beat in eggs and extracts until well blended. In a small bowl, combine flour,

baking powder, baking soda, and salt. Stir flour mixture into creamed mixture, alternating with sour cream. Pour half of batter into a greased 9-inch tube pan. Spoon cranberry sauce over batter. Top with remaining batter. Bake 55 to 60 minutes or until a toothpick inserted in center of cake comes out clean. Cool in pan 10 minutes.

For glaze, combine all ingredients in a small bowl, blending well. Remove warm cake from pan and drizzle with glaze.
Yield: 14 to 16 servings

MULLED TEA BAG

- 2½ teaspoons loose tea leaves
- 1 teaspoon coarsely crushed cinnamon stick
- ½ teaspoon dried orange peel
- ¼ teaspoon dried lemon peel
- 3 whole allspice berries
- 2 whole cloves
- 5-inch square of fine-mesh cheesecloth
- Cotton string

Place tea leaves, cinnamon pieces, orange peel, lemon peel, allspice, and cloves on cheesecloth square. Bring corners together and tie with string to form a bag.

To brew tea, place bag in a mug and add 6 ounces boiling water; steep 4 to 5 minutes.
Yield: 1 tea bag

Tea lovers will enjoy curling up with a cup of hot spiced tea made with our Mulled Tea Bag. For a cute gift, include a basket of cinnamon sticks decorated with paint.

For someone who's nuts about peanuts, try these treats: Kids will flip for Peanut Butter Spread *(clockwise from left)* served with graham cracker bears. Grown-ups will savor creamy Miniature Honey-Roasted Peanut Cheesecakes; we wrapped one in cellophane and tied it with a bright ribbon. Peanut Butter-Cheese Shorties combine two favorite flavors. For unique gift tags, use a paint pen to label shiny glass ornaments.

PEANUT BUTTER SPREAD

- 1 jar (16 ounces) peanut butter
- 1 cup miniature semisweet chocolate chips
- 1/2 cup chopped miniature marshmallows
- 1/2 cup chopped salted peanuts
- 2 tablespoons honey

    Graham cracker bears or vanilla wafers to serve

Combine all ingredients in a microwave-safe container, blending well. Microwave on high power 1 minute and gently stir to swirl mixture. (Do not overcook; chocolate will soften when stirred.) Spoon into gift container. Serve with graham cracker bears or vanilla wafers.
Yield: about 3 cups of spread

MINIATURE HONEY-ROASTED PEANUT CHEESECAKES

- 2 cups crushed chocolate-covered graham crackers
- 3 packages (8 ounces each) cream cheese, softened
- 1 1/2 cups honey
- 1 cup peanut butter
- 1 cup whipping cream
- 2 teaspoons vanilla extract
- 4 eggs
- 1 cup chopped roasted peanuts
- 1 cup miniature semisweet chocolate chips

Preheat oven to 325 degrees. Line bottoms of four 5-inch springform pans with aluminum foil. Lightly grease pans and foil. Press 1/2 cup graham cracker crumbs into bottom of each pan; set aside.

In a large mixing bowl, beat cream cheese until smooth. Beat in honey, peanut butter, whipping cream, and vanilla. Beat in eggs until well blended. Stir in peanuts and chocolate chips. Divide mixture evenly between the four pans. Bake 40 to 45 minutes or until centers are set. Cool to room temperature. Cover and refrigerate overnight.

To remove each springform, use a knife to loosen sides of cheesecake from pan; remove sides. Store in refrigerator.
Yield: 4 cheesecakes

PEANUT BUTTER-CHEESE SHORTIES

- 8 ounces mild Cheddar cheese, grated
- 1 1/4 cups all-purpose flour
- 3/4 cup smooth peanut butter
- 1/4 cup butter or margarine, softened
- 1/4 cup water
- 1/2 teaspoon salt

Preheat oven to 400 degrees. In a large mixing bowl, combine cheese, flour, peanut butter, butter, water, and salt until well blended. On a lightly floured surface, use a floured rolling pin to roll out dough to 1/8-inch thickness. Using a pastry wheel or knife dipped in flour, cut dough into 1/2 x 2-inch strips. Transfer strips to lightly greased baking sheets. Bake 10 to 15 minutes or until golden brown. Cool before removing from pans. Store in an airtight container.
Yield: about 9 dozen shorties

POTTERY TEA CAKES

COOKIES

    1   cup butter, softened
    1   cup granulated sugar
    1   egg
    2   teaspoons vanilla extract
    3   cups all-purpose flour
    1   teaspoon baking powder
  1/2   teaspoon salt
  1/2   cup milk

ICING

    2   cups confectioners sugar
    1   egg white
    2   teaspoons water
        Blue paste food coloring

For cookies, cream butter, sugar, egg, and vanilla in a large mixing bowl. In a medium bowl, combine flour, baking powder, and salt. Stir flour mixture into butter mixture, alternating with milk. Wrap dough in plastic wrap and refrigerate overnight.

Preheat oven to 375 degrees. Trace pattern onto tracing paper and cut out. On a lightly floured surface, use a floured rolling pin to roll out dough to 1/8-inch thickness. Place pattern on dough and use a sharp knife to cut around pattern or use cookie cutter to cut out dough. Transfer cookies to lightly greased baking sheets and bake 8 to 10 minutes or until cookies are lightly browned around the edges. Remove from pans and cool on wire racks.

For icing, combine confectioners sugar, egg white, and water in a small mixing bowl. Divide icing in half and add blue food coloring to half of icing. Ice cookies with white icing; allow to dry. Referring to photo, use a pastry bag fitted with a small round tip and filled with blue icing to pipe designs. To make sponged cookies, use crumpled plastic wrap to stamp blue icing on cookies.

Yield: about 9 dozen cookies

These little cookies make very special gifts: Flavored with brown sugar and pecans, tiny Heart Cookies are packaged in a decorated Shaker box. "Painted" with icing to resemble old-fashioned stoneware, pretty Pottery Tea Cakes can be presented in a miniature crock tied with a raffia bow.

HEART COOKIES

  1 1/4   cups all-purpose flour
    1/2   cup butter, softened
    1/2   cup ground toasted pecans
    1/3   cup firmly packed brown sugar
      1   teaspoon vanilla extract

Combine all ingredients in a medium mixing bowl, blending well. Wrap dough in plastic wrap and refrigerate 1 hour.

Preheat oven to 350 degrees. On a lightly floured surface, use a floured rolling pin to roll out dough to 1/4-inch thickness. Using a 1-inch-wide heart-shaped cookie cutter, cut out dough. Transfer cookies to ungreased baking sheets. Bake 10 to 15 minutes or until golden brown. Remove from pans and cool on wire racks.

Yield: about 6 dozen cookies

A pretty presentation makes a gift of food even more memorable. Scrumptious Cranberry Muffins, tucked in a reusable holiday tin, are perfect for breakfast or an afternoon snack. Nestled on a lacy paper doily and topped with a ribbon rose, rich Fudge Pound Cake is an elegant gift.

CRANBERRY MUFFINS

MUFFINS
    3   cups all-purpose flour
  3/4   cup granulated sugar
    1   tablespoon baking powder
  1/2   cup milk
  1/2   cup butter or margarine, melted
    2   eggs
    1   tablespoon vanilla extract
1 1/2   cups chopped fresh cranberries
  3/4   cup chopped pecans
    1   tablespoon grated orange peel

TOPPING
  1/4   cup granulated sugar
1 1/2   teaspoons grated orange peel
    1   teaspoon ground cinnamon
  1/4   cup chopped pecans

Preheat oven to 375 degrees. For muffins, combine flour, sugar, and baking powder in a large mixing bowl. Make a well in center of mixture and add milk, butter, eggs, and vanilla. Stir just until all ingredients are moistened (batter will be lumpy). Stir in cranberries, pecans, and orange peel. Fill greased or paper-lined muffin cups two-thirds full with batter.

For topping, combine sugar, orange peel, and cinnamon in a small bowl. Stir in pecans. Sprinkle topping over muffins. Bake 25 to 30 minutes or until muffin springs back when gently pressed.
Yield: about 2 dozen muffins

FUDGE POUND CAKE

  1/2   cup butter or margarine, softened
1 3/4   cups granulated sugar
    2   teaspoons vanilla extract
    3   eggs
1 3/4   cups all-purpose flour
  2/3   cup cocoa
    2   teaspoons baking powder
  1/2   teaspoon baking soda
    1   cup sour cream

Preheat oven to 325 degrees. In a large mixing bowl, cream butter, sugar, and vanilla. Beat in eggs.

In a small bowl, combine flour, cocoa, baking powder, and baking soda. Stir flour mixture into butter mixture, alternating with sour cream. Pour into a greased 9 x 5 x 3-inch loaf pan. Bake 1 hour 20 minutes or until a toothpick inserted in center comes out clean. Cool 10 minutes in pan; remove from pan and cool completely.
Yield: 12 to 14 servings

SANTA BREAD

BREAD
4 1/2 cups all-purpose flour, divided
1/2 cup granulated sugar
2 packages dry yeast
2 teaspoons grated orange peel
2 teaspoons ground cinnamon
1 teaspoon salt
1 cup milk
1/2 cup butter or margarine
1/4 cup plus 1 tablespoon water, divided
2 eggs
1 egg white
Red paste food coloring

ICING
2 1/2 cups confectioners sugar
3 to 4 tablespoons hot water

1/2 teaspoon vanilla extract
Raisins and candied cherry halves

For bread, combine 1 1/4 cups flour, sugar, yeast, orange peel, cinnamon, and salt in a large mixing bowl; set aside.

In a small saucepan, heat milk, butter, and 1/4 cup water just until butter melts. Add milk mixture to dry ingredients, beating until smooth. Beat in 2 eggs and 1 1/4 cups additional flour. By hand, stir in enough of remaining flour to make a stiff dough. Turn dough onto a floured surface and knead until smooth and elastic, about 8 to 10 minutes. Place dough in a greased bowl, turning once to grease top. Cover and let rise 1 hour or until doubled in size.

Preheat oven to 350 degrees. Punch down dough; divide in half and refer to photo to form two Santa heads. Place on greased baking sheet. In a small bowl, combine egg white, remaining 1 tablespoon water, and food coloring. Use pastry brush and food coloring mixture to paint hats. Bake 40 to 45 minutes or until bread sounds hollow when tapped. Remove from pan and cool on wire rack.

For icing, combine confectioners sugar, water, and vanilla in a medium bowl. Ice beards. For eyes and noses, use dots of icing to attach raisins and cherries.
Yield: 2 loaves of bread

Sweet Santa Bread is sure to delight both children and grown-ups! And because every loaf rises differently while baking, each Santa will have his own distinct personality.

Share these goodies with friends and family: A cheese pastry complements the sweet filling in Apple-Cheddar Turnovers *(clockwise from top left)*. Delicately flavored with almond, the creamy filling of our Ricotta Cream Cornets is sprinkled with chocolate bits. Crispy Orange Cookies with Chocolate Filling are a yummy snack. A layer of marshmallow is nestled beneath the frosting of our Mississippi Mud Brownies. Lemon Curd Tarts are a popular English teatime dessert.

APPLE-CHEDDAR TURNOVERS

CRUST
1 1/3 cups all-purpose flour
 1/2 teaspoon salt
 1/2 cup butter, chilled and cut into pieces
 1/2 cup finely grated mild Cheddar cheese
 2 tablespoons ice water

FILLING
 2 apples, peeled, cored, and chopped
 6 tablespoons butter or margarine
 1/3 cup firmly packed brown sugar
 1 tablespoon all-purpose flour
 1/2 teaspoon ground cinnamon
 1/4 teaspoon ground cloves
 1 egg yolk
 1 teaspoon water
   Butter or margarine

For crust, sift flour and salt into a mixing bowl. Using a pastry blender or two knives, cut butter into flour until mixture resembles coarse meal. Stir in cheese. Sprinkle ice water over dough, mixing quickly just until dough forms a soft ball. Wrap dough in plastic wrap and refrigerate 1 hour.

For filling, sauté apples in 6 tablespoons butter over medium heat, stirring frequently until apples are soft. Stir in brown sugar, flour, cinnamon, and cloves; stirring constantly, cook 1 minute. Remove from heat and cool completely.

On a lightly floured surface, use a floured rolling pin to roll out dough to 1/8-inch thickness. Cut dough into 4-inch circles (we used the ring from a 4-inch pastry pan with removable bottom). Combine egg yolk and water. Brush pastry circles with egg yolk mixture. Place 1 heaping tablespoon of filling in the center of each circle and dot with butter. Fold pastry over filling, pressing edges to seal. Brush outside of pastry with egg yolk mixture. Cut slits in tops of turnovers for steam to escape. Refrigerate 30 minutes.

Preheat oven to 350 degrees. Bake 20 to 25 minutes or until golden brown.
Yield: about 8 turnovers

LEMON CURD TARTS

Pretty gumdrop roses top these tangy lemon tarts. Simply roll half of a red gumdrop between two sheets of waxed paper and roll into a rose shape. Roll out a green gumdrop and use a sharp knife to cut out small leaf shapes.

CRUST
- 1¼ cups all-purpose flour
- 2 tablespoons granulated sugar
- ¼ teaspoon salt
- ½ cup butter, chilled and cut into pieces
- 3 tablespoons ice water

LEMON CURD
- 6 egg yolks
- 1 cup granulated sugar
- ½ cup fresh lemon juice
- 6 tablespoons butter, cut into pieces
- 1½ tablespoons grated lemon peel
- ⅛ teaspoon salt

Sweetened Whipped Cream to serve (recipe on page 129)

For crust, sift flour, sugar, and salt into a mixing bowl. Using a pastry blender or two knives, cut butter into flour until mixture resembles coarse meal. Sprinkle ice water over dough, mixing quickly just until dough forms a soft ball. Wrap dough in plastic wrap and refrigerate 1 hour.

On a lightly floured surface, use a floured rolling pin to roll out dough to ⅛-inch thickness. Cut dough into circles about ¼-inch larger than tartlet pans. Press dough into pans; trim excess around edges. Refrigerate 30 minutes.

Preheat oven to 400 degrees. Place small pieces of aluminum foil on dough and weight foil with dried beans or pie weights. Bake 10 minutes. Remove weights and foil and bake 3 to 5 minutes or until very lightly browned. Cool completely before removing tart shells from pans.

For lemon curd, combine all ingredients in a heavy non-aluminum saucepan over medium-low heat. Cook, stirring constantly, until butter melts and mixture thickens slightly. Do not allow mixture to boil. Remove from heat. Transfer mixture to a bowl to cool. Cover and refrigerate at least 2 hours before serving.

To serve, fill tart shells with lemon curd and top with a small amount of Sweetened Whipped Cream.
Yield: about 16 tarts

RICOTTA CREAM CORNETS

PASTRY
- 1 sheet (from a 17¼-ounce package) frozen puff pastry dough, thawed
  Metal cornet molds
- 1 egg white
- 1 teaspoon water

FILLING
- 1 cup ricotta cheese
- ¼ cup confectioners sugar
- 1 teaspoon vanilla extract
- ½ teaspoon almond extract
- ½ cup miniature semisweet chocolate chips

Miniature semisweet chocolate chips to garnish

Preheat oven to 350 degrees. For pastry, cut dough into about ¾ x 10-inch strips. Beginning at tip of one mold, wrap a strip of dough around mold without stretching dough. (The strip will only cover about three-fourths of mold.) Repeat with remaining strips and molds. Combine egg white and water. Brush over dough. Place molds on a baking sheet. Bake 20 minutes or until golden. Carefully remove pastry from molds and cool on a wire rack.

For filling, beat ricotta cheese, confectioners sugar, and extracts in a medium mixing bowl until smooth. Stir in ½ cup chocolate chips.

To serve, use a pastry bag or spoon to fill pastries with filling. Garnish with chocolate chips.
Yield: 8 to 10 cornets

ORANGE COOKIES WITH CHOCOLATE FILLING

COOKIES
- 1 cup vegetable shortening
- 1 cup granulated sugar
- 2 eggs
- 3 tablespoons orange juice concentrate
- 2 tablespoons grated orange peel
- 1 teaspoon vanilla extract
- 4½ cups all-purpose flour
- 1 teaspoon baking soda
- ½ teaspoon baking powder
- ½ teaspoon salt
- ½ cup buttermilk

FILLING
- 1 cup semisweet chocolate chips, melted
- 2 tablespoons whipping cream
- 2½ teaspoons orange extract

For cookies, cream shortening, sugar, eggs, orange juice concentrate, orange peel, and vanilla in a large mixing bowl. Combine dry ingredients and stir into creamed mixture, alternating with buttermilk. Divide dough in half and wrap in plastic wrap. Refrigerate at least 2 hours or until well chilled.

Preheat oven to 375 degrees. On a lightly floured surface, use a floured rolling pin to roll out dough to ⅛-inch thickness. Using 2-inch round cookie cutter, cut out dough. Transfer cookies to a lightly greased baking sheet. Bake 6 to 8 minutes or until very lightly browned around edges. Remove from pans and cool on wire racks.

For filling, combine all ingredients, blending until smooth. Spread a thin layer of filling on bottoms of half of cookies and place remaining cookies on top of filling. Chill 5 minutes or until chocolate hardens.
Yield: about 4 dozen cookies

MISSISSIPPI MUD BROWNIES

BROWNIES
- 1 package (19.8 ounces) fudge brownie mix
- ½ cup water
- ⅓ cup vegetable oil
- 1 egg
- ¼ cup all-purpose flour
- 1½ cups miniature marshmallows

FROSTING
- 1¾ cups confectioners sugar
- ½ cup semisweet chocolate chips, melted
- ⅓ cup milk
- 2 tablespoons butter or margarine, softened

Purchased tubes of red and green decorating icing (optional)

Preheat oven to 350 degrees. For brownies, combine brownie mix, water, oil, egg, and flour in a medium mixing bowl; stir just until blended. Pour batter into a lightly greased 10 x 8 x 2-inch baking pan. Bake 25 to 30 minutes or until center is set. Top with marshmallows and bake 2 minutes longer.

For frosting, combine confectioners sugar, melted chocolate chips, milk, and butter. Beat until smooth and spread over brownies. Cut into bars.

If desired, use decorating icing to pipe small red and green bows onto tops of brownies.
Yield: about 20 brownies

Lads and lassies will love these adorable Anise Shortbread Scotties! Cut in the shape of this beloved dog and adorned with an iced holly "collar," the light, crispy cookies have a delightful licorice flavor. For a true Highland treat, present them in Shaker boxes covered with tartan plaid fabric.

ANISE SHORTBREAD SCOTTIES

1 cup butter, softened
1/2 cup confectioners sugar
1 1/2 teaspoons crushed anise seed
1 teaspoon vanilla extract
1/4 teaspoon ground cinnamon
2 cups all-purpose flour
Granulated sugar

Purchased tubes of green and red decorating icing

Cream butter and confectioners sugar until light and fluffy. Beat in anise seed, vanilla, and cinnamon. Stir in flour.

Trace pattern onto tracing paper and cut out. On a lightly floured surface, use a floured rolling pin to roll out dough to 1/4-inch thickness. Place pattern on dough and use a sharp knife to cut around pattern. Transfer cookies to ungreased baking sheets. Sprinkle with granulated sugar. Chill cookies 30 minutes before baking.

Preheat oven to 375 degrees. Bake cookies 5 minutes; reduce heat to 300 degrees and bake 10 minutes more. Remove from pans and cool on wire racks.

Use green and red icing to pipe holly leaves and berries onto cookies.

Yield: about 4 dozen cookies

(Left) A loaf of dessert bread is always a welcome gift, especially when you deliver it in a decorated basket. Drizzled with creamy frosting, Cinnamon-Banana Bread is enriched with brown sugar and pecans. (Right) A bottle of fruity Raspberry Wine is sure to be a "berry" merry gift.

CINNAMON-BANANA BREAD

BREAD
1 cup firmly packed brown sugar
1 cup butter or margarine, divided
2 ripe bananas, cut into small pieces
1/2 cup chopped pecans
1/2 cup granulated sugar
2 eggs
1 3/4 cups all-purpose flour
2 tablespoons ground cinnamon
1 teaspoon baking powder
1/2 teaspoon baking soda

FROSTING
1 1/4 cups confectioners sugar
1 package (3 ounces) cream cheese, softened

Preheat oven to 350 degrees. For bread, combine brown sugar and 1/2 cup butter in a medium saucepan over medium heat, stirring until butter is melted. Add bananas and pecans, stirring until well coated. Cool to room temperature.

In a large bowl, cream remaining butter and granulated sugar until fluffy. Beat in eggs. In a small bowl, sift together remaining ingredients. Stir dry ingredients into creamed mixture. Stir in banana mixture. Divide batter evenly between 2 greased 3 1/2 x 6 3/4-inch loaf pans. Bake 45 to 50 minutes or until a toothpick inserted in center of bread comes out clean. Cool in pans 10 minutes. Transfer to a wire rack to cool completely.

For frosting, combine confectioners sugar and cream cheese in a medium bowl. Using medium speed of an electric mixer, beat until smooth. Drizzle frosting over bread. Store in an airtight container.
Yield: 2 loaves of bread

RASPBERRY WINE

3 cups frozen unsweetened raspberries, thawed
1/4 cup granulated sugar
1 bottle (750 ml) dry white wine

In a large bowl, combine raspberries and sugar, stirring until well coated. Stir in wine until sugar is dissolved. Cover and chill 5 days. Strain wine through a fine sieve; discard raspberries or save for another use. Store wine in refrigerator. Serve chilled.
Yield: about 3 cups of wine

173

CHRISTMAS TREE COOKIES

½ cup vegetable shortening
½ cup butter or margarine, softened
1½ cups firmly packed brown sugar
1 egg
⅓ cup evaporated milk
½ teaspoon vanilla extract
3½ cups all-purpose flour
1 teaspoon baking powder
½ teaspoon ground cinnamon
½ teaspoon ground cloves
½ teaspoon ground ginger
½ teaspoon salt
18 6-inch-long wooden skewers
18 apples

In a large bowl, cream shortening, butter, and brown sugar until fluffy. Stir in egg, evaporated milk, and vanilla until smooth. In another large bowl, sift flour, baking powder, cinnamon, cloves, ginger, and salt. Add dry ingredients to creamed mixture; stir until a soft dough forms. Cover and refrigerate at least 1 hour.

Preheat oven to 350 degrees. On a lightly floured surface, use a floured rolling pin to roll out dough to ¼-inch thickness. Use a tree-shaped cookie cutter to cut out cookies. Transfer cookies to a greased baking sheet. Insert a skewer into bottom of each cookie, leaving 2 inches of skewer exposed. Bake 8 to 10 minutes or until golden brown. Cool completely. Insert a skewer into top of each apple.

Yield: 1½ dozen 5-inch cookies

Festive cookies make merry gifts! For wholesome snacks or delightful party favors, spicy Christmas Tree Cookies *(left)* are perched atop rosy red apples and adorned with bows. The Country Santa Cookies are maple-flavored triangles decorated with colorful icing.